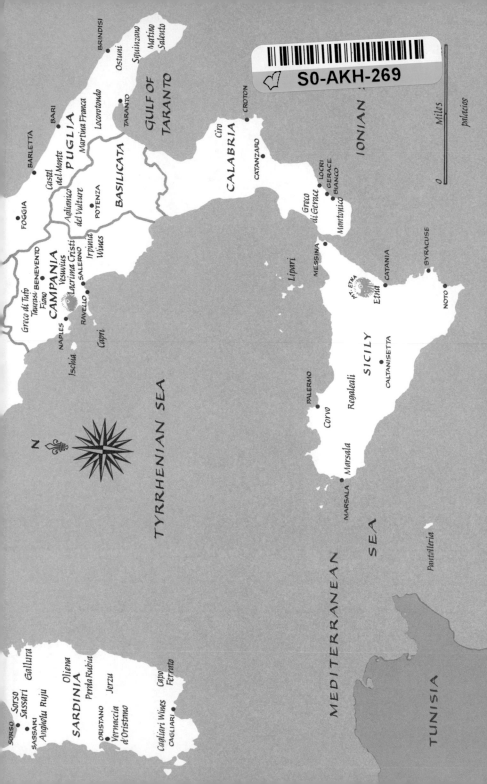

S0-AKH-269

*The
Great Wines
of Italy*

PHILIP DALLAS

The
Great Wines
of Italy

Doubleday & Company, Inc., Garden City, New York
1974

ISBN: 0-385-01553-4
Library of Congress Catalog Card Number 73–79658
Copyright © 1974 by Philip Dallas

For my wife Ninnixedda and my sister Geraldine

Contents

Part One

CHAPTER ONE

A Discourse on Italian Wine

Back in the fifties, I suggested to the editor of an American magazine that I should write an article on Italian wines. The reaction of this lady was, to me, somewhat of a shock. She expressed surprise that anyone should wish to write about anything so second-rate. However, she offered to publish my article if I were able to prove to her readers that Italian wine was not poison and that it even had some merits. My article must have been among the first ever written in praise of Italian wines to appear in a major magazine. Her attitude was harsh, but I found her opinion widely held and to be widely held even today. I shall, therefore, bear it in mind during the writing of this text.

Italy's reputation for making a poor product has still not wholly been overcome, and it may be some time before it is. But how did this reputation arise, and how much truth is there in it? Is it a reputation won in the eighteenth century, or is it a justified contemporary criticism? Or did it come from a completely different quarter and for completely different reasons? Was it the Borgias, the Mafia, or the Triple Alliance that did the damage? Of course there are a variety of factors, including Fascism, that have culminated in this widespread denigration; otherwise I should not have asked these rhetorical questions.

Perhaps the first factor is that relatively little fine Italian wine is exported. Chianti in a raffia-covered flask—a modest, young, and cheerful wine—became Italy's representative abroad. This was to Italy's misfortune, because it had to stand comparison with the great Burgundy and Bordeaux wines. Chianti in a flask never pretended to be anything but an inexpensive and pleasing luncheon wine, but most people quite reasonably pronounced French wines better. The battle would have been fair if the aged reserve Chiantis, which are bottled in ordinary Bordeaux bottles, had been compared with the French wines; these old Chiantis, after a few years in the barrel and a few in the bottle, can make any connoisseur sit up and take notice. But unfortunately these were not, and are not, widely enough known. There are, in fact, some fifty very distinguished producers of aged Chianti, most of whom belong to the Tuscan landed aristocracy and almost none of whom have heard of modern marketing methods.

Even today, after tens of millions of foreign tourists have visited Italy, there is still a tendency to compare inexpensive Italian wines with expensive French ones. This is chiefly the fault of the Italian producers, who have not tried sufficiently hard to make their best wines well known at home or abroad, or succeeded even in making them widely available in hotels and restaurants in Italy. It is also the fault of hotel and restaurant owners and their headwaiters, who are remarkably unaware of the kaleidoscopic arc of Italian wines offered from the Aosta Valley, in the Alps, to the island of Pantelleria, off Tunisia. But it is also due to the fact that visitors to Italy come mostly in summer, which is not the season for enjoying Italy's best in wine and food: strong red wines and roasts are winter fare.

The French, for over a century, have nursed the reputation of their wines: they have encouraged every initiative that could add luster and mystique to their best wines and every initiative that caused their drinkers to demonstrate a sensibility superior to that of *hoi polloi*. Italy, on the other hand, ignored the world and cheerfully sold its wine almost entirely at home and mostly without even a label: after all, the competition was too much to overcome, so why try?

As in any commercial activity, a solid domestic market for a branded product is the springboard for exports and an international reputation, but a solid domestic market for a non-essential product that is not inexpensive, requires a big, comfortably off middle class with aspirations and good taste. France had this to a considerable extent even a hundred years ago and a good market just across the English Channel to help out, which was soon followed by one for expensive wines across the Atlantic. Only in the postwar period has the Italian middle class grown sufficiently important to justify a whole wine industry aiming to satisfy its greater exigencies and thus supply the essential springboard for looking abroad. Previously, there was always fine bottled wine available for those connoisseurs who wanted it and could afford it, but the market for fine Italian wines, both in Italy and abroad, was limited.

Italy's wine production was always very large, and the Germans turned to Italy in the immediate postwar years to import large quantities, though certainly not of the best. They usually bought in bulk, in tankerloads, which went by road over the Brenner Pass.

Then there was an upheaval: the Germans condemned large quantities as unfit for consumption; they demanded that their wine should be chemically, clinically pure. Nobody, in any country, had ever before made such a demand. Perhaps the only wine that really came into that category was champagne; for the rest, they mostly had natural sediment and additives containing harmless foreign and native bodies. After all, it wasn't pasteurized milk that was being sold. Wine is a liquid that evolves and matures and then deteriorates.

This upheaval changed the course of wine production in all Europe and produced unending legislation from the Common

Market headquarters, in Brussels, which, at the time of writing, in early 1973, has not yet finished. Of this technological revolution, one can ask the following questions: what wine is cloudy? What wine ferments in the bottle after you have brought it home? What wine turns out to be vinegar when opened? What wine turns sour if left open for a couple of days? The answer is, of course: very little; but, only two decades ago, the answer would have been different. This change, then, is due to technology, the Germans, the Common Market regulations, and the demands of today's wine buyers, who, unlike, let us say, a member of London's literary-gourmet society, the Saintsbury Club, are not interested in seeing how a particular wine in particular circumstances turns out, but insist that every wine be precisely according to what is written on the bottle or in the producer's catalogue. The wines most likely to bring a surprise when opened, be it a pleasant one or a disappointment, are the very finest, which have, due to their generous alcoholic strength and full body, been allowed to mature naturally in the cask and in the bottle, with all the risks that this entails.

I am rather in accord with the Renaissance statesman-historian Francesco Guicciardini, who said, "When I consider how many risks of sickness, mishap, and of violence there are to which life is, in numberless ways, subject and how many things must coincide in the year so that the harvest is good, there is nothing that amazes me more than seeing an old man or a fruitful year." He might well have added, ". . . and a bottle of wine."

But the fact, today, is that all Europe's exported wines meet the specifications laid down by Common Market regulations. This currently means that about 20 per cent of the total production has passed the tests. Italian wines, by law, cannot be of lower chemical quality than French or German ones, but the prejudice against them lingers on. One can cogitate on the possible reasons for this: perhaps it is a throwback to the pre-World War I anti-Italian propaganda or to that of the 1930s and 1940s, which, though now forgotten, I am assured by Italian marketing experts has left a subconscious resistance to Italian products, be they plastics or shoes, which sell better if their origin is not publicized.

Perhaps the prejudice against Italy and Italian things and the Italian way of life is something much deeper. There has been a reaction against the corruption and high living of the Italians since Renaissance times that has never really died. Northern Europe was fascinated and disgusted with Italy. The bare austerity of the North was too markedly in contrast with the luxury and creative arts of Italy to be happily tolerated. But the Americas and the Indies were opened up, giving northern Europeans a new civilization that not only suited their hardy temperament better but, at the same time, turned the Mediterranean into a backwater and Italy into a country bypassed by the new trade routes. This, for the northern Europeans, was highly satisfactory not only economically but morally. Not only did Italy collapse into bankruptcy, but Italy and the Papal States underwent a profound campaign of derision from the world, which, the more they fell into disrepair, became the more justified. The derision of the old Italy, its art and its philosophy, in a sort of cultural revolution, which was to bring on the modern world with Rousseau, the French Revolution, the new mercantilism, and the growth of practical science and industry, has still not run its course, though changing times have put Italy back onto the trade routes and made of her an industrial country.

Often today, professional journalists, who should know better, are left aghast when, for the first time, they are confronted with modern Italy. The expectation of seeing the ramshackle, the outdated, something with which to commiserate or to chuckle over, is too often destined to disappointment. But this does little for a country's reputation: disappointment can produce resentment rather than delight. Equally, there are admirers and lovers of Italy, who see Italy through the pince-nez glasses of fifty years ago, who are upset when they come across a petrochemical plant bigger than any they have ever seen before. There are, I feel, few people who see Italy for what it is, or who wish to see it for what it is.

I first came to live in Italy in 1947, after seven years in the East, when the country was still at the bottom of its fortunes. I recall Rome's Via Veneto almost without traffic, and I recall a distinguished journalist friend observing a formidable open Alfa-Romeo touring car (which today is probably literally a museum piece) and being morally offended that an Italian should possess such a jewel after losing a war, while he, a successful writer in England, was still on the waiting list for a utility motorcar. But neither he nor I knew who was the owner of this monster Alfa-Romeo; it could well have been a foreign diplomat. In all events, to my complete astonishment, this incident caused my friend to cut short his visit to Italy the next morning, never to return to this day. Bewildered by this visceral reaction, I went on my way toward Sicily.

There, in Taormina, I recall drinking every day for over a year a golden Etna wine that was always served at a perfect cellar temperature and turned the simple food available at that time into a banquet. The price of a carafe of that delectable liquid would, today, not buy five cigarettes. However, in the normal run of things in those days, to find a really satisfying wine that was crystal clear and was not in a labeled bottle was very difficult. Most of the local wines were made with little skill, and particularly the whites went wrong: cloudy and bitter; the reds seemed to stand up to the rough production methods better, though this was hard to understand, as it is more difficult to make a red wine than a white. Only later did I discover that contact with the air has a more ruinous effect on whites than on reds, and that now many wines are stabilized under sterile conditions undreamed of by Pasteur and other scientists and enologists of the past. When living in Amalfi subsequently, I found the local barrel wine usually close to vinegar, but by good fortune there was an inexpensive bottled wine from the hinterland of Salerno available.

Recently I again tasted Etna white, which is now made by modern technological methods. Inevitably I was disappointed. But, then, how could it bring back my youth? Perhaps if I go back to that old hotel with its magnificent view of Etna, the *madeleine* story will come true for me—if the real McCoy is still being made.

Also in Taormina, when I had a little house, I used to buy demijohns of red wine from a landowning English friend. It was a very strong wine, always rather cloudy, but wine as nature made it, with no chemicals and less than a year's aging in the cask. I recall that not only did it go down remarkably well, but it produced a great warmth of friendship, goodwill, and often high spirits at the same time. Nowadays nobody would drink such wine. Heaven knows, the feet of my friend's peasants were filthy when they trampled the grapes, but I always like to think that the dirt went to the bottom of the barrel and the fermentation burned up any germs; I do not want anybody to disillusion me on this issue. I still have the last bill, unpaid, for this wine—five dollars for a demijohn (fifty liters at ten cents a liter)—which has always been on my conscience. But my friend died years ago, leaving a fortune, and I never paid the estate this outstanding debt. Perhaps it doesn't matter: it is all rather out of a past world.

But returning to the subject of prejudice, Sicily has played its part in harming Italy's image, particularly in the United States but also in Great Britain, due to the criminal propensities of the Mafia and Cosa Nostra. Some, therefore, of anti-Italian prejudice is justified, though a great deal is no more than hearsay, in the sense that one will hear people condemn baroque art who could scarcely identify a piece or name an artist of the period, unaware that they are repeating anti-papal propaganda of the late-seventeenth century! If you doubt my word, remember how long it has taken the pre-Bach Italian composers to be recognized by the modern world; only in the past two decades have Monteverdi, Frescobaldi, and Vivaldi, for example, returned to favor after

centuries in the doghouse. It is hard to recall that the painter
Caravaggio was rehabilitated only twenty years ago.

Although books written by Italians often wax lyrical over the
virtues of Italian wines, most of the English language books
I have read either damn them with faint praise or entirely ignore
them. The most flattering quote written by a non-Italian that I
ever came across was in Cyril Ray's admirable treatise *The Wines
of Italy,* in which he says (in the text and in a footnote), "Barolo
ages as well and as long in the bottle as a good claret (longer than
a Burgundy). . . . Indeed—as will be observed, too, of the finest
Tuscan wines—these full Italian red wines have an immense
capacity for aging in the bottle."

The best Italian wines do not come from Taormina or Amalfi,
delightful as those resorts are, but rather from Piedmont, Tuscany,
the Alto Adige (South Tyrol), from Lombardy's Valtelline, from
the Veneto, and from the Friuli region. It is there one finds the
greatest skill in wine making and the best grapes for fine wines, as
well as a climate that is not so torrid in summer as that of the
South, which tends to produce very alcoholic or overly sweet
wines; this criticism, however, is fast becoming outdated, since
southern Italy, Sicily, and Sardinia are now producing remarkably
sturdy dry table wines of considerable note. Names of southern
wines such as Torre Quarto, Cirò, Greco di Tufo, Greco di
Gerace, Perda Rubia, Oliena, Taurasi, and Corvo are already in
the notebooks of Italian wine lovers, and they will be in the notebooks of Frenchmen, Englishmen, and Americans as the years
pass. This notable improvement in southern wines, in some cases,
may be due to a discovery of fairly recent date that if the grapes
are picked a little early, before they have their full sugar content,
the wine they produce is more elegant and "northern." Also, an
increasing use of *pergola* cultivation instead of the traditional
southern *alberello* (bush) vines produces a lighter wine.

Although there is a prejudice against Italian wines, it should
be noted that over three million bottles of the sparkling spumante
are sold by Piedmont to France every year; that Switzerland,

which has the wine-growing areas of France and Italy equidistant from its doorstep, purchases more from Italy than from France. Surprisingly, France has replaced Germany in the past two years as Italy's best customer, multiplying her wine imports from Italy by the incredible figure of fifty times as much—5,000 per cent— as well as importing considerable quantities of pinot grapes for making sparkling wines. Excluding vermouths, Italy sold over $100 million worth in 1969, $350 million in 1971, and $400 million in 1972 on foreign markets, but this is little in comparison with what it could sell if there were, in Italy, a competent publicity and marketing organization such as France and Germany have.

Much is made of the "sophistication" cases by the national and international press; and this is added to by the lumbering methods of Italian justice, which does not make known to the press and the public even the charges being pressed or the evidence to hand, while the case often takes five years to come to court . . . and sometimes never does. This inevitably causes the embroidery of fantastic tales as to the possible contents of Italian wine: wild accusations alleging that it is made with banana skins, old boots (for the tannic acid!) and chemical coloring produce headlines. The Italian government recently stated that "sophistication" has been sharply curtailed and that if there is a thimbleful of phony wine for every fifty liters of good wine, that is a lot. It should also be remembered that the firms that have tampered illegally with their wines were, in any case, working in the cheapest, non-appellation category, which is not normally exported, and where a profit is hard to make. Even the use of sugar to enhance the alcoholic content of a wine or the addition of standard, branded chemicals to prevent a second fermentation—both normal practices in the rest of Europe—can cause an Italian winery to be closed down for "sophistication." These two practices are made use of to cut costs; but, for reasons unclear, they are not approved by the Italian Ministry for Agriculture. When a winery is closed down, the worst is always assumed, though in fact nothing worse than following standard European practice has been done, albeit illegally.*

For decades, the growers and producers have had their own associations, consortiums, and federations to discipline themselves and their rivals—the Chianti group was first set up by the Grand Dukes of Tuscany back in the eighteenth century—which mostly issue numbered bottle neck labels in proportion to the quantity of wine that each member-producer announces as his crop for the year.

* At the time of proof correcting, I have read an article saying that the anti-fermentative product recommended in this book as an economical means of preventing a second fermentation in wine, but which is prohibited —I suggest, ureasonably—in Italy by the Health Ministry, has been banned in Germany as of April 1, 1973. It seems that the fears of Swedish scientists that this anti-fermentative forms the cancer-producing "urethan" were published in *Science* magazine in 1971. Subsequent studies by the FAO and the WHO did not disprove these fears, so the federal government, in late 1972, decided that the use of the chemical should be discontinued within four years. After an article in the weekly *Zeit*, the German government altered the date to April 1, 1973. Plainly, the federal government was not concerned with an active danger to health; in fact, our doctors and scientists have uncertain ideas as to what causes cancer.

Equally, I recall some few years ago that it was announced that Paris consumed a quantity of Beaujolais equal to that produced by the delimited zone. It was respectfully asked what the rest of France and the world were drinking under the same name. But the scandal lasted a day and there was no apparent financial loss or prestige damage to the good name of Beaujolais.

Had either of these unhappy circumstances arisen in Italy, the press— and particularly the Italian press—would have been vitriolic; wine would have been stopped at foreign frontiers by health authorities; importers would have canceled their orders; and individuals would have gone into hospitals all over the world swearing they'd been poisoned by Italian wine. One cannot, therefore, but admire the French and German talent in handling their embarrassments and deplore the insouciance of the Italians. A recent scandal, in early 1973, which cost Italian wine producers a fortune in money and international prestige, was caused by twenty-four peasant wine producers near Frascati, who at best sold their wine in buckets locally, using a harmless but illegal anti-fermentative similar in effect to the one now banned in Germany.

However, the West German action will require that a brilliant chemist produce a new chemical anti-fermentative to replace the one banned, or the German producers will be constrained to follow the Italian model and sink vast sums of money into the wine-making machinery mentioned in Chapter Four.

The past few years have seen appreciable changes. Laws have been passed that align the discipline of Italian wines to the French-controlled system under Common Market regulations. That is to say, worthy wines or groups of closely allied wines have been allotted their production zones, and the law insists that the processing of such wines shall be such as not to diverge from approved methods to obtain a specific style of wine from specific types of grapes. The present-day concept of being able to produce and bottle precisely what is laid down by law is a far cry from the past, both distant and recent. The attainment of this remarkably high state of the art has taken well over two thousand years.

CHAPTER TWO
A History of Wine Making

Every wine writer has his own theory as to where wine was first born; mine is that wild vines, such as are still cultivated in New York State, grew throughout the Mediterranean, the Near East, and even in India and China in prehistoric times. As the various civilizations rose, they experimented and learned about wine; as they fell, they forgot about wine. Wine is something essentially connected with civilization, with continuity and with peace, rather than with barbarity. Plato called wine the gods' greatest gift to man.

The first record of *Vitis vinifera* (the grape-bearing vine), allegedly goes back to Noah, who expressed a noted preference for wine over water when, after the Flood, he planted a vineyard on Mount Ararat and overindulged in the first crop. Others say that he invented beer, and this sounds more likely; his grain, damp from the flood waters, fermented. After all, if you plant a vine it will be several years before you get a bottle of wine from it.

Wine was well known, however, to the early Egyptians, the Sumerians, the Phoenicians, and the Minoans. The Greeks, in historic times, domesticated the vine and took their wine-making skills to Sicily. The oldest known bottle of wine was excavated at Ephesus and was reckoned to be two thousand years old. I say it was reckoned to be two thousand years old, because it exists no more, since a photographer got too close to it with his flash and this ancient bottle of fragile glass disintegrated. The contents, dry and gummy, turned out to be wine mixed with honey and resin. The Romans, in their turn, took their wine-making know-how to all the provinces of their empire, and subsequently wine became the essence, along with bread, of the Christian faith. In fact, Jesus Christ is the first person named in history (*pace* Noah) as having made wine, even if the Cana miracle did rather dodge the processing.

Wine was a luxury in earliest Roman times to such an extent that legislation was passed prohibiting women from drinking it. With the passing of the centuries, wine production leaped. By the second half of the first century A.D., the Emperor Domitian was constrained to pass laws preventing farmers from giving up corn growing and cultivating only the vine. Greek wines, preferably from Chios, were still considered the best, but this was perhaps because the Romans were great wine snobs and liked the idea of imported goods as much as we do today. As far as imported Greek statues were concerned, they were certainly right; as for the wine, we can never know. In all events, there were, at an early date, major vintages from crops in the Rome and Naples areas, in Sicily, in the Veneto and the Aosta Valley. The Falernian, the Caecuban, the Mamertine, and the Rhaetic were to become famous wines through the writings of Pliny, Horace, Martial, and Petronius. It would seem that this generous supply was still insufficient for Roman thirsts. Cargo ships sailed from Rome, coasted to Elba, crossed over to Marseilles, and coasted down to Spain to load up with wine. Many of these ships foundered at Elba and are now being excavated by frogmen: amphoras full of wine mixed with honey have been brought to the surface.

The Romans boasted of drinking hundred-year-old wines that

had retained their body, taste, and aroma. So strong were these wines that water or even salt water was added to them. Hundred-year-old wines, to me, seem something of an exaggeration if we think in terms of today's aged wines, of the difficulty of aging wines, of the care and even rebottling that must go on, and of the often modest or even disastrous results. If we are to believe the Romans, they filled an amphora with wine, sealed it with sealing wax, and put it away in the attic for a century. This is just too good to be true.

The Romans inevitably found difficulty in stabilizing their wines, as we do today; however, quite remarkably, they discovered a rudimental technique of pasteurization without knowing it. They learned, over two thousand years ago, that submitting wine to heat stabilizes and matures it. This, however, is not a system for making wine last a hundred years. The fact that they put their wines in the attic and not in a cellar is also proof that they knew what they were doing. In this way, for several summers the wine would ferment, like a Tuscan "vin santo," and rest during the cold winter; and, like a vin santo, would have a naturally long life, though not one of a hundred years.

They also made spiced wines, as did Hippocrates in Greece in 400 B.C. Hippocrates brewed wine with honey and almonds for medical purposes. The Romans boiled down their wine with absinthe blossom (not the toxic leaves) and honey: and since *Wermut* is the German and wormwood the English name for the absinthe plant, we can deduce roughly that they produced a sort of highly potent vermouth, which would indicate how they obtained the concentrated wines that retained their characteristics over the decades and that, being even stronger than vermouth, required the addition of water and even salt water if the wine had become too sweet.

The practice of watering these old wines is well documented. At a Roman banquet, for example, a venerable amphora of wine was brought in and an "arbiter" elected, who had to stay relatively sober for the whole feast. It was his duty to decide on how much water should be added to the wine to keep the party happy but within bounds; from our knowledge of Roman history, it would seem that the arbiters were more often broad-minded than hidebound.

Throughout history, then, man has produced wine. If he has produced good wine, it has not been by the grace of God, but due to his own hopeful efforts. Professor Maynard Amerine of California has observed that if you leave wine to nature, it is clear that what God intended was vinegar. Such modest technical skills as the ancients had learned were mostly forgotten during the Dark Ages, but fortunately not all, nor throughout all Europe. Many enclaves were missed by the barbarians (Amalfi among them), and many a barbarian acquired a taste for wine. The Benedictine and Cluniac monks were, of course, the main ganymedes over the dark centuries, since they required wine not only for keeping up their spirits in hard times, but also for sacramental purposes. Those lands, such as Sicily, that were conquered by the abstemious Moslems had their wine production decimated, but their vineyards continued to produce grapes and raisins.

Among the Goths with a taste for wine was Theodoric, whose minister, Cassiodorus, records that his emperor gave instructions for the protection of vines and wine making. Theodoric is said to have had a liking for the Recioto of Verona, though we cannot know much more than that. King Roatri of the Lombards in the early seventh century also encouraged wine production, and this practice was carried on by Charlemagne, who viewed the planting of vineyards as being as praiseworthy as the building of a church. Scholars have noted that a remarkable number of abbeys, convents, and churches have been sited on good wine land, rather than a large number of poor vineyards being sited near church property. All in all, wine succeeded in reaching the year 1000 A.D. without the world's forgetting how to make it. The world did not come to an end, as so many people expected and from then on things looked up enologically.

Salerno became the greatest center of civilization in Europe at the turn of the millennium. It had had for some time a reputation for scholarship in philosophy and theology (St. Thomas Aquinas taught there), and the arrival of an African monk began its fame as a medical center, at a time when next to nothing was known about medicine. This medical school and hospital is traditionally said to have been founded by an Arab (presumably Constantine, the monk), a Jew, a Greek, and a Latin. The school rose to international fame and declined in the thirteenth century. Its counsels spread throughout the civilized world, and even as late as 1607, an English poet, Sir John Harington, considered it worthwhile to publish a translation of their good-natured and often humorous advice in verse form. The school even invented the "hair of the dog that bit you" theory. They counseled, "If the evening libation harmed you, drink again in the morning: it is the best medicine!"

What is remarkable is the extent to which wine is involved in their medical thinking. Though ". . . if you lack medical men," they said, "let these things be your medicine . . . good humor, rest, and sobriety." Another maxim is "Love wine and women and all recreation," but another warns that "wine, women and baths, used or abused, do men much good or harm." They were very concerned about "humors," as were the English in the eighteenth century, and have all manner of recommendations about the right food and wine for every psychological malady. But ever returning to wine, they say: "The better wines do breed better humors, the worse ones are cause of unwholesome tumors."

Renaissance times brought into being the businessman-cum-gentleman-farmer, particularly in Tuscany. Successful merchants set up a country villa and, using their wider experience of the world than that of the local farmers, produced an agricultural renaissance as well as an artistic and humanistic one. The production of wine was so large that, for the first time in history, perhaps, it came within the reach of everybody's purse.

Almost at the same time, wine production started up in

Piedmont, in the Valtelline, around Verona and Lake Garda, in the Emilia Romagna and in the Roman hills, particularly toward Montefiascone. As early as the thirteenth century, the first book in "modern" times on enology was published: Pier de' Crescenzi's treatise was translated from the Latin into Italian, German, and Polish; a hundred and thirty-two manuscripts and sixteen incunabula editions are known.

Distilling of a primitive sort was developed during Renaissance times, though its actual introduction into Italy dates back to the twelfth century, when the Moslems were known to have had the art, though, because of their Islamic faith, they did not drink the resultant liquids. It took two centuries for the Italians to realize that distilled wine was an excellent beverage. This invention of brandy led to the production, at a modest level, of liqueurs, but it was not until the nineteenth century that these were brought to perfection, when it became possible to produce delicate neutral spirits as their base. However, the "rosolios" of Padua were the start: they consisted of distilled wine combined with attar of roses and honey. Around 1530, when Catherine de' Medici left for France to become the wife of the future King Henry II, she not only took her Florentine cooks but also a group of her rosolio experts along with her.

With the extension of trading in the East, the Maritime Republics of Venice, Pisa, Genoa, and Amalfi started bringing back oriental spices such as cardamom, nutmeg, ginger, myrrh, and cloves. These, too, were used as aromas, along with native mountain herbs, for the rosolios. From here, and bearing in mind the spiced and cooked wines that had existed in ancient Greece and Rome, the leap was not far to the Turin vermouths and the fine liqueurs of the monastries of France and Italy.*

There seems little doubt that the Italian Renaissance, and particularly its Florentine efflorescence, was floated on wine. The references to wine and Bacchus in paintings, sculpture, and literature, as well as in a mountain of private correspondence, are

* See Appendix C—A Note on Monastic Rosolios and Elixirs, p. 384.

uncountable. At the court of Florence, whether under the Medicis or later under the grand dukes, banquets are recorded at which culture and wine were mingled with no inconsiderable success.

There was Chianti, then called Florence Red or Vermiglia, though it was not the same wine as that later "invented" by Baron Bettino Ricasoli: I think it must have been more of the nature of a straight Sangiovese, a Brunello, or Vino Nobile of Montepulciano, but in any event it was a strong, full-bodied red dry wine and, as such, a rarity and profoundly appreciated by connoisseurs. The regular wine-of-the-country was white: Trebbiano, slightly sweet, was the most important, but there were also the Greco, the Malvasia, and the Vernaccia.

When I say that the Renaissance was floated on wine, this statement can be supported by statistics: in 1320, in Florence alone, over five million gallons—not bottles—of wine were taxed to purchase the land and to build the Signoria Palace!

Although the Bettino Ricasoli Chianti mixture of four types of grape was not standardized till the late-nineteenth century, the Florentines had already invented the *governo* system for wine making. This unique practice consisted in harvesting a small quantity of grapes a few days before the grand harvest. These grapes were left in the sun to dry and sweeten, and when the harvest was in and the grape juice already fermented in the casks, these grapes would be pressed and added, skins and all, to the barrels. The result was to produce a rounder wine and to give it that special prickly effect for which a young Chianti is famous. It was a brilliant idea for speeding the maturing of the wine and reducing the risk of its turning to vinegar.

Though Tuscany enjoyed a superabundance of good wine, these wines did not travel well—not even to Rome. The Tuscans, however, became even more refined in their tastes: they popularized the wineglass rather than the silver or pewter mug for drinking. After all, there were the master glass blowers of Empoli nearby, who were also producing the famous round flasks. Among other refinements were special flasks called *rinfrescatoi* and *can-*

timplori, which had pockets blown into their sides into which
either warm water or ice could be put to raise or lower the
desired temperature of the wine. These had a particular period of
fashion when the primitive thermometer was invented in the early-
seventeenth century by a pupil of Galileo, a Venetian named
Sagredo. The *termoscopio,* as he called it, filled with distilled
Chianti instead of mercury, accurately measured the ambient
temperature or the temperature of a liquid such as wine.

One of the curiosities of the history of wine is that whites,
though easier to make, were and are particularly unstable, especially during the hot weather of their first summer, when they
are inclined to start fermenting again. There seems little doubt
that, back in Renaissance times, the Florentines had discovered
that a little sulphur in the cask served to calm the wine down.
However, this treatment had and has its disadvantages: you could
smell the sulphur and it could give you heartburn. There was and
is little you can do about the heartburn except take a magnesia
pill, but the smell of the sulphur can be hidden by chilling the
wine. The rinfrescatoio and the cantimplore flasks, with their
built-in pockets for ice to cool the wine, were plainly designed
also for the purpose of reducing the smell of the sulphur. This
refinement seems to have been forgotten, and then reinvented in
Bordeaux in 1892, when the Phylloxera bug had destroyed most
of the red wine grapes. Normally, at that time, white Graves were
sold locally, as they had no reputation in either London or Paris.
But one shipper reinvented the Florentine elegance of "drinking
cool," propagandized it, and, succeeding in selling dry white wine
for the first time on a large scale in London, saved himself from
bankruptcy.

From the sour Amalfi whites of the postwar period to the wines
of Rome today, you will still find whites that need chilling; but, on
the whole, sulphur is no longer used in aggressive quantities to prevent that second fermentation: filtering and sterile or hot bottling
are used to do this job. Chilling, with ice or in the refrigerator, not
only disposes of the smell of sulphur but also of much of the

bouquet and taste of the wine, as any chilling system inevitably does to food and drink. Since the smell of sulphur is no longer—or rarely—present, at least in Italian wines, chilling is no longer necessary. Of course, nobody will stop chilling white wine just because it is unnecessary; it is an accepted formula and shibboleth and also pleasing in its way, particularly with some whites. But if you drink a white wine at cool cellar temperature, you will find that it offers all sorts of charms that were previously hidden, and that there are possibilities of marrying whites to a far wider range of dishes; this is particularly true for the full-bodied and strong white wines of Italy.

Although there was and still is the risk of cellarmen turning into alcoholics and inviting their friends to help them with their daily tasks, the seventeenth-century Tuscan cellarmen brought their local wines to a stage of perfection that was not again reached till the nineteenth century. The major snag was the pouring of olive oil onto the surface of the wine to seal off the air. This practice was fairly satisfactory if the flasks had to travel only a short distance by mule cart, but disastrous if the wines were to be shipped, when the oil mixed with the wine. In Tuscany the wine arrived in good trim, and the cellarmen, even if drunk, knew just how to remove the oil with an expert flick of the wrist, leaving the wine unspoiled. In London, for example, this skill was not widely spread, and the result was far from being the wine that had left Florence. From this, perhaps, arose the reputation that Italian wines have for "not traveling," which is of course today quite ludicrous, though one often still hears it.

A second major snag was that, though the use of the cork became known in the seventeenth century, it was not until 1877 that finally a reinforced flask was produced that could take the pressure of the new corking machines, after which Chianti, then a newly perfected wine, quickly made its reputation throughout the world. However, it is both curious and notable how an apparently negligible lack of technological know-how held back wine exports for more than two centuries, despite unending hopeful but frustrated attempts.

By 1877 the French were already in the saddle, and for the Italians the game was lost. But even so, the dry Tuscany red wines made great progress, since their special tannic tang appealed to men's palates.

After almost inventing wine as the drink of modern Europe, the Italians lost the advantage for the sake of a cork, or perhaps the lack of a bottle with a strong enough neck to take one. One can only, by way of excuse, suggest that with foreign armies trampling and looting the country, know-how took second place to *sauve qui peut*. But if only Leonardo da Vinci or Galileo had put their minds to corking wine bottles, the history of wine would have been very different.

Very discreetly and over many centuries from the Middle Ages onward, German bishops set up little wine-growing fiefs for themselves on the South Tyrol, now called the Alto Adige, the production of which went, equally discreetly, straight home to the bishopric. Only relatively recently, since the wines of Bolzano and Trento have become famous, has the wisdom of these prelates been fully appreciated.

Owning a slice of Italy has always been something desirable: this sunny land of fine cities, which literally flowed with wine, became too great a temptation for the French, the Spaniards, and finally the Austrians. From 1600 on, Italy was a battlefield and a colony—worse, it was split up into many colonies and principalities, none of whose rulers were particularly concerned to add to the gross national product of their slice of Italy, but preferred to export all the wealth they could lay their hands on or spend it living high on the hog. This period was crowned by Napoleon explaining to his ragged and half-starved army of "mustaches" that just over the mountains lay the "fat" Valley of the Po, where they could solve all their temporal inconveniences and lacks. Napoleon conquered all Italy, though he oddly forgot to include Sardinia; perhaps as a blood brother from the adjacent island of

Corsica, he knew that the pickings would be small and that mounting an amphibious invasion would not be worth the candle. The good name of Italy and of the papacy, which had been transferred to France in preventive custody, reached an all-time low; and the quality of Italian wine did likewise, though the wine was still abundant.

After Napoleon's defeat and a return to normalcy in Italy, which included the return of Savoy, with its capital at Chambéry, to the dukes of Piedmont, Italian wines started to regain their reputations. Carlo Alberto, Duke of Savoy, King of Sardinia, and ruler of Piedmont, set up a rigid military state, that aimed at and finally succeeded in removing foreign dominance from most of northern Italy: the Austrians held from Milan to Venice and Trieste in an iron grip. But soldiers need strong wine, and officers are rather more discriminating. Count Camillo Cavour, prime minister of Piedmont, saw the possibility of making Italian wine of top quality for both his officers and his troops, and invited an enologist, Louis Oudard, from Rheims, to take over his lands and plant the vine. Monsieur Oudard succeeded admirably. He made Barolo and Barbera. Carlo Gancia, noting the availability of great quantities of Muscat grapes in Piedmont and, presumably, the lack of French champagne on the Italian market due to the Phylloxera pest in France, went for two years in the early 1890s to study at the Piper Heidsieck winery at Rheims, and on his return to Piedmont, started making sweet Muscat champagne; a decade later, he imported Pinot vines to make champagne. It was only in the year 1919 that the use of the name "champagne" was prohibited.

Also in the second half of the nineteenth century, Baron Bettino Ricasoli launched Chianti as we know it today, but it was traditional Tuscan malignity that invented the story about his being a jealous old husband of a beautiful young wife. The tale goes that his wife danced too many times with a handsome young officer at a ball in Florence; the Iron Baron, as Ricasoli was disrespectfully and ironically nicknamed, called for his coach, bundled his wife aboard, and they drove all night to Brolio Castle, near Siena, where, to pass the decades usefully, Ricasoli perfected the enology of Chianti, a wine, like Bordeaux, made from four different types of grape.

In Sicily, the Marsala wine made its name earlier, in 1773, when two gallons of distilled wine was poured into a barrel of wine in the hope that this would help it travel to England: it did. It is one of the principles of enology that the stronger the wine, the better chance it has of traveling and aging, but spiking wine with spirits is a trifle rough-and-ready. Soon after, a highly successful Marsala industry, with British capital and know-how from the port and sherry industries, was founded. The British were not only the major initiators of the Port, Sherry, Madeira, and Marsala industries, but also prominent in promoting Cognac and Bordeaux.

In the late-nineteenth century came the vine blights, Oïdium, mildew, Peronospera, and Phylloxera. The destruction of European vineyards was very grave, and a two-millennium dilettantism in wine production came to an abrupt end. The capital investment in wine producing was already becoming very large, and, as such, could not afford to take such losses from bugs, sloppy processing, ignorance, and sheer wastage. The modern scientific world, which at last began to understand fermentation and the other strange reactions that occur in the barrel and in the bottle, had arrived. The French led the way in the eighteenth century, and finally Pasteur, in the nineteenth, gave us a sterilization system and studies that were to be the basis of the new enology by which we learned how to kill off harmful microbes either by filtering them away or pasteurizing the wine by heating it, already bottled, to 60° C. This pasteurization, though effective, was not entirely satisfactory, since it left a taste of "cooked" wine if not done to perfection, i.e., according to the strength of the wine, the type of grape, etc., all of which have to be taken into account for the time and intensity of the heat required to halt the activity of the microbes.

An improvement, called hot bottling, was invented in Germany in the 1930s, whereby the wine is heated for only about a minute, while passing through heated stainless-steel pipes. This does less harm to the bouquet of the wine than Pasteur's system, and in fact it is close to impossible to pronounce with certainty from its taste that a particular wine has been hot bottled. This system also retains all the advantages of a quick maturing of the wine, but has the disadvantage that the wine will have a limited life span and must be drunk young.

Pasteur did not find out all the answers. He believed that oxygen was essential to wine making and that any amount of it could be allowed to make contact with the wine during vinification. Only in recent years has it been discovered that he was right only in part. Air, certainly, is needed, but in the most minuscule quantities: the amount that can seep through the seams of a well-bunged cask is enough. For the rest, wine—and particularly white wine—needs sterile conditions if it is to stabilize properly. And this is best done either by the most painstaking traditional methods of filtration, with particular attention to every closure, faucet, and pipe joint being airtight, or by hot bottling under stringent vacuum conditions.

It is said that enology was not sufficiently advanced to make stable dry red wines before the year 1700 (the Florence reds of Renaissance times were the nearest approach) and that white wine was much more commonly in use. The difference between making red wine and white wine is that, in the former case, the grapeskins remain in the cask during the fermentation, to give color to the wine. These grapeskins are either floating or immersed in either open or closed barrels or tanks. All these systems require considerable care or the wine turns to vinegar; plainly, in the past there was no sure rule, and too often the wine soured. White wine, however, was made without the grapeskins and did not present these problems. Producers therefore often took the easy way out. They even made fine white wine from red grapes lightly pressed. They would also stop the fermentation by filtering the wine one or more times while there was still sugar unburned in it, thus ensuring not only stabilization but a sweetish wine; one, however, that at least would not turn sour. Certain grapes also do not have sufficient yeasts to burn out all the sugar and stop fermenting of their own accord, resulting in a sweet wine.

After 1800 and Count Chaptal's "invention"† of the device for measuring the amount of sugar in the grape juice, it became possible to add a precise quantity of sugar if the natural sugar content was too low to make a good wine. Later it was learned how to add extra, specially cultivated yeasts to ensure a complete conversion of the sugar into alcohol.

By the middle of the nineteenth century, red wine, too, was fairly reliable, though not yet in the modern sense. This would seem to be borne out by the difficulties experienced by the Tuscans, who had given up the struggle in favor of the French, who had made much greater headway. There is almost nothing written, either in France or in Italy, about fine vintage red wines before 1850; and even in the quarter century afterward, there is continuous reference to failed years, mildew, and ill-balanced wines, interspersed with great vintage years. Nevertheless the

† Chaptalization is a most valuable method of increasing the alcoholic strength of a wine, which in turn allows it to travel and keep, without damaging its essential characteristics, provided it is used within rigorous limits: that is to say, to enhance the alcoholic content by one or at most two percentage points. It is also vastly less expensive than the use of cutting wine or neutral-aroma wine concentrates.

If, however, it is abused to give greater strength, the side effects are immediately noticeable: chiefly, the bouquet becomes aggressive, particularly on opening the bottle, and the wine, on drinking, is a heady and drunk-making potion.

After the sugar has dissolved in the course of a few hours in the must before fermentation, it is impossible to distinguish it clinically from the natural sugar of the grape. Though analytical chemists may be fooled, professional wine tasters are not.

Chaptalization was perfected around 1800, during Count Chaptal's tenure in the Ministry of Agriculture, and was named after him.

French were so far advanced in comparison with the Italians that Carlo Gancia went to Rheims, and Cavour called Oudard to stabilize his Nebbiolo grapes, despite the vine diseases that were then destroying French crops.

Historically, though the Catholic Church over the centuries was the standard-bearer of the vine, Napoleon's expropriation and sale of church lands was more important in making wine the standard drink of France and Italy by putting wine production into lay hands, which were more effective than those of the ecclesiastics. The Church had stressed the production of white wines, which were used for sacramental purposes; the new, lay owners of the vineyards were more interested in producing reds.

It can be noted that the connoisseurs, between 1870 and 1925, say, wrote that claret, for example, was not always a dry wine, but sometimes one full of sugar. The only wines with a longer history by contemporary or near-contemporary writers are port and sherry, and these wines were and are stabilized and fortified with brandy, thus dodging most of the trials and troubles of wine making. These same connoisseurs began to express disappointment with the clarets of their later years when they found that those of the late 1920s and '30s were dry, with no sweetness, covert or overt, either in the hail or with the farewell; they felt cheated. They submitted that something had changed in the soil, in the grape, in the weather. They did not know that it was intentional and that the enologists had finally brought the technology of wine making under control. The day of reliable, fine, dry wines, produced from Phylloxera-resistant American vines, had arrived, though the connoisseurs were, oddly enough, not aware of it. Enologists had learned not only about the quantity of sugar needed, but the amount of acidity required to age wine, the quantity of tannin to give it robustness, and all the other residues, yeasts, and by-products of fermentation that affect the taste and quality of wine. They also had learned to pump wine into vats and barrels from the bottom instead of the top, thus avoiding

contact with the air. The only thing they still lacked was a completely sterile system of stainless-steel pipes, pumps, and faucets.

In this wine-fancying business, one continually treads on rakes.
Recently, reading a book about wine bibbing by a certain Bertall,
who, it would seem from his text, was a painter of no great re-
nown in Paris during the middle of the past century (he was
youngish during the 1848 insurrection), I gathered that the vine
was brought to Marseilles in almost prehistoric times by the
Phocaeans, a great maritime people of western Asia Minor, and
that the famous and holy St. Martin of Tours not only preached
the gospel to the people of the Loire in the early-fourth century,
but also taught them viticulture and wine making. These two
snippets of history are fair enough and we can accept them at
face value. Then he goes on to say that the wines of France are
divided into three major categories: white wines, red wines,
and blue wines! "Just like the colors of the French flag," he adds.
For further elucidation, he continues:
"White wines, for the most part, are luxury wines and not in
common use; they range from the Chablis and the Saumur, which
one sips with oysters and which grace the most refined tables
and put everyone in fine humor, to the champagnes which froth
at galas and to the great Sauternes whose amber tints shine only
at the most important receptions.
"White wine is the wine of the rich. Red wines are French
wines par excellence, all in common use and much appreciated.
The blue wines are the wines of the poor, of the workers and of
those who do not like to work; they are ordinary table wines
which heat the stomach and have a sour taste. . . ."
This, of course, gets us out of kilter, since we are convinced
that claret and Burgundy were always the great wines of France.
It would seem that this book by Bertall was written in a transi-
tional period just before the art of making red wines of top
quality was mastered. Before that, white wines were for the
rich.

He adds a recipe from the School of Salerno that had not yet come my way and adds glory to that noble institution: "It is good to get drunk once a month." But, of course, on wine: hard liquor had not been invented in Medieval times.

Bertall also tells a sad tale of one of his models, Thomas the Bear, an enormous ex-Foreign Legionnaire, who was thrown out of the Legion because he ate as much as twelve men. Worse, however, was that he drank as much as twelve men, customarily consuming twelve liters of wine at a sitting, with no ill effects. Lacking money, he would make do with twelve liters of water. His unending problem was to find enough money to eat and drink. Only once in his life did he reach a state of blissful satiety over any appreciable length of time: that was when he stormed the kitchens of the Tuileries in the 1848 revolution and held them against all comers. This was the sublime climax of his life. Shortly after, having been dislodged from his culinary fortress and weak from lack of food, the bear with which he wrestled in the streets of Paris (hence his nickname) to earn his dozen meals a day (and, presumably, those of the bear also) hugged him too lovingly and too long.

Returning to the rakes trod in this field of wine scholarship, one comes upon the interesting hypotheses of Maxwell Campbell, an expert on claret whose drinking extended from the 1860 vintages right through to the immediate post-World War II period.

He suggests that wines were better before the 1880s and 1890s, the period when the American Phylloxera bug did its profound damage throughout France, and that the disease robbed the wines of the power to impart a strong personality. These are strong words and perhaps should be read in a relative sense only, but that there was a drop in quality after the 1970s seems correct, as he goes on to say that producers were even constrained to pasteurize their claret, presumably because it was weak and unstable or because the new American vines had not yet acclimatized themselves.

He recalls the famous cricketer P. G. H. Fender, who became

on retirement a wine expert, saying that a certain bourgeois claret was so sweet that it might almost be a *bourgeoise*. He recalls a Château Lafite that when uncorked, exhaled an unmistakable whiff of sulphur dioxide. Perverse and unacceptable characteristics such as these are so completely out of the question today, certainly for Italian wines, that we must acknowledge that we can make better and far more reliable wines now, even if they have less character than in 1860.

Recently I came across a Garibaldi story I had never heard before: In 1859, while traveling in Piedmont, he overnighted in Biella, a fine Nebbiolo wine-growing area. Everybody was distraught, as the grape crop was going to fail. Garibaldi went to the bishop and explained the use of sulphur; the bishop promptly delivered a sermon on the virtues of sulphur and its utilization, and the vintage was saved. But the peasants were never really convinced that it was not the bishop's exorcising of devils that saved the day. Garibaldi, being from Nice, had certainly seen the French using sulphur: though the Florentines used sulphur centuries before, plainly the process had not reached all Italy, particularly at a time when Italy was divided up into principalities and intercommunication was difficult.

In support of our French painter's theory that white wine was for the rich, Maxwell Campbell writes that, in the mid-eighteenth century, the Benedictines were producing at Carbonnieux considerable quantities of Graves and that its reputation had spread even to teetotaling Moslem Turkey, where it was imported for the Sublime Porte—discreetly labeled CARBONNIEUX MINERAL WATER.

The "modern" history of wine making in France and Italy is as different as the "ancient" history. Whereas, in the latter, France had the better fortune, in the former, Italy was able to take advantage of France's bitter experience and save herself from a similar fate.

With the modest import of American vines, mostly for study

purposes, into France in the 1870s, the Peronospera mildew
spread, doing untold damage. It reached Italy, but not in such a
total way. Though this malady was most widely spread and, in a
way, more destructive than the later Phylloxera, it was finally
halted (though never extirpated) first with sprayed lime, and
later and more effectively with copper sulphate, though I gather
that in the past decade this, too, has been superseded, by a zinc
derivative called zineb, which is not only cheaper but more satisfactory.

Next came Oïdium mildew, also from the States, which equally
played havoc, rather in the style of the potato blights of Ireland.
The cure for Oïdium was found to be sulphur, which kills the
incipient fungus. This plague was followed by the Phylloxera bug,
also from the United States, which made it necessary to uproot almost every vine in Europe. However, this did not hit all Europe
simultaneously. The Phylloxera is a minute louse with a taste for
European vines and none for American vines. It travels not only
on vines being transplanted from one area to another, but also in
the mud on boots, animal hoofs, and the wheels of vehicles. The
effect in France was disastrous, chiefly because it was something
completely new; nobody had any previous experience upon which
to draw; and by the time the prophylactic was discovered, the
damage was done.

Among the things learned was that the American vine was
immune to the Phylloxera bug's attentions. The best defense,
then, was to graft traditional vines onto American roots. The
snag here was that there were three major types of American
vines, and it took the agrarian and enological experts some time
to test these in various conditions and produce hybrids more
suited to the various wine types. These were the bad, bad years.
Today, in Italy, there are a dozen American hybrids in general
use, according to soil and the wine to be produced. Fortunately,
the American vine is most prolific and offers an enormous amount
of "wood" each year for planting; this cut the change-over period
appreciably for the French.

During the 1872–74 period of the disaster in France, the French wine trade bought every drop of wine they could find in Italy, Spain, and Portugal, where the Phylloxera had not yet arrived. Particularly, they bought the powerful cutting wines of southern Italy to restore their sad crops of low-alcohol-producing grapes. The imports were massive; such quantities were not reached again until 1972—almost a hundred years later.

The Phylloxera first recorded in Italy was in 1905, at Como. It quickly spread to Piedmont and other parts of Italy, but the Italian Ministry for Agriculture was not caught unprepared, as the unfortunate French had been. The Italians had done their homework and were ready and expecting the plague. As soon as it arrived, decrees, rather like those for foot-and-mouth disease in England, were promulgated. It became a crime to transplant a vine from one vineyard to another if it was not an American vine. A system of injecting half a liter of carbon disulphide in gas form into the ground every five yards between the vines was effective in killing the bugs, but cost more than the vineyards were worth; it was therefore discontinued. The Italian experience was the same as that of the French, but the former managed to contain the menace, each time it arose, within very modest limits. The sick vines were uprooted and replaced with American vines purchased from French nurseries; these by then had been cultivated and crossed and generally brought to perfection by the French experts. Simultaneously the Italian Ministry for Agriculture set up vine nurseries that went further ahead in the hybrid field to meet the various Italian conditions more precisely. These ministerial vine centers not only succeeded in containing the Phylloxera pest, but gave the farmers Phylloxera-resistant vines to plant at no charge.

Everything came to a halt during World War I in the agricultural sphere, even the Phylloxera. In 1920 a campaign was started to uproot all old-style vine roots and replace them with American vines; this was done even in areas where the Phylloxera bug had never set foot. By this time the agricultural experts and the enologists were not working in the dark: they knew precisely which hybrids to plant in every case, and the change-over was completed satisfactorily by 1940 with no loss of quality or characteristics in the resulting new wine production.

Italy may not thank France for having passed on these three plagues, but she can at least be grateful for French expertise in the field, which saved Italy from a similar disaster. And, after all, the three plagues could just as well have arrived at Naples on American vines destined for a Neapolitan farmer whose brother had emigrated to the United States.

One curiosity regarding the importance of wine to Italy is that after the great wine "drought" of the 1870s and '80s, France continued buying major quantities of Italian wines. But, slowly, the Algerian production of cutting wines rose, and France herself got in a stronger position in table-wine production by the early years of the 1900s; consequently, the need for Italian imports grew less.

After the Entente Cordiale, in 1904, when fears of war with Germany were rising, it was decided that Italy should be encouraged to break off her participation in the Triple Alliance with Germany and the Austro-Hungarian Empire—an accord signed in 1882 but scarcely remembered by any Italian; certainly it was not a treaty that anybody intended to honor in the extreme case of European war: it is often forgotten that the Austrians held the Alto Adige, much of the Veneto, and Friuli-Venezia Giulia, including Trieste, territories Italy regained during the First World War. The means of pressure against Italy was the cutting off of purchases of wine, and cutting wines in particular. The result was another wave of emigration of southern Italian farmers and farm laborers to the United States and, as we all know, the entry of Italy into the war on the side of the Allies.

The new success in wine making, which started in the last quarter of the nineteenth century both in Italy and in France, produced the need for regulating and controlling the production. In Italy a law was proposed in 1904, but it took till 1963 to get it (or, rather, something better) through both houses of parliament.

The French and the Italian laws are by no means identical. The Italian law,‡ coming later, is stricter and more detailed, but does not delegate as much authority to the controlling commissions. One of the differences, for example, is in the most important issue of yield per hectare. In Italy, let us say eighty quintals per hectare is permitted for a certain wine; if the yield goes 20 per cent above this, the wine is automatically disqualified as DOC. In France, in a land of lower yields, the permitted production is forty quintals per hectare, let us say. However, if during an unusually favorable year eighty or one hundred quintals are produced per hectare, this is not disqualified as AOC unless the controlling commission so decides.

France got its first wine law through in 1905, but it did not serve the purpose. It was updated and made stricter in 1919. In 1927 a few legal loopholes were filled, and finally, in 1935, the law was settled in principle, though continual modifications were added after 1945.

Here again we arrive at the between-war years as those of the first great awareness of wine technology, the era when a reliable wine could be produced year after year from Phylloxera-resistant vines, when plant diseases could be nipped in the bud and farmers finally got around to spraying their vines to prevent mildew and keep off bugs and bacteria. The only real risk to the producer lay in thoroughly miserable weather and a consequently poor crop, as in 1972; but once even a modest crop was in, there was negligible risk of a failed year. Today, even a crop battered by late-summer hail and eaten by insects can be sterilized and restored sufficiently to make a sound, if unimpressive, cheap table wine. Such wines can never bear an AOC, DOC, or VQPRD qualification for a dozen good reasons, but they may be sold locally and, unfortunately, also internationally provided they are given a very broad, generic brand name.

‡ See Appendix B—An Explanation of DOC Legislation.

The era of truly serious wine production on a large scale in all Europe came after World War II. France had her productive structure well settled and only in part destroyed by the war: her defined zones and her legislation were not upset by the new laws passed by the Common Market. Italy, on the other hand, found herself in a series of new circumstances from the highest to the lowest levels. She found herself with a new and large production of fine wines and insufficient outlet until a whole series of structural alterations were made to her economy, internal laws, approved growing areas, and control mechanisms. Only then could Italy enter as a fully fledged wine producer-exporter with all her cards in order. The first matter was agreement on the zones: to date, there are some seventy already approved by the Ministry for Agriculture; a total of around a hundred is likely to be the final figure. The types of wines, characteristics and methods of production, and the raw materials had to be defined. This list of approved wines was something of a surprise, as all sorts of names of wines have popped up that were all but completely unknown outside of their own provinces, though some of them had a great history but had nearly vanished from production: among these, for example, are some Piedmontese wines such as Sizzano, Fara, Boca, Lessona, and Caluso. Equally, there are other controlled zones, which have no history of any importance, whose names are quite unknown and likely to stay that way.

The first effect the law had was to increase the value of the land that had been delimited. Italian farmers in the past, to a great extent, had been in the habit of doing mixed farming, thus giving themselves two or three cash crops as well as growing what they needed for themselves. This mixed farming meant growing, let us say, cabbages between the vines. This practice now is not only severely frowned upon by the authorities, but it is also unrewarding, provided the fine-wine business is successful; in any event, growing cabbages on valuable vine land is not good sense.

Also, the farmers, and wine producers too, did not all necessarily cultivate the vines that were approved. This meant plowing up whole areas and replanting if there was to be a profit from the new zoning laws. An investment of this nature is no small sacrifice: for the farmer it is, say, five years before he sees any return on his investment; for the producer who grows his own grapes and processes them into fine wine, it may be eight, ten, or even fifteen years before he sees anything coming back into the till. He should of course have a capital gain, but that depends on there being a prosperous economic situation, which is difficult to prophesy ten years ahead of time.

It has been a major upheaval, made particularly difficult by an increasing lack and an increasing cost of agricultural labor. The cost of grapes has inevitably risen, but chiefly in the hilly and terraced land, where mechanization is either difficult or impossible; on rolling land, where tractors and pneumatic grape croppers can be used, the price is tending to stay level. However, since the better wines come from "difficult" land, these will tend to become —at least apparently—disproportionately more expensive.

The DOC zoning in Italy will now mean that some 15 per cent of Italian wines are controlled, in comparison with around 25 per cent of France's: DOC (Denominazione di Origine Controllata) is the Italian equivalent of the French "Appellation d'Origine Controlée" (AOC). One of the curious criticisms of Italian wines, which has every aspect of plausibility, is that France has more vineyard acreage (1.2 million hectares, a hectare being about 2½ acres) than Italy (1.1 million hectares), and yet Italy produces more wine. Logically, a large part of Italian wine must be made of chemicals and other fermentable substances, it is wrongly concluded. If you look at the statistics and the permitted crops per hectare, you will find that Italy produces, on the whole, almost twice the quantity of grapes per hectare as France and, in some parts, far and away more than twice as much. This is due to nothing else but a more favorable growing climate. But the best wines tend to come from areas, both in France and Italy, where the crop per hectare is relatively small. Incidentally, both France and Italy have, in the past decade, reduced their vineyard acreage, yet both have increased their gross production through improved yields.

There have been considerable administrative tangles during the course of the Common Market accords. For example, Italy is unhappy about France and Germany using sugar to enhance their wines while this is forbidden by law in Italy. France tends to look askance on Italy, which insists on the right to use irrigation in certain zones where three-month droughts are a commonplace and the vines would dry up and die without the use of sprinklers on summer evenings. Each country ceded the other's point. Germany, particularly, gained all sorts of minor privileges, but nobody has fussed about them, since, basically, German production is very small compared with that of France or Italy and the wines are fairly high-priced and not directly competitive except in the luxury field. Both France and Italy are more interested in having the German market wide open on any reasonable terms for their big production of quality table wines than in quibbling over minor advantages.

The surprising result of the Common Market is that we already have wines with all their characteristics laid down by law according to the European Common Wine Policy. This, to the wine lovers of the past, would not only have seemed impossible, but sacrilege and taking half the fun out of being a connoisseur. However, within tighter limits and particularly with the finer wines, the delights of being an old-style connoisseur are not only possible but perhaps require an even greater discernment, to distinguish between wines that are close cousins. Although the DOC law may be respected, there is still a difference between one winery and another, between a regular wine and the *superiore* and *riserva* made from a choice of the same grapes and aged in the wood and the bottle. The DOC law has done a lot to improve the quality of and standardize wines, but there is still plenty of room for discrimination, good taste, and judgment in a search for the best.

Another of the major structural tasks Italy belatedly faced, in

1970, to conform with Common Market regulations, was to produce a Doomsday Book of every inch of Italy on which a vine grew. Among the first surprises to arise from this was the fact that the enormous quantity of surplus cutting wine believed to be produced in Puglia and Sicily was not by any means as much as was thought, and in fact the French buyers found far less than they needed when they came to Italy to buy instead of acquiring in Algeria, as in the past.

Cutting wines, it should be made clear perhaps, are wines of a high alcoholic content, deep color, and much body. The addition of a small amount of these to a pale and thin northern wine or a second-pressing wine gives the sort of boost that adding sugar will never do. This is not permitted with AOC-DOC wines, but it may be used for the rest. This lack of surplus cutting wines in southern Italy, due possibly to the greater demands of the Turin and Milan vermouth industry and the greater acreage being turned over to table-wine production, may upset the balance of things in Europe, since Algeria has already started plowing in some of her vineyards, neglecting others, and leaving only the best with a view to selling their produce (even to the USSR) as table wines rather than as bulk cutting wines, of which France used to take over 300 million gallons a year and now takes none.

The unending controversy over cutting wines can be told fairly briefly. Italian law has always tried to give economic support to the handicapped South of Italy, even if these efforts so often turn out only to make the North proportionately richer. In all events, the principle stands and, in fact, particularly in the past twenty years, much of southern Italy, Sicily, and Sardinia has progressed and changed beyond recognition. With regard to cutting wines, the law said that the northern wine producers that had a poor crop could not use sugar to increase the alcoholic content of their wine, but must buy cutting wines from the South and could add at most 10 to 15 per cent to their own wines; all this to support the southerners.

The years have passed and the enologists have been improving southern wines until, though this should be said in a whisper, they are often better than the wines they are meant to improve. I recall a season when a certain wine from Lazio was improved out of all recognition, and I learned from my wine seller that this was due to a heavy importation of wines from Sardinia that year. For the record, it should be recalled that the idea of mixing wines for their various advantageous characteristics to produce a specific named wine is common practice throughout Europe. The point about cutting wines, whether from Italy or Algeria, is that they are not produced within the controlled zone of the specific final product and cannot, therefore, be used for DOC-AOC wines. They may only be used for non-controlled wines. It was expected that southern Italy would suffer from all these changes, but it does not seem to have occurred: the Common Market regulations have successfully discouraged France, by the complicated FEOGA tax system, from importing cutting wines from Algeria as long as a similar product is available in Europe, which, in this case, means the "Mezzogiorno" of Italy.

It is northern Italy, no longer permitted to use either cutting wine with its DOC wines or sugar, that has suffered and complains bitterly that in poor years it is at an economic disadvantage vis-à-vis its French rivals, who can use sugar. Northern Italy's way out of the difficulty is a relatively expensive system of boiling down, in vacuum conditions, some of the same grape must as is used for the wine being produced, until it is mostly sugar, and adding it to the wine as it ferments. Logically, particularly since the southern problem has resolved itself, Italy might just as well approve the use of sugar within the limits permitted in France. However, perhaps it is too late. The Common Market has already divided itself up into zones, some of which are permitted chaptalizing privileges, according to the prevailing climate, to produce a satisfactorily alcoholic wine. This classification is instructive: it shows that the natural sugar content is below requirements in northern Europe and increases, going south, till in the Midi of

France and northern and central Italy the optimum is reached, where no chaptalization is needed or permitted.

Since it is not obligatory for French and German producers to put the alcoholic content of their wine on the label, as it is in Italy, perhaps it could be useful to give a rule of thumb on this matter so that the reader can understand better the Common Market zoning which follows.

In Italy, wine that cannot legally reach 10 per cent of alcoholic content would not be bottled except as a sparkling, non-DOC wine: it would be sold locally and cheaply or sent for distillation to make industrial alcohol or vinegar. An 11 per cent wine is a light, young table wine, not considered fit for aging. A 12 per cent wine is fairly robust and, according to the grape from which it comes, could be matured in the cask and the bottle to be a fine wine. Wines of 13 per cent and 14 per cent (except in the South) are essentially from selected grapes and can be considered to have the ideal alcoholic gradation for making a strong, long-lived wine. Wines from 15 per cent to 17 per cent, of which there are few, can be outstanding, but not necessarily better than a 13.5 per cent wine. With normal climatic conditions and with first pressings, these alcoholic quantities are reached naturally in Italy. A poor year may mean a degree less of alcohol.

The Common Market's Zone A, which consists roughly of Luxembourg and all Germany except the Baden area, is considered the chilliest and may chaptalize (i.e., add sugar in liquid form) to the extent of increasing the volume of the wines by 10 per cent for controlled wines and 15 per cent for others. If this enhancement is done by adding concentrated must (the boiled-down wine already mentioned), the added volume may reach only 11 per cent in either case, but by special permission it may reach 15 per cent in poor years. In Germany, specific Italian cutting wines of 12–15 per cent alcohol may be used to the extent of 15 per cent of the total volume to "improve the color of the wine": this, however, only till 1979.

Ordinary table wines must have a natural alcoholic content of

5 per cent and may have this hiked by 3.5–4 per cent by chaptalization and/or the use of cutting wines. VQPRD wines (the Common Market quality-control symbol) must have a basic 6 per cent alcohol. If these do not reach 6 per cent naturally, they may be turned into sparkling wines and chaptalized up to 8.5 per cent. No Italian wine comes into this category of low alcoholic strength: a natural 10 per cent is considered the bottom in Italy; anything less is scarcely considered wine. However, we must remember that all these figures are for minimums. A careful choice of grape, picked at the right moment and then semi-dried, may well give considerably more alcoholic content than the minimum required even in Zone A, though the price of the wine will be high.

Zone B consists of the German Baden area on the French border, Alsace-Lorraine, the Jura, Savoy, the Loire, and the Champagne departments of France, which, winewise, means Champagne, Burgundy, Chablis, and Beaujolais, to mention the more important. Here the Common Market considers that the climatic conditions for wine making are better than those of Germany and permits the addition of dry sugar only, rather than liquid syrup, to enhance the alcoholic content of the wines. If the increase of alcohol is done by adding concentrated must, the volume of the resultant wine may increase by 8 per cent or, in exceptionally miserable years, by 11 per cent. Table wines in this area, however, must start with a basic alcoholic content of 6 per cent which may be hiked to 8.5 per cent; the controlled wines must have a basic 7 per cent and may be increased to 9.5 per cent. But, irrespective of the starting point, no white may be forced above 12 per cent or red above 12.5 per cent.

Zone C.1 is made up of central, central-west and southwest France, which, in practical terms, means the whole range of clarets, Sauternes, and the products of the Cognac and Armagnac areas. In this category, chaptalization is not permitted: the table wines should reach 7 per cent and the controlled wines 8 per cent without artificial help. However, these wines may be enhanced with concentrated must to a maximum of 6.5 per cent of the total volume. This inversion of Bordeaux and Burgundy is a surprise, since most of us think of Burgundy as being a more robust wine, produced under more favorable climatic conditions, than the more subtle claret. Though there are formal limitations on chaptalization of French wines in the Bordeaux Zone, C.1, this practice is broadly permitted when needed.

Zone C.2 covers the Midi of France (with the exception of small areas of the Var, the western Pyrenees, and Corsica, which fall into the next category) and all northern and central Italy, down to Rome. This grouping, in effect, includes Châteauneuf-du-Pape, the Rhône Valley, and the bulk of the best-known Italian wines. Here we find that no sugaring is permitted and that table wines must have a natural minimum alcoholic content of 8 per cent and the controlled wines of 9 per cent. Here it is permitted to increase alcohol by two percentage points by the use of concentrated musts, as long as this does not increase the volume by over 6.5 per cent or bring the alcoholic content to over 13 per cent.

Zone C.3 takes in Corsica, some parts of the western Pyrenees, the Var, and parts of Italy south of Rome, including Sardinia, Sicily, and other islands such as Pantelleria. Here we are dealing with wines of a naturally high alcoholic content, and sugaring is, of course, prohibited, and as far as Italy is concerned, unnecessary. The table wines must have a basic 8.5 per cent and the controlled wines 9.5 per cent alcohol. If concentrated must is added, it may not increase the volume more than 6.5 per cent. The maximum content permissible, when enhancement is used, is 13.5 per cent. Many of the wines of southern Italy by nature go considerably higher. This regulation, therefore, is considered absurd in Italy, but perhaps it is good for the western Pyrenees. An overall rule of thumb is that the producer does not have the right to reach the top alcoholic limit by any and all means: he has only the right to reach the minimum by licit practices.

In the case of southern Italian wines, the problem is not to get them to reach the minimum, but to prevent their going over the top. This is a tricky legal matter, as wines with natural 15–17 per cent alcohol are not recognized as yet as being within the scope of the Common Market arrangements if there is any sugar content still not burned up and turned into alcohol during fermentation; and there are plenty of these sweet, dessert wines. Dessert wines, for the EEC, must have over 17 per cent alcohol, which means either heavy chaptalization or the addition of wine alcohol. Such wines, incidentally, also come into the higher bracket of excise duties for Great Britain and pay as though they were fortified wines such as sherry and port, irrespective of whether they have been fortified. As things stand, the 16 per cent Italian dessert wine—a Tuscan vin santo or a Nasco from Cagliari—cannot be marketed in Europe but must be sold in Italy, since it comes into the EEC category of "wines to be processed into table wines," which is nonsense, since instead of being too weak, it is too strong and, in any case, quite unsuited and too costly for processing into table wine. The correction of this anomaly is said to be under consideration in Brussels.

There is now a fascinating list of qualifications for wines. In Italy there are Simple DOC (controlled name of origin), DOC, and Guaranteed DOC. At the time of writing, the first category is still virgin, and no Italian wine has been included in the last category, though Barolo, Brunello, and Vino Nobile di Montepulciano will be the first; classic Chianti (Chanti classico) should follow. In France there are table wines, Simple VDQS, and the AOC (controlled origin) categories. On top of this, we now have VQPRD (quality wines produced in specific regions), which is the Common Market guarantee of quality rather than zone: this is due to a German legislative quirk. Also of German origin is the new division of wines into three types: wine *tout court,* even if it has only 3 per cent alcohol; wine fit to be processed into table wine, which must have the minimum alcoholic content laid down by law (starting with 5 per cent in Germany, which may be hiked by as much as 100 per cent by licit methods); and finally table wines, which may or may not be of controlled origin. The Italians are horrified at the way the Germans bump up the alcoholic content of their wines, and ironically say that it is not certain if one is drinking wine or sugar-beet syrup. However, rather than make a fuss, they look the other way and pretend it isn't happening.

The average wine drinker and even connoisseurs are finding all this uphill work, but no doubt we shall all learn in due course. But things are likely to get even more complicated with the new official consortiums' decision to stick numbered labels on the bottles to add to the confusion, since they may in many cases (Chianti, for example) double up the already existing labels of the commercial consortiums.

Let me explain: Another of the structural changes required by the new Common Market legislation is that, within each controlled area, the wineries must set up consortiums; in the large areas, there may be many consortiums, each with, say, twenty firms, while in the smaller areas, only a few. However, it is not compulsory for the wineries to be members of a consortium; it is only better that they are. Better in the sense that it demonstrates a greater confidence in the wines they are purveying and their willingness to be inspected by their peers. Each consortium will keep tabs on the technical, qualitative, and quantitative sides of the production of each member and will have the right to elect specialists as "judicial police" with full powers of inspection, sampling, testing, and if necessary, making formal charges of abuse of the zone's practices, which must be heard in a court of law.

The reliability and impartiality of this locally elected enological policeman has been put into some doubt by certain parties, but on the whole the principle seems to be accepted; and since there is a Federation of the Consortiums, there is the possibility of exchanges of policemen so that private interest can be neutralized. However, having a private policeman does not free the consortium members from the risk of the knock on the door from the real government anti-fraud police. And the likelihood of such attentions is much greater for those firms that decide not to join a consortium. In the meantime, the ultimate guarantee of quality comes from the sampling done by the Italian government, when wines are exported, and by foreign governments' sampling, when wines are imported.

Up to now, the requirements of Italian law with regard to the chemical enological data for each specific wine have been modest but sufficient to cover the essential characteristics and purity of the wine. The tests required by the Common Market legislation include analytical and organoleptic checks on color, clarity, sediment, odor, taste, stability (fresh-air and refrigeration tests), microbiological characteristics, density, alcohol content, total dehydrated residue, sugar and ashes content, volatile and fixed acidity, alkalinity, SO_2 content, and, in the case of sparkling wines, either the pressure (presumably in atmospheres) or the quantity of carbon dioxide. This, needless to say, is quite a demand, and even the equipment for doing all these tests is by no means easily available. However, the Italian producers set about meeting this problem, as they have already met all the others.

The main point about all this would seem that, within the limitations and presumably a modest permitted flexibility, VQPRD wines must reach standards that are to all intents and purposes identical—though reached by a variety of methods according to the geographical latitudes of the wineries. And it seems that, by nature, Italian wines are far closer to the Common Market optimums than any others.

What has happened in the past twenty-five years to all that *vin du pays,* that cloudy red wine from Taormina, that acid white from Amalfi, and all the other peasant brews that sometimes were a sheer delight and too often a disaster?

Though you will still find hand-made (and foot-made) wines in the countryside, most of the barrel and demijohn wine you come across will have been produced by one of the seven hundred or so co-operatives that now flourish and make nearly 25 per cent of Italy's total wine production. These co-ops, usually called

cantine sociali, with the help of low-interest loans from the government have grown from being just local suppliers of inexpensive
wines to, in some cases, producing most distinguished ones. Initially they tended to make nameless brews of all the grapes
offered by their member farmers, but, with the passing of the
years, their technical advisers have become more demanding, and
many co-ops are now making DOC wines, sparkling wines, and
even laying down their best vintages. The trend for their future
lies in yet further division of their production into a greater variety
of qualities and types of wine, much in the way of the German
co-operatives, each of which produces a quite remarkably large
number of different wines and engages in several processes. The
demand in Italy for such a *cru* system on a mass level does not
yet exist, but it will grow during the decade.

One distinguished Italian wine writer of recent years has taken
up and propagandized the view that machine-made wine isn't
the real thing; and that, to be chic, you should drive off into the
country on Sunday morning and come back with the car loaded
with flasks—preferably unwashed and amateurishly corked—of
peasant wine that has been made the way nature meant wine to
be made. Large numbers of Italians follow his advice and no
doubt drink cloudy, acid wine and curse his name the while,
noting also that the wine has even managed to pick up an overtone of sump oil during its storage time in the garage. There is
the added risk that the peasant is not the honest John he seems—
and this should surprise nobody. Often, through ignorance and
lack of equipment and of capital, he will use stabilizing methods
that are illegal and harmful.

The price of being fashionable is, at that cost, too high. In any
case, the vast bulk of wine offered throughout Italy is now made
in up-to-date wineries by well-qualified technicians. Of this bulk,
a useful proportion is made inside controlled areas and is of DOC
standard. Though the VQPRD symbol means a guarantee of
quality, the same quality may be offered outside the controlled

zones, and the French also find that the VDQS group sometimes offers equal quality and lower prices.

The VQPRD is, in fact, a symbol guaranteeing the use of a specific grape from a particular area and certain resultant chemical and biological results. That is to say, it is a sort of clean bill of health. But the certificate does not say if the subject is male or female, blond or brunette, tall or short, fat or thin, any more than the VQPRD gives a description of the wine. It can be red or white—but not blue!

The VQPRD can be considered also as a sort of pedigree certificate that covers a wide variety of beasts, let us say from horses to bulls to dogs. Though each of these animals can be pronounced in perfect health, it is difficult to judge which is better, an Angus bull or a King Charles Spaniel. In wine terms, it is difficult to compare a dark-red 17 per cent tarry dry wine from the Sardinian mountains with a delicate Rhine wine of low alcoholic content. This is, of course, taking the matter to extremes, but the Buxbaum rules for evaluating wines do break down as those of Cruft's would if, instead of dogs, you had to judge horses with them.

The Buxbaum rules are as follows: two points for clarity, two for color, four for bouquet, and twelve for taste. Thus, twenty out of twenty means perfection. However, even the Office International du Vin has concluded that the system of judging prize bulls and racehorses together and by the same rules does not make sense and has proposed that wines be divided into categories, since it is equally unreasonable to judge a Bardolino and a Barolo by the same standards as it is to judge a Beaujolais and a Lafite-Rothschild. To date, neither the categories nor the names of the wines to go into the categories have been announced; and since this is an invidious task on an official level, certain to arouse rancor, complaints, and bitterness as well as suits for defamation . . . it is unlikely ever to occur. This writer, on the other hand, is beholden to nobody and can go out on a limb just as far as he wishes and make a few comparative statements about wines.

First, collectors' wines. For Italy, the best long-lived wines are Barolo, Gattinara, reserve Chianti, Brunello, Vino Nobile of Montepulciano, Venegazzù, Barbaresco, and perhaps a Cirò from Calabria: these should be treated much as you would a good claret. However, you will find a strong tendency for the Italian producer to hang onto his fine vintages and leave them for more years in the cask before bottling and marketing them, in contradistinction to the Frenchman, who prefers to bottle early and invites the connoisseur to mature the wine in the cellar himself. The main reason for this is that the French use small, two-hundred-liter barrels which mature the wine more quickly than the Italian three- to five-thousand-liter casks. Later bottling has the advantage that there is less sediment, since it will have largely precipitated in the barrel: Italians do not like sediment.

Few white wines have a reputation for aging really well. Noted in this category are the Sauternes of France and, in Italy, a good Vernaccia from Oristano, a Pinot Grigio or Traminer from the Trentino or Friuli, or even a Roman "Fiorano" are the best bets; and such little-known joys as the Greco di Tufo, from Avellino, or the 16 per cent Greco di Gerace, from Calabria. However, the bad name white wines have for aging I have discovered to be not well founded, though I have equally believed it. Certainly only white wines made from certain grapes age well, but there are quite a number of these; these wines will age well, however, only if they are specially selected and given the most loving care. In these circumstances, even the homely Trebbiano will live fifteen years to acquire an unexpected elegance. And I think that, with the new sterile, air-free system of processing and bottling, we will find that a lot of whites are aging as they never have in the past.

The making of comparisons is almost impossible but must be done, even if with reservations. When one says, for example, a Barbera di Alba, one has in mind a superior wine produced by one of the better wineries and aged in the wood and in the bottle. The reader might well have found a similarly named product in the supermarket, and pronounce me a fool. I propose, therefore, to make a list not only of the DOC and other noted wines of Italy, giving a description of each, but also—and this, to me, seems of vital importance, just as much as it is to know the names of the châteaux or négociants from which French wines come—a select list of the producers that have a first-class reputation, and to mention trade name, cru, or other indication they use that may help the reader to make a swift and sure recognition of the recommended house and its wine.

Buying what the French call estate-bottled or château-bottled wine of repute is the surest way of getting good wine. Wine bottled elsewhere justly arouses all sorts of doubts. Only, I think, the British wine trade, which has bottled French wines for generations, has succeeded in maintaining a reputation for sea-green incorruptibility. In fact, there is no obstacle in most non-wine-producing countries to importing wine and bottling it and calling it what you like. You can, no doubt, quite legally import Chilean wine into Canada and bottle it as Château Frontenac, and you can equally import Moroccan wine into Belgium and call it Cru Tokay or Château Ypres. It is only when you start calling it Premier Cru Pinot or Château Yquem that a sharp-eyed French lawyer will knock at your door. Only recently has Italy aroused itself from its Rip Van Winkle lethargy to sue those who have been for years marketing Lake Garda Bardolino, Valpolicella Extra, Michelangelo's Chianti, and suchlike brand names made from the cheapest wines available in Spain, Greece, and Algeria, which have been doing untold damage to Italy's reputation as well as robbing her of a major export market in the Benelux countries.

This list, therefore, will prevent the reader's being led astray by such jokers and lead them to the labels that are reliable. Such a list, to the best of my knowledge, has never been compiled by any writer, and only the Bolaffi book on European wines has an Italian list, but a very limited one. It seems to me that this lack of

advice, of knowing where to turn, has been the cause of many
disappointments for those who, with all the goodwill in the world,
have searched for Italian fine wines.

I told a senior functionary who was involved in the marketing
of Italian wines abroad that I proposed to make such a list, and he
profoundly recommended that I do nothing of the sort. "Why go
out on a limb?" he asked. "Who makes you? The firm may go
broke; the owner may die and it may fall into the hands of
scoundrels. Where is your reputation then?" A fair argument,
but not a decisive one, since my reputation can be more harmed
by the reader's buying what comes to hand as Italian wine rather
than following my list, which carries a far lesser risk of disappointment.

The structure of the wine trade in Italy is not the same as in
France. Négociants in the traditional French sense do not exist
in Italy; there are several very large firms that buy wine, process
it, and bottle it under their famous names. They are looked on
askance by connoisseurs in Italy, but they usually save their
reputations by maintaining one or two lines of top-quality wine.
In the past, they often did not even own an acre of land; nowadays
they have mostly bought themselves a vineyard to show off to
visiting firemen even though it would not make up 1 per cent or
even .1 per cent of their total sales. In Italy, only the producer
who grows his own grapes, makes his own wine, bottles it, and
puts it on the market, gains full respect. Such men are personally
involved, even psychologically, with their product: if you like their
wine, it is a personal compliment; they might even blush with
pleasure.

Then there are the co-operatives, which vary widely in their
standards: some, like the CAVIT, of Trento, are most distinguished. Here one should worry chiefly if the price is too low;
and often the price they ask is too low for good wine.

The producers usually put aside their best grapes for making a
red for aging; their second-best for their regular table wine, though
they might first make a little rosé with their second-best. With

their best white, they make a vintage-dated white and, with the poorer grapes, perhaps a hot-bottled wine for local consumption. The truth is that all these can get into the Common Market controlled category: even the last mentioned, provided it has enough alcohol. The wine lover therefore should look for *cru* names, *superiore, riserva, vecchio,* and other guarantees when he is after the flower of a vintage, as these will give him far greater security.

Returning to the invidious task of comparisons, the immediate question is, Which Italian wine is most like a French wine, or With which Italian wine would the Frenchman feel most at home? The answer, according to the Frenchman's imports, is that he gets along very well with Valpolicella, an admirable, smooth, well-balanced red wine from near Verona. But Valpolicella is by no means a prime example of Italian wine. One of the greatest pleasures of discovering Italian wines is to discover their variety: from the moors of Piedmont and the valleys of the Alps to the torrid vineyards of Sicily and Sardinia, they come in over a hundred distinct types and a thousand variations. France, over the decades, has stabilized how she considers good wines should taste, and these are produced, unlike in Italy, in a climate that, with the exception of the Midi, the land of Châteauneuf-du-Pape, is much the same. Italian wines are not commensurable with French wines except in a few cases. It is perhaps rather like comparing Périgord and Umbrian black truffles with Alba and Acqualunga white truffles. The enthusiasts for the black denigrate the white as too masculine and overwhelming, while those who—like myself—consider that the white Alba truffle is among the greatest gifts of God, enjoy a black truffle but do not rate it very high.

However, I wish to persuade nobody on this point, as white truffles already cost over sixty dollars a pound around Christmas, and any further competition for the modest quantities put on sale would not be welcome; and so with Italian wine: I hope that the best will not all be exported and the prices go beyond my reach.

The only real means of comparison is to say that in Italy one drinks X wine with roast chicken as one would drink Y wine in France.

From the Italian viewpoint, the finest wines are taken with four-legged game such as venison, chamois, or wild boar; this includes all the previously mentioned long-lived wines: the Barolos, Gattinaras, Brunellos, the austere Chiantis. The next category, in the Italian view, is of wines suited for drinking with game birds or perhaps a jugged hare; this includes Nebbiolo, Barbaresco, Lessona, Sizzano, Grignolino, Ghemme, from Piedmont; Inferno, Sassella, and Grumello, from the Valtelline; the Vino Nobile of Montepulciano, from near Siena, and perhaps the Taurasi, from Avellino.

Next in order come the wines for roasts. Here again we require a strong, well-matured wine that is both elegant and full of character; we could include a Tuscan Nipozzano or Uzzano, a Dolcetto from Piedmont, a Merlot from Venezia Giulia, a Donnaz from the Aosta Valley, a Boca, Fara, or Barbera or a fine Black Pinot from the South Tyrol. The choice is munificent and the list incomplete. And since age is of the essence of this type of wine, one must always remember that, at a certain point, a well-aged Barbaresco or Black Pinot will be a more formidable wine than a youngish Barolo or Chianti.

This is an Italian view of usage. It requires that the person who tries the comparison with similar French usage choose wines of a similar vintage and of equally high quality. It requires also that the wines be treated with similiar courtesy; that is to say, one should not come from a shop window where it has been burned by the sun and shaken by the traffic while the other has been cradled in a silent and cool cellar. Wine tasting is not golf: there is no handicap system.

One profound divergence of opinion between English and Italian gourmets and wine lovers arises: it is that the former's preferred menu to accompany their best wine, inevitably French, has as its main course a saddle of mutton and Worthing beans. The Italian, at this point, throws up his hands, pronouncing obscure epithets and expressing the view that the only drink fit to marry with a saddle of mutton is Scotch whisky, which he likes, but in this specific context he looks on it as a first-class anaesthetic to the taste of roast mutton. To the Italian, the finest wines require a roast, but preferably a wild boar or a pheasant; in all events, something more noble than the lowly sheep, which, in Italy, is eaten only very young and looked upon with horror as food, once fully grown.

CHAPTER THREE
On Choosing Italian Wines

In the choosing of wines, the vintage is an important consideration. But the bulk of wines are, after a winter in the cask, ready to be drunk; and this is precisely what happens to them. Some of the whites improve with a few years' nursing, first a while in the cask and then in the bottle. A larger number of reds enjoy a longer life span, of, say, five to ten years, after which they, like the whites, fade away: these are usually the superiore or riserva wines. Only the noblest of reds and whites last a decade or more. It is, therefore, essential to know into which category the wines fall and how long they are likely to last so you drink them in good time if they belong to you or avoid them, if too old, when offered on a wine list.

Within the limits of the expectation of life of a wine, I think there is a far less notably erratic graph of quality than there was a few decades ago. Certainly in France and Germany a sunless summer can produce a sad crop, but the other and more customary risks, such as bugs and mildew, are now things of the past; mildew used to taint wine so consistently that an Irish wit invented a new wine, Château Mildew, and even acquired a taste for it.

I think that dud years are now almost non-existent in comparison with the 1880s and 1890s, when they were almost the rule rather than the exception. And, as I said earlier, once even a modest harvest is in, technology can save it, whereas previously it still had many risks ahead. Therefore, vintage charts should be viewed as a recommendation on the especially favorable years rather than a warning against the duds. Let us say that the curves of the vintage graph nowadays are much smoother than in the past and are likely to level out even more. In Italy the climate is more reliable than in France and Germany, and the vintage years are less important, but only relatively. There have been exceptional years recently, such as 1947, 1952, 1961, and 1971, and these are the ones that have mostly been laid down for longer maturing. But in Italy, as in France, "exceptional years" do not necessarily mean that the year is exceptional for all wines. The year 1947, for example, was a good year for Piedmontese Barolo, but the Alto Adige wines were not of the best. In truth, the value of vintage charts in any country can be easily vitiated by bad weather coming during the harvest; i.e., the first part of the crop might be exceptional and the second half second-rate, having been damaged by rain and hail. The classic example of this was the 1964 Bordeaux vintage.

Here follows an Italian vintage chart made up by Marco Trimani of Rome:

The producer of fine wines usually markets a vintage with which he is not satisfied as a prêt-à-porter wine; that is, a wine for immediate consumption. Sometimes this decision can be taken immediately, when the producer sees the grapes; sometimes he allows the wine to rest in vats all winter before reaching his decision. He stocks away only the fine years and puts them on the market when brought to optimum condition through years in the cask and as much as they need in the bottle. Finding that a wine is improving well in the barrel, he keeps it there, racking it once a year. This moment of racking—and perhaps filtering—is the moment when an old wine can die of exposure and bronchitis, just like a human being, if exposed to cold air and harsh treatment. It is much for this reason that the Italian producers prefer to do the aging of their wines themselves, trusting their own experts and distrusting the technical ability of the amateur wine lover to carry out these difficult tasks of racking a barrel or changing a cork, because of his lack of machinery and skill. This also explains why, say, a seven-year-old Barolo has little or no sediment: it has already precipitated in the barrel.

Italy is often criticized for not having the cru system: but you will find that producers, if cornered, will admit that their reserve wine comes from a special hillside that gets the most sun and has the best soil. The cru system exists, but Italian producers are just not forthcoming in publicizing the fact.

In fine, Italian vintages are of relative import only, for the very good reason that only the better years and the best crus are chosen for aging; that is to say, the old wines available are inevitably good years and you are consequently saved the trouble of remembering the whole vintage chart. You also are relieved of the risk of the wine not aging well: when you buy it, it has already aged well.

In fact, the chart is interesting, but no more than interesting, because in great part it is nonsense. In many cases, either there is none of the wine available (even if it is still good) or it has long lapsed from being of drinkable quality. In concrete terms, a twenty-five-year-old Frascati white is a contradiction in terms: to know that 1946 was a good year is information of no practical use. Frascati is essentially a young wine and therein lies its charm. If there exists a 1946 Frascati, it is a miracle; at the most, a twelve-year-old bottle might still be around, though it would not necessarily be any better for not having been drunk earlier. Most of it is hot-bottled nowadays anyhow, which makes nonsense of any vintage years for Frascati. At the same time, it is not useful to know that 1970 was a fine year for Brunello, since it won't

ITALIAN VINTAGE YEARS*

VINO	'45	'46	'47	'49	'50	'51	'52	'53	'54	'55	'56	'57	'5
Albana	6	8	6	10	8	4	8	8	6	2	10	10	
Barbacarlo	6	4	8	6	4	6	8	6	4	8	6	6	1
Barbaresco	8	6	6	4	6	8	8	2	4	6	4	8	
Barbera d'Asti	6	6	8	4	8	4	2	6	6	8	2	6	1
Barbera d'Alba	6	4	8	4	6	6	6	2	4	8	4	6	
Bardolino	6	6	8	6	7	6	6	6	4	4	6	10	
Barolo	8	6	10	4	6	8	8	2	6	6	4	8	1
Boca	8	4	10	6	8	2	2	4	6	6	8	2	
Bonarda dell'Oltrepo	6	4	8	4	6	6	8	6	4	8	6	6	1
Botticino	6	6	8	6	8	4	6	4	6	4	4	6	
Brunello di Montalcino	10	8	9	7	9	8	8	5	6	10	6	8	
Cabernet Trentino	4	6	10	10	4	4	6	2	6	4	4	8	
Caldaro o Lago di Caldaro	2	4	4	10	4	2	10	4	8	4	2	4	
Capri	6	6	8	4	8	4	4	10	4	8	6	6	
Castel del Monte	4	6	4	4	4	10	4	8	4	2	6	6	
Cellatica	6	6	6	6	6	4	6	4	6	4	4	6	
Chianti	8	6	6	6	6	8	6	6	8	8	6	6	
Chianti Classico	6	4	8	8	6	2	8	4	4	8	4	8	
Cirò	6	2	6	6	6	6	2	2	6	4	6	6	
Clastidio	8	4	6	6	6	6	10	6	6	6	4	6	
Cortese di Gavi	7	8	6	2	4	2	10	4	6	8	4	4	1
Dolcetto della Langhe	6	4	8	4	8	8	6	2	4	8	4	6	
Franciacorta	7	8	6	6	6	4	6	4	6	4	4	6	
Frascati	8	10	4	6	6	4	6	4	6	4	4	6	
Frecciarossa Rosso	8	6	10	4	4	2	4	2	2	8	8	6	
Freisa d'Asti	10	4	8	6	4	4	8	2	8	6	6	4	
Gattinara	8	8	6	6	8	2	10	4	6	8	4	6	
Ghemme	4	2	10	2	2	4	8	2	2	4	8	8	
Grignolino	6	4	8	4	6	6	6	2	8	8	4	6	
Inferno	6	4	10	4	4	4	10	2	8	4	4	8	
Lagrein	2	4	4	10	4	2	10	4	8	4	2	4	
Lambrusco di Sorbara	4	4	6	4	4	6	8	4	4	6	2	4	
Lugana	6	6	4	6	8	4	6	4	8	2	4	8	
Marzemino	4	6	10	6	2	2	10	2	6	2	2	8	
Merlot Trentino	4	6	10	6	2	2	6	2	6	2	2	8	
Montepulciano d'Abruzzo	4	4	4	4	4	4	4	4	4	2	8	8	1
Montecarlo Bianco	5	5	10	6	2	6	5	4	8	10	6	6	
Moscato Naturale d'Asti	6	6	6	4	6	4	4	6	6	8	4	6	
Pinot d'Oltrepò	6	4	10	6	6	6	8	4	4	8	4	6	1
Soave	2	6	4	4	4	4	8	6	6	6	4	8	
Teroldego	4	6	6	6	2	2	6	2	6	2	2	8	
Torgiano Rosso	6	2	4	4	4	4	6	8	6	4	8	4	
Valpolicella	6	8	6	6	6	4	8	8	4	8	6	8	
Verdicchio di Jesi	6	6	8	6	6	6	4	6	8	8	6	6	1
Vernaccia di S. Gimignano	6	6	7	6	6	6	5	6	8	8	6	6	
Vino Nobile Montepulciano	6	4	8	6	4	6	8	4	8	4	4	6	1

* The 1972 figures have not been included, not because this was a poor year on the whole in many parts of Europe, but because they are not re-

LEGEND:

10 = Exceptional 6 = Good
8 = Excellent 4 = Average

'59	'60	'61	'62	'63	'64	'65	'66	'67	'68	'69	'70	'71	VINO
6	4	10	4	4	6	6	8	6	8	4	10	8	Albana
2	4	8	10	2	10	4	4	6	6	10	8	8	Barbacarlo
2	2	8	8	2	10	6	2	6	6	6	10	10	Barbaresco
2	4	10	6	2	8	2	2	6	4	6	6	6	Barbera d'Asti
2	2	8	6	2	8	4	4	8	6	6	6	8	Barbera d'Alba
2	2	4	2	10	8	4	6	8	6	10	6	8	Bardolino
6	6	10	8	4	10	8	6	8	6	6	8	10	Barolo
8	2	10	8	2	8	2	2	2	2	8	8	8	Boca
2	4	8	8	4	6	4	6	6	6	6	8	8	Bonarda dell'Oltrepo
4	6	4	2	4	6	2	4	4	4	6	8	6	Botticino
8	6	10	7	5	10	6	8	8	6	4	10	—	Brunello di Montalcino
0	2	6	4	6	10	2	6	6	4	10	10	8	Cabernet Trentino
8	4	8	6	6	2	8	4	6	8	10	6	6	Caldaro o Lago di Caldaro
2	10	10	2	4	8	4	6	4	10	4	8	8	Capri
2	6	6	4	4	4	10	8	6	10	6	6	6	Castel del Monte
4	6	6	4	6	8	2	4	4	4	6	6	6	Cellatica
4	4	4	8	2	6	4	6	6	6	6	8	8	Chianti
2	2	4	8	2	8	6	6	8	8	8	8	10	Chianti Classico
2	8	8	4	8	4	6	6	6	10	2	6	6	Cirò
4	6	8	6	6	10	8	6	6	8	8	10	10	Clastidio
6	8	10	6	4	10	4	4	4	2	4	6	6	Cortese di Gavi
2	2	8	8	2	8	6	4	4	4	2	6	8	Dolcetto della Langhe
4	6	6	4	6	8	2	4	4	4	6	8	8	Franciacorta
4	6	8	10	2	6	4	6	6	8	6	8	8	Frascati
4	8	10	10	6	10	6	6	10	8	10	10	8	Frecciarossa Rosso
4	2	10	4	6	8	4	2	6	4	4	8	6	Freisa d'Asti
4	4	8	6	2	10	6	4	6	8	8	8	8	Gattinara
2	2	6	8	2	8	2	2	6	4	6	8	8	Ghemme
2	2	8	4	2	6	4	4	4	4	6	8	8	Grignolino
8	2	8	4	4	10	2	4	6	4	8	8	8	Inferno
8	4	6	4	4	6	4	6	6	8	10	8	6	Lagrein
4	4	10	2	6	2	4	2	4	6	6	8	10	Lambrusco di Sorbara
4	6	6	4	4	8	4	4	4	4	8	6	6	Lugana
0	2	8	6	2	8	2	6	6	4	10	8	8	Marzemino
0	2	8	6	2	8	2	6	6	4	10	6	8	Merlot Trentino
6	6	6	6	8	2	8	6	6	10	2	8	8	Montepulciano d'Abruzzo
6	2	10	8	2	8	4	8	6	4	8	8	8	Montecarlo Bianco
4	6	6	4	2	6	4	4	4	2	4	8	8	Moscato Naturale d'Asti
2	4	8	10	4	8	6	6	8	6	6	10	8	Pinot d'Oltrepò
4	4	8	6	8	6	8	10	8	6	10	8	8	Soave
0	2	8	6	2	10	2	6	6	4	10	6	8	Teroldego
4	4	2	8	8	6	6	10	8	10	8	10	10	Torgiano Rosso
6	4	8	8	4	8	4	6	8	6	8	8	8	Valpolicella
2	8	8	6	4	4	6	2	4	6	4	8	8	Verdicchio di Jesi
6	8	6	10	2	8	10	8	6	6	6	8	10	Vernaccia di S. Gimignano
2	4	6	8	2	8	2	6	10	8	6	10	10	Vino Nobile Montepulciano

liable, since many first prognostications have turned out to have been exaggerated as the wine passes its first winter.

be on sale for another six years and producers recommend another ten years in the bottle before broaching.

But who will say, categorically, how long the various wines last? The answer is, Nobody. You will get a variety of answers such as: As long as you like, Depends on the year, Depends on the cellar, the acidity, the processing, Depends on the alcoholic content, Depends on the aftercare. It is all rather like asking how long is a piece of string. It is doubtful even if anyone will give you an optimum period for any specific wine's condition, though this should be easier, for even this is difficult and depends on the ambient conditions in which the wine lives and many other factors, in which luck also plays its part.

How, then, can we get onto firm ground? Marco Trimani is of the seventh generation of wine merchants in Rome and has remarkable experience. His cellars include the best wines from all over Italy (let the canard finish that in Italy you can only find the wines of the immediate region: not only does Trimani have a magnificent selection of the world's wines, but in all the cities of Italy nowadays you can find a very wide selection of Italian and French wines). To continue, one might risk saying that what Trimani has not got is either not worth having or produced in minimal, non-commercial quantities, though he is always searching out new wines from producers worthy of note. He takes the view, as does this writer, that wines should not be pushed to the limits of age before being drunk: almost all fine wines reach their peak of maturity in their first decade of life.

But let us look at the wine chart again and see what vintages he still had available in 1972 and conclude that either he or the producers had considered that earlier years either were all consumed or were no longer valid as table wines.

Here, then, is the chart again; this is a pragmatism that can produce howls of disagreement from those who have secret stores or supplies of vintage wines. But since they are not likely to be putting these on the market, it is of purely abstract interest that, let us say, fifty years ago there was a wonderful year for Black

Pinot from the South Tyrol. We are not aiming to drink academic enological theory; we are aiming to drink wine. I think that this pragmatic view could be considered equally valid for other wine-producing countries of the world. "Abstract" enological theory, of course, becomes fascinating when you do lay hands on an old and rare bottle.

This pragmatic view is a de facto view looking backward at what is today available. Many of the years struck out do not mean that a wine does not age more than shown, but rather that there is none left. Looking to the future and the laying down of wines, the range is much broader and the first chart again becomes valid as a guide to buying. Since the chart is not by any means complete, the notes about wines which follow will also help in counseling for laying down for the future. A useful rule of thumb is that a wine considered worthy of being aged in the barrel for, say, two or three years is going to be equally worthy of being aged in the bottle. Here, then, is the up-dated chart:

The chief conclusion to be drawn from the charts is that we have six major areas that produce long-lived wines: Piedmont and Tuscany, the Valtelline, the South Tyrol, and the small zones of Brunello and Montepulciano; there are several other, minor areas dispersed throughout Italy.

It is as important to know the price of wine as its characteristics; and also to know how a wine increases in price with aging. Up to mid-1972, this was easy. Since then, the market for fine wines, which was traditionally slow and unimpressive, has changed and, like the world's currencies, is fluctuating, and for much the same reasons. However, let us first look at what it was like before this new fluid money and wine market arose.

The Barolo, which is a magnificent wine for aging, surprisingly did not rise much in price with the passing of the decades; on the Rome market, a 1949 Barolo sold for less than ten dollars and a 1937 for only twenty dollars. At five years of age, when put on sale, it cost as much as a fine French wine of similar age. Barbaresco equally started with a relatively high price, but did not

ITALIAN VINTAGE YEARS

VINO	'45	'46	'47	'49	'50	'51	'52	'53	'54	'55	'56	'57
Albana	6	8	6	10	8	4	8	8	6	2	10	10
Barbacarlo	6	4	8	6	4	6	8	6	4	8	6	6
Barbaresco	8	6	6	4	6	8	8	2	4	6	4	8
Barbera d'Asti	6	6	8	4	8	4	2	6	6	8	2	6
Barbera d'Alba	6	4	8	4	6	6	6	2	4	8	4	6
Bardolino	6	6	8	6	7	6	6	6	4	4	10	
Barolo	8	6	10	4	6	8	8	2	6	6	4	8
Boca	8	4	10	6	8	2	2	4	6	6	8	2
Bonarda dell'Oltrepo	6	4	8	4	6	6	8	6	4	8	6	6
Botticino	6	6	8	6	8	4	6	4	6	4	4	6
Brunello di Montalcino	10	8	9	7	9	8	8	5	6	10	6	8
Cabernet Trentino	4	6	10	10	4	4	6	2	6	4	4	8
Caldaro o Lago di Caldaro	2	4	4	10	4	2	10	4	8	4	2	4
Capri	6	6	8	4	8	4	4	10	4	8	6	6
Castel del Monte	4	6	4	4	4	10	4	8	4	2	6	6
Cellatica	6	6	6	6	6	4	6	4	6	4	4	6
Chianti	8	6	6	6	6	8	6	6	8	8	6	6
Chianti Classico	6	4	8	8	6	2	8	4	4	8	4	8
Cirò	6	2	6	6	6	6	2	2	6	4	6	6
Clastidio	8	4	6	6	6	6	10	6	6	6	4	6
Cortese di Gavi	7	8	6	2	4	2	10	4	6	8	4	4
Dolcetto della Langhe	6	4	8	4	8	6	6	2	4	8	4	6
Franciacorta	7	8	6	6	4	4	4	6	4	4	6	
Frascati	8	10	4	6	6	4	6	4	6	4	4	6
Frecciarossa Rosso	8	6	10	4	4	2	4	2	2	8	8	6
Freisa d'Asti	10	4	8	6	4	4	8	2	8	6	6	4
Gattinara	8	8	6	6	8	2	10	4	6	8	4	6
Ghemme	4	2	10	2	2	4	8	2	2	4	8	8
Grignolino	6	4	8	4	6	6	2	8	8	4	4	6
Inferno	6	4	10	4	4	4	10	2	8	4	4	6
Lagrein	2	4	4	10	4	2	10	4	8	4	2	4
Lambrusco di Sorbara	4	4	6	4	4	6	8	4	4	6	2	4
Lugana	6	6	4	6	8	4	6	4	8	2	4	8
Marzemino	4	6	10	6	2	2	10	2	6	2	2	8
Merlot Trentino	4	6	10	6	2	2	6	2	6	2	2	8
Montepulciano d'Abruzzo	4	4	4	4	4	4	4	4	4	2	8	8
Montecarlo Bianco	5	5	10	6	2	6	5	4	8	10	6	6
Moscato Naturale d'Asti	6	6	6	4	6	4	4	6	6	8	4	6
Pinot d'Oltrepò	6	4	10	6	6	6	8	4	4	8	4	6
Soave	2	6	4	4	4	4	8	6	6	6	4	8
Teroldego	4	6	6	6	2	2	6	2	6	2	2	8
Torgiano Rosso	6	2	4	4	4	4	6	8	6	4	8	4
Valpolicella	6	8	6	6	6	4	8	6	4	8	6	8
Verdicchio di Jesi	6	6	8	6	6	6	4	6	8	8	6	6
Vernaccia di S. Gimignano	6	6	7	6	6	6	5	6	8	8	6	6
Vino Nobile Montepulciano	6	4	8	6	4	6	8	4	8	4	4	6

59	'60	'61	'62	'63	'64	'65	'66	'67	'68	'69	'70	'71	VINO
6	4	10	4	4	6	6	8	6	8	4	10	8	Albana
2	4	8	10	2	10	4	4	6	6	10	8	8	Barbacarlo
2	2	8	8	2	10	6	2	6	6	6	10	10	Barbaresco
2	4	10	6	2	8	2	2	6	4	6	6	6	Barbera d'Asti
2	2	8	6	2	8	4	4	8	6	6	6	8	Barbera d'Alba
2	2	4	2	10	8	4	6	8	6	10	6	8	Bardolino
6	6	10	8	4	10	8	6	8	6	6	8	10	Barolo
8	2	10	8	2	8	2	2	2	2	8	8	8	Boca
2	4	8	8	4	6	4	6	6	6	6	8	8	Bonarda dell'Oltrepo
4	6	4	2	4	6	2	4	4	4	6	8	6	Botticino
8	6	10	7	5	10	6	8	8	6	4	10	—	Brunello di Montalcino
8	2	6	4	6	10	2	6	6	4	10	10	8	Cabernet Trentino
8	4	8	6	6	2	8	4	6	8	10	6	6	Caldaro o Lago di Caldaro
2	10	10	2	4	8	4	6	4	10	4	8	8	Capri
2	6	6	4	4	4	10	8	6	10	8	6	6	Castel del Monte
4	6	6	4	6	8	2	4	4	4	6	6	6	Cellatica
4	4	4	8	2	6	4	4	6	6	6	8	8	Chianti
2	2	4	8	2	8	6	6	8	8	8	8	10	Chianti Classico
2	8	8	4	8	4	6	6	6	10	2	6	6	Cirò
4	6	8	6	6	10	8	6	6	8	8	10	10	Clastidio
6	8	10	6	4	10	4	4	4	2	4	6	6	Cortese di Gavi
2	2	8	8	2	8	6	4	4	4	2	6	8	Dolcetto della Langhe
4	6	6	4	6	8	2	4	4	4	6	8	8	Franciacorta
4	6	8	10	2	6	4	6	6	8	6	8	8	Frascati
4	8	10	10	6	10	6	6	10	8	10	10	8	Frecciarossa Rosso
2	10	4	6	8	4	2	6	4	4	8	6		Freisa d'Asti
4	4	8	6	2	10	6	4	6	8	8	8	8	Gattinara
2	2	6	8	2	8	2	2	6	4	6	8	8	Ghemme
2	2	8	4	2	6	4	4	4	4	6	8	8	Grignolino
8	2	8	4	4	10	2	4	6	4	8	8	8	Inferno
8	4	6	4	4	6	4	6	6	8	10	8	6	Lagrein
4	4	10	2	6	2	4	2	4	6	6	8	10	Lambrusco di Sorbara
4	6	6	4	4	8	4	4	4	8	6	6		Lugana
8	2	8	6	2	8	2	6	6	4	10	8	8	Marzemino
8	2	8	6	2	8	2	6	6	4	10	6	8	Merlot Trentino
6	6	6	6	8	2	8	6	6	10	2	8	8	Montepulciano d'Abruzzo
6	2	10	8	2	8	4	8	6	4	8	8	8	Montecarlo Bianco
4	6	6	4	2	6	4	4	4	2	4	8	8	Moscato Naturale d'Asti
2	4	8	10	4	8	6	6	8	6	6	10	8	Pinot d'Oltrepò
4	4	8	6	8	6	8	10	8	6	10	8	8	Soave
8	2	8	6	2	10	2	6	6	4	10	6	8	Teroldego
4	4	2	8	8	6	6	10	8	10	8	10	10	Torgiano Rosso
6	4	8	4	4	6	8	6	8	8	8	8		Valpolicella
2	8	8	6	4	4	6	2	4	6	4	8	8	Verdicchio di Jesi
6	8	6	10	2	8	10	8	6	6	8	10	8	Vernaccia di S. Gimignano
2	4	6	8	2	8	2	6	10	8	6	10	10	Vino Nobile Montepulciano

appreciate much with the years. Reserve Chianti, however, would seem to have had a greater demand: a 1961 (eleven years old) cost three dollars, a 1943 cost twenty dollars, and a 1934, fifty dollars. The Vino Nobile and the Gattinara kept modest prices, while the Brunello behaved more like a French wine; though the rising graph began at much the same point, the sharp upturn came later. A 1964 cost around seven-fifty, a 1955 leaped to over thirty dollars; then, the curve ran up to one hundred twenty dollars for a 1945, one hundred eighty dollars for a 1920, and four hundred dollars for an 1891. Already the world had woken up to Brunello, and to Biondi Santi's Brunello in particular.

The prices asked for well-matured fine vintages of lesser known wines were so low that they could not pay for the time and trouble taken; they could only have been a labor of love on the part of the producer, and if there was any commercial intent, at best it was prestige publicity. For example, a Torgiano Rubesco 1964 for one dollar or a Cirò 1964 at the same price, while a Chianti of the same year was only earning two dollars. Such derisory prices were, I am sure, purely abstract ones: nobody, and certainly no cost accountant, had investigated the real cost of laying down a wine for three or more years and then keeping it in a bottle for two more before marketing it.

Except for the Brunello, there had not been much economic pressure of demand and consequent shortage to make laying down stocks for the distant future a tempting or lucrative enterprise, either for the producer or for the amateur. The Italian producer only faced tying up capital and accepting all the risks of his wine oxidizing in exchange for very little, while his costs were as high as his French colleagues', who had a lively market. At the same time, the wine lover could always find matured wines at his wine store at inexpensive prices without the trouble of laying them down in his cellar. However, with the sharp rise in the price of fine French wines of recent years, many farsighted amateurs in Italy began to buy for the future.

In the year 1972–73 several important factors have altered the Italian domestic wine market. First, the amateurs have grown vastly in number and have been buying much more, and more expertly. Secondly, the poor crop of 1972, the devaluation of the Italian lira, and generally rising prices, have aroused them—and perhaps speculators too—to buy more heavily in the wine market, confident of an increase in wine prices and a good investment. The result has been that the modest stocks in the cellars of the dealers have been depleted and prices have, in fact, risen. Prices for matured wines have risen from 15 per cent to 25 per cent according to provenance and age, but no clear pattern as yet can be seen: nobody would put out a handsomely printed price list of Italian wines any more than anybody would carve in marble today's going rate for an ounce of gold. However, this 15–25 per cent rise, after years of no increases at all and with the general sharp rise in costs and wages in Italy, is no great shock or surprise. It means, however, that fine wines have, at long last, entered the market economy, but I still doubt that, in real terms, the producers are benefiting very much, mainly because they did not have a very large backlog to sell.

However, though the demand for and the prices of fine Italian wines have now, for the first time, increased, there is no shortage of good wine. The major effect has been that wine lovers have started to look more broadly at the scene and discover wines other than Brunello, Barolo, and Reserve Chianti.

Just as many non-Italians are looking to Italian wines, due to the increased cost of French wines, Italians are now learning to appreciate wines they had previously ignored. Today, for example, a matured Carema sells for around three-fifty in Rome, whereas, only two or three years ago, not half that price could have been asked. And there are dozens of such Italian wines, which are music to the ear of the experienced Italian wine lover, just as those of Bordeaux and Burgundy are to lovers of French wines.

For decades, the French have been drinking large quantities

of Italian sparkling wines, but in the past few years they have started taking a connoisseur's interest in the rest, and during this period of awakening for Italian wines, there have been numbers of American and British importers traveling Italy, negotiating with producers who have never exported a bottle of wine before in their lives.

If you look at the wine list of any good restaurant or at the offerings of your wine merchant, you will see that the bulk of the French wines are from the past ten years and that even many of these leap to prices that exclude the bulk of humanity as potential purchasers. If one moves to the decade before, the prices are often ruinous. My point, however, is that in the case of both French and Italian wines, the vintages chiefly available are those of between four and ten years before. This usually means a well and completely matured wine.

Continually one hears people saying that Italian wines do not age: where this theory came from I do not know, but the second chart disproves it, as do the words of Cyril Ray quoted at the beginning of this text.† On the other hand, some Italian wines do not age, and, equally, some French ones do not age either. But the French have a considerable financial incentive to make the necessary investment in maturing in the wood, which is the basis of a long life in the bottle. With Italian wines, the incentive is less, but this, too, is changing. There are more mature wines on the market and their prices are beginning to move upward, and this trend will continue. The Italian government is now appropriating funds to loan to producers, chiefly to co-operatives, so that they can afford to lay down their finest wines.

In the case of the wine list at the good restaurant, let us assume that the French wines will all age magnificently beyond the ten-year period and that the Italian offerings will not. Here we arrive at the same false situation of comparing a middling Italian wine (the export of fine Italian wines to the United Kingdom or the United States is not large) with a thoroughbred

† See p. 10.

French one, at vastly different prices. Nobody ever seems to talk of the middle run of French wines. And, in all good faith, drinking of wines in optimum condition is done inside the first decade of their life: longer life is a luxury for a small number of experts and connoisseurs who can afford to pay the high price asked, a price closer to rarity value than real value. It is doubtful if any wine really improves after its twelfth year. It will begin its decline into an elegant, delicate, graceful old age: full of subtleties, but ethereal rather than virile. The human emotion toward a very old wine is admiration rather than a physical love.

The use of French wine as an investment certain to produce a better capital growth than real estate, philately, or modern art, is now the fashion. This shift of French wines from being something to drink to something on which a 400 per cent‡ profit can be made by shrewd buying and selling is one of the reasons that wine lovers who prefer to drink wine rather than see a cru accrue profits are hopefully and often successfully investigating Italy as an alternative supply. The liquid assests of Italy are untold.

Italy's lack of commercial talent in the wine business was brought embarrassingly to the fore recently. With the new Common Market arrangements, Italy was convinced that France wished to push Italy into the position of supplying inexpensive table wines to the North while France and Germany hung on to the quality market to the exclusion of Italy. At all events, Italy took no action of any note to do anything, but was horrified to find the French filling the Italian supermarkets and grocery stores with *appellation contrôlée* wines at prices hard to rival and often below those of local wines. This shock was followed by another, a highly efficient public-relations campaign designed to persuade

‡ With regard to selling one's aged wines, which have increased in value, at a profit, U.S. law broadly permits citizens to sell such wines privately to friends or back to the wine store. Illegality enters in only, it would seem, if one, without a license, offers wine on the open market, systematically, repeatedly, and in appreciable quantities; in this case one's action would constitute illicit trading and a public activity. In any event, before engaging in the selling of wine, one would be wise to check the local state laws.

the Italians to eat Italian style but to drink French wines. The utter incompetence of the Italian producers, authorities, and interested agencies to combat this and do something practical to defend Italian wines was plain for all to see.

An export policy that made it possible for the average Italian to drink appellation French wines at a lower price than those he could buy from the local co-operative was and is remarkable. However, all at once the tables are yet again turned and we are no longer talking about Médoc, Côte d'Or, or Châteauneuf-du-Pape; we are no longer talking about wines that, if cellared for a couple of years, will be worth twenty dollars a bottle. And if one talks with the confused Italians, it is even more difficult to know what we are talking about. The Italian wine world was left aghast by the competition, and it would seem that they have been so shocked into immobility that they have not even opened a bottle of French supermarket wine and tasted it to see what is actually being offered for sale. Perhaps they know it doesn't matter. However, one can be sure that the wines are modest ones, helpfully chaptalized and produced on a major industrial scale in a manner that I shall explain further on in this book; this, at least, is my finding after trying a couple of bottles.

It cannot be said that the French jumped the gun. They moved into Italy efficiently and well after the gun had been fired. The Italians, on the other hand, were still in the locker room discussing abstract future prospects when the French were halfway to the finish line to pick up not only the luxury market, which was already theirs, but also the cheap one the Italians were convinced was to be their sad fate to supply if they did not do something to protect themselves. While discussing what they thought was theirs for sure, they lost this too—at least in part.

This is among the sadder tales on land and sea, because Italian wines are very good. They start with a basic raw product that is ideally suited to making both fine matured wines and high-quality table wines without the pick-me-ups of sugar and cutting wines, and their enormous variety is an endless fascination to all who start on an investigation of them.

Aside from the great names, one finds such delights as Perda Rubia, from Sardinia, which is the strongest dry red wine in Europe and suitable for drinking with the local wild boar; there is Torre Quarto, from Puglia, a stern, masculine wine; there is Gragnano, from the Sorrento Peninsula; the Sangiovese of the Romagna (a wine of which I am particularly fond), which marries happily even with seafood dishes; the rich and strong reds from the Alto Adige, such as the Pinot Noir, or Blauburgunder as it is called locally; the Refosco, of Friuli, a vigorous dry red wine that seems to demand that one take action, either combative or amorous; and a Santa Maddalena, with its bouquet of Alpine flowers. These are names that come to mind writing, but there are dozens more, the Castel Chiuro, for example, a magnificent full-bodied red from the Valtelline; the Venegazzù, a unique long-aged red from Treviso; a Torgiano Rubesco from Perugia, a pink Lacryma Christi "champagne" from Vesuvius, or an almost unknown Taurasi, a formidable red from Avellino.

Plainly a situation of commercial ineptitude cannot exist permanently or throughout an entire country like Italy, which has the largest production of wine in the world. And, in fact, it doesn't. The cellars of the wineries of Sardinia are empty: the wine has been sold in bulk to France. How wise the French are! as the Sardinian wines are superb, strong, and full-bodied.

But also on an international level, it would be impossible for holding companies and conglomerates not to want to put their finger in the pie of such a large industry. Just as the highly efficient Martini and Rossi vermouth company owns its own distillery in Scotland, even if it does not announce this on the label of the Scotch in question, major international companies such as Nestlé, Seagram's, Crosse & Blackwell, and FIAT have been buying into the Italian wine business, though, like Martini and Rossi, usually without plastering their name on the bottle. One trembles at the thought of what will be thought up in corporation board rooms on the sixtieth floor of skyscrapers for the future of Italian wine. One cannot but fear that operators in the food-and-drink sphere will never understand that wine is not like a soft drink, in that if you increase your output at short notice the quality must go down: you must use grapes you would previously have used for a secondary wine. I have heard that one major international firm is buying up cheap wine and selling it not as a DOC wine, which it isn't, but as, let us say, Italian Sunshine Wine. It is the equivalent of the wines with which the French have flooded the Italian supermarkets, perhaps worse.

Many big companies are sinking new capital into old wineries to produce DOC wines and to establish up-to-date organizations with export outlets through sister companies of the investing-holding companies. This will mean that a wider selection of DOC Italian wines, apparently inexplicably, will suddenly become available in Europe and the United States; not because a great propaganda drive has been mounted and public demand been aroused, but because the holding companies are extending their domains. This may not be the most elegant entrance for Italian DOC wines onto the international scene but, at least and at last, wine writers will not be able to ignore Italian wines totally, as they have in the past.

One of the world's most distinguished connoisseurs and writers about wines and foods, in a listing of wine-producing countries, mentions the vineyards of Kenya and of Chile, and those of Brazil, Uruguay, New South Wales, the Lebanon, and Armenia, but omits Italy. At a later point in the same book, having damned Barolo with faint praise, he goes on to invent a wine called "Barolino" (at least, I have never traced it), which he describes as "distinctly inferior." The other highlight of Italian wines in this book is the description of Chianti as "an excellent thirst-quencher and acceptable with oily or highly spiced foods. It is claimed," he goes on, "that it helps digestion and prevents

constipation, but it is not claimed to rival the red wines of
Bordeaux and Burgundy . . . there are wide differences in quality—or the lack thereof—from one straw-coloured [sic!] flask
of Chianti to another."

There is plainly a vast lacuna of communications if an expert
who is familiar with the wines of Armenia and Chile has not
had it brought to his notice that reserve Chianti is bottled in
Bordeaux-type bottles and is often aged for five years before
being marketed and has been so for a century and that this is the
Chianti on which the real reputation of Tuscan wine stands.

As anybody can see, Italian wines have not only a great deal
to do to gain a reputation, but also to bury the damage, intentional or unintentional, done to their reputation over a very
long period during which the Italians were quite uninterested
in what anybody said and quite happy to plod along as they
always had, producing fine wine for those who wanted it and
wanted it sufficiently to find out where it was available and then
go out and get it, and local wines for local sale.

This attitude of self-sufficiency still exists: you still have to
work from your own notebook to remember the names of small
producers of "big" wines, though, Part Two of this book will help
obviate this for the future.

Times have changed radically. The more internationally aware
section of Italy is now very concerned about her world repute,
especially since the huge restructuring of the wine-producing industry, which is capable of offering very large quantities of high-
quality wine. But nobody knows how to sustain a prestigious
name, and even if anybody had coherent ideas on how to do it,
there are no funds currently available with which to do it. The
producers and experts agree that the government-sponsored effort
at DOC wine propaganda, mounted in 1970, was a failure and
just wasted good money. Groups of producers then stepped in, to
no great effect. There is talk of the government having appropri-
ated a huge budget for wine propaganda, but, as yet, nobody can

decide how to use it: it therefore remains idle in the bank—all $2 million of it.*

This self-satisfaction and unwillingness to raise ambitions is well founded. After all, the Italians are a good wine-drinking people, and the domestic market is improving both quantitatively and qualitatively. Certain foreign markets have been steady over the years, so why fuss? The Trentino Alto Adige has always trucked some $15 million worth of wine to Germany, Switzerland, and Austria. The Chianti zone could rely on over $10 million of exports to the United States, Great Britain, France, Switzerland, and Belgium. Verona wines (Soave, Bardolino, and Valpolicella) to the value of over $6 million went to Switzerland, the United States, and Germany, while over $1 million of Puglia cutting wines were regularly sold to France, Germany, and Switzerland, and $.5 million of Frascati went to the United States and Switzerland. And when you add $5 million of sparkling spumantes leaving Turin every year for France and Germany, you cannot say that it is not a successful business; and all this with scarcely any appreciable effort.

When, in 1970, the Common Market trade barriers came down, things changed: the export figures started rising, equally with no appreciable effort, sometimes doubling, and in the case of French imports they increased precipitously, fifty times. Gross world sales of Italian wine for 1971 shot up to $220 million, of which $150 million went to Common Market countries.

On top of this, with Algeria being written out of the picture by a stroke of the Common Market pen, Italy has picked up an increased share in the bulk and cutting-wine market of northern Europe and also the market supplying the distilleries of northern Europe. Though the export figures for Italy are appreciable and

---

* If ever this money is put to work, it will be to publicize DOC wines only, and regrettably those made by co-operative (cantine sociali) in particular. Thus, though it may well have the effect of increasing sales of quality and bulk DOC wines, it will in all probability have little effect on the connoisseur market or produce the prestige for Italian wines that, as in France, a relatively small number of distinguished producers have worked a lifetime to attain.

rising, they are still not in proportion to Italy's position in the market. But as long as nobody is up to the task of giving Italian wines the prestigious image they merit, Italian producers will have to satisfy themselves with this steady but growing market they have and with supplying bulk wines that turn up, after further processing, with foreign labels and perhaps even buy them back elegantly bottled. Perhaps Italy should have worried more about being put into the position of main supplier of bulk wines than being offended by possible downgrading to purveyor of inexpensive table wines. But the co-operatives are quite happy with the more modest role, as long as they can clear their production every year and manage to pay their farmer-members a steady sum (even if the minimum acceptable) to keep the boat afloat and justify their existence.

Common Market regulations do not encourage producers to set themselves up as makers of fine wines: they guarantee with hard cash, through the FEOGA system, that the producers of uncontrolled wine shall get a guaranteed return for their efforts, based on the alcoholic content. This is such as to discourage the Italian producers, whose wines are mostly of high alcoholic content, from embarking on the risks of international commerce but to satisfy themselves with a sure minimum. The odds on selling bulk wine above the FEOGA protection level are very good, both at home and abroad. And it is so much easier to load a tanker ship or tanker truck than to fuss with publicity, foreign agents, traveling salesmen, unending accountancy and billing, customs problems, and perhaps even bad debts.

CHAPTER FOUR
The World Status of Italian Wines

It is very difficult to get an all-over view of wine production throughout the world and Italy's position in it. By good fortune I was shown the few relevant pages from a booklet entitled *Agricultural Commodity Projections 1970–1980,* printed rather than published by the UN's Food and Agriculture Organization, which gives its predictions for the decade's wine production throughout the world.

It is a highly competent document, and with some editing and paraphrasing here and there I print it almost complete, as it is a remarkably informative and, needless to say, impartial statement of fact and current trends:

"During the 1960–70 period, the area under vines remained stable at approximately 25 million acres throughout the world. However, wine production increased by about 25 per cent from 240 million hectoliters to 300 million hectoliters [a hectoliter is one hundred liters]. This is explained by three different factors: in Western Europe, the land under vineyards has in fact decreased, but there has been an increase in production because of an improvement in technology and often relocation of vineyards to more suitable terrain. In Italy, for example, the average yield per acre has increased as much as 40 per cent [presumably due also to the abandoning of mixed farming]. In Eastern Europe, the increased yield is mostly due to an expansion of plantations, though also an improvement in yields has been noted. During the decade, viniculture has become more firmly established in the Southern Hemisphere: Australia, the Republic of South Africa, and the South American republics.

"In northwest Africa (Algeria, Morocco) there has been a 50 per cent fall-off in production due to loss of traditional markets in France and other Common Market countries and a consequent aging of the vines, with no replacements and a deterioration of viticulture skills. However, the Soviet Union, from 1968, has become a major importer of Algerian wines and one of the major wine importers of the world.

"World consumption has continued to rise: the bulk of this increase is in the producer countries. In France and Italy, individual consumption seems to have reached a ceiling, and the drinking of *vin ordinaire* has begun to decline in favor of quality wines. In Spain and Portugal, wine drinking reached a peak in the middle of the decade and declined due to a rise in prices and less generous crops. A reduction in trade barriers with northern Common Market countries led to greater wine consumption, while higher excise taxes in Great Britain slowed down imports. The Common Wine Policy of the Common Market, which has facilitated trading in wine, has also had a favorable effect on Spain's, Greece's, and Portugal's general trading.

"It is estimated that there will be a 25 per cent increase in demand between 1970 and 1980. The 'developed market economy' countries are expected to increase their consumption by 20 per cent, while the European 'centrally planned economy' countries could show a 50 per cent rise (bringing their per head intake of wine from ten to thirteen liters per annum) over the next ten years. Demand in the "developing" countries is expected to rise by almost 30 per cent, thus accounting for 13 per cent of the 1980 world market.

"High-income and large-consumption countries such as France and Italy will have a leveling off of consumption at around 120 to 125 liters per head per annum. Future demand will most likely be stronger in certain other southern European countries, where wine is a customary drink but has been restricted by low income: it is therefore expected that Greece and Yugoslavia will show a rise of almost 50 per cent in consumption. Spain and Portugal will not show such remarkable advances, since they have already had a preliminary increase, during the 1960s.

"High rates of increase are estimated for countries with high incomes and, at present, a low intake of wine: the United States is expected to increase over-all consumption by 50 per cent, with the annual per-head wine intake going from 7½ to 10 liters. A comparable trend is becoming evident for the Scandinavian countries, the United Kingdom, and other northern Common Market countries.

"Of all the developing countries, those of South America are expected to have the greatest increase in demand. Already their consumption is 80 per cent more than that of North America and is expected to increase beyond the standard 25 per cent during the decade. African countries are expected to follow the trend too, with East Africa showing an increase of 60 per cent and West Africa of 40 per cent, but the total quantities involved will still be be very small. Consumption in Asia, even if it should increase greatly, will also be globally negligible.

"Among the European countries with centrally planned economies, where the aggregate demand is expected to rise by about 50 per cent, the Soviet Union is outstanding both for the size of its market and for an estimated increase of almost 60 per cent. Consumption in non-wine-producing countries of this group, particularly Poland and East Germany, is expected to attain very high rates of expansion.

"Italy is likely to be in 1980 the leading producer, with an output increase of 14 per cent, and to reach 82 million hectoliters. Portugal, Spain, and Greece are each likely, with new technology, to be able to increase their production by 30 per cent, while the Comecon countries will increase theirs by 45 per cent and the Soviet Union by 60 per cent.

"North America, principally California, is expected to produce 16 million hectoliters, or 20 per cent more than in 1970, while Australia is expected to show a production increase over the decade of 37 per cent and South Africa one of 29 per cent.

"By 1980, the balance between demand and production will have changed. At present, there is more wine than demand. By the middle of the decade, despite increased production, demand will run slightly ahead of supply.

"The main import markets are West Germany, France, and the United States. France and West Germany will draw their supplies chiefly from Italy, which should have a surplus of 9 million hectoliters. France would be an importer of 8.5 million hectoliters; the Common Market as a whole, of 11 million hectoliters. It must also be recalled that France is an exporter of 2 million hectoliters of quality wines. Despite increased home production, the United States will experience a shortfall in supply of over 8 million hectoliters by the end of the decade, which would have to be made up in imports.

"Greece, Yugoslavia, Portugal, Australia, and South Africa, despite marked increases in production, are unlikely to have much surplus to export after satisfying home consumption. The Eastern European countries, however, could have 3 million hectoliters of surplus (in particular, Bulgaria, Hungary, and Romania), and the Soviet Union may, by 1980, have surpluses for export. Since there will be, toward the end of the decade, a shortfall of supply on a world basis of around 3½ per cent, there will be a similar rise in price to bring supply and demand into balance."

What can we deduce from this admirable United Nations document? This projection assumes a decade of peace and the success of the Common Market, and though written before the actual entry of the United Kingdom, Ireland, Denmark, and Norway, recognizes a trend toward greater wine consumption, which will inevitably be accentuated with the lowering of tariffs.

These projections are based on trends. These trends would be altered by an active government policy, such as Morocco re-investing in its vineyards and finding new markets or the U. S. Government putting high tariffs on wine imports; by a policy, in France and Italy for example, of distillation of surplus wines to maintain high price levels, or even a major prohibitionist policy aimed at the reduction of alcoholism. The Soviet Union, in fact, in 1972, after already having doubled the price of hard liquor, started yet another prohibitionist campaign in which beer and wine are encouraged and vodka production is further reduced. Yugoslavia recently prohibited the sale of alcohol in bars between four o'clock and seven o'clock (in the morning!), since there were too many accidents and incidents in the factories. I recall a Communist word-of-mouth propaganda campaign against wine in the early 1950s, which failed. I am therefore happy to note that they have finally seen the light.

Presumably the increase in population will mop up most of the greater production, but, except for Italy and France, where individual input of wine is already high, there will be a per-head increase too. My feeling is that the Italian statistics do not fully reflect the situation, and perhaps the French ones are also mis-leading, though to a lesser extent. There are, for example, some twenty million tourists who visit Italy each year, and it is proba-ble that their drinking habits hike the Italian per-head average somewhat. Italy probably could drink more wine without any risk of national alcoholism: it is said that Italy had a per-head consumption of wine in 1908 of 150 liters. It is often said, offi-cially, that France could not drink more wine, since, being richer than Italy, she also has an appreciable consumption of harder liquors and *apéritifs* and that any sharp increase in wine con-sumption might be met with a government anti-drink campaign and increased taxation on alcohol. At present, France has a per-head consumption of 120 liters, Italy 115 liters, Portugal 98 liters, and Spain 60 liters.

In early 1972 the results of the first statistical check on Italian wine production, based on Common Market rules, were published. These showed that there were just short of two million vineyards in Italy and that 55 per cent of Italian farms had their own vineyards, that over 3 million acres were entirely devoted to wine production, and that there were 1.7 million acres where grapes were cultivated along with other plants. These figures, especially the 55 per cent, go to show how deeply ingrained in the Italian character is the production of grapes and wine. And one can assume fairly safely that many of the other 45 per cent, which have no vineyard, are sited unsuitably or have unsuitable soil; otherwise they, too, would have one.

Another early-1972 statistic has been something of a surprise. In 1969, before the liberalization of wine trading in the Common Market, Italy sold 2 million hectoliters to fellow Common Market countries, this making up half of Italy's total exports. With the freeing of this market, Italy's sales jumped to 4 million hectoliters in 1970 and to over 8 million in 1971. The most remarkable trend has been that Germany is no longer Italy's biggest customer, as it has traditionally been. France has taken first place. Now the Common Market absorbs 80 per cent of Italy's wine exports. It seems that the Common Market has already become the cozy protectionist area it was planned to be, whereby each country specializes rather than tries to make itself self-supporting in every item of agricultural production, with non-Market countries kept well at arm's length.

Wine, and Italian wine in particular, seems to have a glowing future. But, in view of the technological and biochemical similarities of all wines, perhaps one can take the example of the automobile industry to make a comparison. With relatively few exceptions of poor construction, a car or truck made in the United Kingdom, the United States, France, or Germany is much the same, inasmuch as it serves the purpose for which it was constructed. Only, I believe, China continues making its cars and trucks by hand, and they are not likely to be better for it. Among the rest, there is only relatively more or less of craftsmanship and more or less of price. France, let us say, produces the Rolls Royces of wine, while Italy provides the Alfa Romeos; sherry and port, perhaps, are the formidable Cadillacs. But each of the producing countries offers a variety of lesser machines than those which have made their world-wide reputations, and here we have to discover what we want, at what price, and for what purpose: this is intelligent discrimination. Buying the top-top is one thing; one cannot be "wrong" socially or practically. But if too many people do it, there is a shortage and the price goes up. But the world does not finish there; if it did, it would be a very pompous, dull, and dead-end one. Who would blaze the trail in a dune buggy to discover Sardinian wines or chug up mountain valleys in a Volkswagen to discover the joys of Bolzano Blauburgunder?

As with motorcars, the various wines have their specific characteristics, and these we should try to know. It is pointless to compare a Mercedes and a Volkswagen without including the factors of price and running costs. The main divisions are between the grand wines and the lesser ones, and between the lesser ones and the inexpensive, commercial wines.

The grand wines are, of necessity, ones of high alcoholic content, produced by a sunny summer, careful selection, and/or semi-drying of the grapes, which makes them able to withstand the various insidious attacks from biochemical quarters. These wines, when young, are often sharp and even undrinkable and become harmonious only after a heavy investment has been made in them by cellaring in good oak barrels. The number of noble vines, which make great and big wines, is reckoned to be not more than a dozen in Europe. But one should equally remember that not every drop of Merlot will last twenty years: many other factors, such as favorable weather, a favorable growing position, and perfect health, will play their parts. The noble reds include

Cabernet, Sauvignon, and Cabernet Franc, the Pinot Noir, the Merlot, and the Italian Nebbiolo and Sangiovese; the noble whites include the Riesling, the Pinot Blanc (Chardonnay), the Traminer, the Sauvignon Blanc, and the Sylvaner. All these, reds and whites, are cultivated in Italy.

In truth, a "noble" vine has only the meaning that if you do all the right things by its grapes, it will return the compliment and give you fine, long-lived wine. In this sense, you can add to the list the Piedmont Barbera, the Alto Adige's Schiava, the ubiquitous Vernaccia, the Sardinian Cannonau, the Pinot Grigio, the Tuscan Trebbiano, the Friuli Tocai, and the southern Greco, Gaglioppo, and Aleatico.

Lesser wines—even if made from noble grapes—after a quiet winter of repose in a sterile resin vat, are ready to drink. If they are treated as grand wines and made to precipitate their sediment in the cask into a second year or more, the cost would not be in line with the result. The sheer tying up of capital in wine in the wood is such as to make a producer think twice before starting it; yet, to avoid it, he must make an enormous capital investment in machinery that will do all the things that the oak barrel and time would, and if not as well, at least in such a way as to assure his reputation as a producer of consistent-quality wines.

If we are to believe the producers of great wines, it is as easy as falling off a log to make them, provided you have a vineyard with the right grapes: well colored, and full of sugar, acids, and tannin, etc. You then gently press the better bunches and pass the resultant liquid and by-products into the cask, after which nature does the rest. The most that the producer might admit to doing beyond this is to add some egg white or isinglass to help the precipitation process and clarify the wine, after which the only thing that can give a little trouble is too much air getting into the wine after the fermentation has stopped; and all this despite Professor Amerine's admonition.*

Academically speaking, aging a wine—in the vat, in the cask,

* See page 17.

and in the bottle—means that it, with time, changes its taste, its smell, its color, through a throwing off of all sorts of acids and yeasts and other micro-organisms, which have served their purpose in the making of the wine and now are no longer required. This natural process is highly complicated and is understood even today only pragmatically rather than in chemical detail; just as electricity is understood and can be used pragmatically, but cannot be fully explained on a scientific level, biological, enzymatic, and physico-chemical transformations take place in the wine during the maturation that are affected in their behavior and time schedules by a thousand incidental factors.

In the case of red wines, for example, it is known that they first precipitate their tartaric acids, and the malic acids transform into prickly bubbles and finally disintegrate: the wine becomes smoother. Next the color softens as some red particles sink to the bottom of the barrel while yellow ones increase their proportionate presence.

After this preliminary clarifying of the wine, begins the growth, with the help of minimal quantities of oxygen, of volatile esters, and a new and delicate aroma replaces the strong vinous one of the young wine. During this period a whole series of complex chemical reactions have taken place simultaneously: oxidation, hydrolysis of the glucosides, condensation, and others.

In the wood, which is porous, there is both an evaporation of alcohol and an ingress of oxygen varying with the physical conditions and the temperature and humidity of the cellar. Ideal conditions are high humidity and a steady 52° Fahrenheit temperature. The evaporation requires that the casks be topped up, preferably with an identical wine, every ten to fifteen days. The wine then takes on some of the personality of the cask in which it has been stored; and it is surprising that the effect of the physical contact of the wood on the wine is proportionate to the size of the barrel. The French, for example, using small, 300-liter barrels for their fine wines, mature the wine more quickly than do the Italians, who use larger, 3000-liter barrels: Italian enologists insist that the slower maturing is better. During the first year, instead of filtering, the wine is passed usually from one barrel to another as much as three or four times, each time leaving behind the sediment. Subsequently, one or two rackings a year of this nature are sufficient; some producers say they don't move their wine at all.

Maturing in the barrel can last from only six months to a year, for whites, up to three for reds, and, for a few rare, mostly red wines, as much as five, after which there are no further advantages to be gained from the barrel. The art lies in bottling at the right moment, before the wine becomes "heavy," taking on too much taste of the wood, or picks up too much oxygen in its travels from one cask to another, which would cause it to oxidize and degenerate before it reached its optimum. The wine matures in the barrel and refines and gains its bouquet in the bottle. The ideal is to find the perfect balance between wood and bottle age for each wine and for each vintage.

There has always been a good, healthy argument pro and contra the virtues of maturing in the wood, and right has been on both sides, though the barrel has not been the winner. French experts have always preferred a short maturing in the wood and a longer one in the nearly airtight conditions of the bottle, particularly as they have a connoisseur market which is prepared to cellar wine for many years and decant it to be rid of the sediment inevitably formed. The Italians still hanker after longer maturing in the barrel, even though it is expensive in comparison with earlier bottling and sale. But they have the advantage of selling a wine with less sediment, which requires no talent to serve properly—only a little delicacy and care.

Nowadays the barrel is coming back into its own, particularly in Italy, because a new factor has been introduced into the argument. Today stainless-steel faucets, tubes, joints, and pumps can be made that are completely airtight. Here, in the past, lay the snag with long maturing in the barrel: wine's great enemy, oxygen, would sneak in through the slightest fissure during the rack-

ing process, and there was little to do about it but bottle the
wine as quickly as possible before it oxidized.

This serene process of wine making, allegedly with no ac-
knowledgments to modern science, one can reasonably assume
was thought up by the cellar committee of a Benedictine monastery
in the Middle Ages and passed from cellar brother to cellar
brother down the ages till it is used by all the makers of fine and
noble wines. Its only disadvantage is that it works only with the
best grapes of great vintage years and then only if the wine is
protected from the air. The invention of topping up with inert
carbon dioxide or nitrogen gas instead of with wine improved the
situation enormously, but this system is really suitable only when
maturing lesser wines in gastight steel or fiberglass containers
rather than in casks.

It is the lesser mortals and the lesser wines, then, which suffer
and have to employ and apply such technology: those who produce lesser wines, which in the past were acid, cloudy, and, in
memory of Monsieur Bertall, "blue," who have to go to quite
incredible acrobatics to make them not only drinkable but often
very good.

Over the past hundred years the French have been ahead of
the Italians in research, experimentation, and practical technology
in wine making, and they still are. Their enological institutes are
consulted widely even for the planning of entire processing plants
and vinification methods. Italy lacks this close collaboration between institutional development and industrial needs and the invaluable teamwork of experts of various disciplines such as
chemists, enologists, microbiologists, agricultural specialists, and
mechanical and hydraulic engineers of diverse provenance that
is customary in France.

However, Italy is in the avant-garde in the production of plant
and machinery used in wine making and has a large and well-
trained body of practical enologists and enotechnicians working
in large and small wineries, which, doubtless following the French

lead—there is scarcely any other—made a striking leap forward in vinification methods during the 1960 to 1970 decade, to the extent that it can be said that all dubious and antiquated practices have been completely abandoned in the light of modern technology.

What, then, is this complex system of making wine, which requires so many specialists and such expensive plant and equipment? Here I can give an answer that a space engineer of NASA gave me when I asked what was the fundamental difference between the US and the Soviet space programs. He replied: "Well, there's the easy way and there's the difficult way." The difficult way puts a man on the moon and the difficult way makes the finer wine. With wine making, there are dozens of intermediate ways, some based on the quality of the wine and its specific characteristics, others of a purely economic nature.

It is difficult to know what system or systems have been used to make a great wine, chiefly because nobody will tell you, nor will you find it written down. With noble wines, the enologists are artists as well as men of science, whose loving care and delicate touches produce great wines. In fact, the cycle and processing can change from crop to crop according to quality, according to end use, according to the vicissitudes of the turbulent transformation from fruity grape juice to harsh young wine. It is difficult for an enologist to tell you, even if he wanted to and even if he thought that you could understand enough of the technical jargon to make it worth his while, how he makes his wine. So he usually says that he makes it as a medieval Benedictine monk would.

The truth is that making wine is not like making a soft drink, in which, once the production cycle has been programmed, that is that forever. With wine, every action is debatable: no two enologists necessarily agree on what to do in every circumstance. What follows, then, should not be taken as gospel, but rather as broad principles to give the reader an idea of what goes on during the production of good table wines.

There are ten basic phases of vinification, which, to the best of my non-scientific ability, I shall try to elucidate.

First, to make a quality wine the best grapes on the vine are chosen and pressed. The pressing should be a light one, taking the juice but not bruising the seeds or splitting the skins: in this way a rosé or even white wine can be made from black grapes. In the case of white grapes, the juice is passed to fermentation vats; with red, both the juice and the skins (which color the wine) are passed to the fermentation vats. Incidentally, fermentation vats nowadays are often, in Italy, made of fiberglass, which is easy to sterilize and quite indestructible.

Phase two is the fermentation, but before this gets under way, the enologist must know the percentage of sugar and of tartaric and tannic acid he has, so he can make certain decisions: within the law, he may add certain quantities of sugar (in concentrated must form in Italy) and acids to balance his wine. With red wines, he must also observe the color and decide how long the grapeskins must stay in the vat to give the right color to the wine.

After, say, twelve hours or at most two days, the fermentation begins, and after a few more days, of its own volition, when the sugar has been turned into alcohol, the grape juice stops bubbling and becomes wine. If the weather is very cold, the fermentation may not start naturally. It then must be started by adding grape juice treated with specially cultivated yeast that is already fermenting, which serves as a reactant. If the weather is too hot, the fermentation can start far too soon and "boil" too much. This is a trouble the southern Italian producers face and that requires very cold cellars or air conditioning to combat.

The wine is then roughly filtered of skins and other matter and passed to another vat, where a second but brief fermentation consumes the remaining sugar, provided enological action is not taken to halt the fermentation and produce a sweet wine.

Phase three is the composition of the wine. Many wines are simple, one-vine wines; others are conglomerates, made up of up to four different vines, one of which, let us say, gives the main character, another the body, another the alcoholic strength, and yet another the bouquet. At this stage, then, the wine is composed in the approved proportions and mixed in the vat.

Phase four is that of deproteinization and deironization, if required. The former process is done by adding Bentonite, gelatin, and carbon, which causes all the floating elements to attach themselves to the additives and to precipitate to the bottom of the vat. Next, if iron must be removed, as it would "rust" in contact with the air and make the wine oxidize, this is done with the aid of ferrocyanide of potassium and casein. The addition of some tartaric acid makes any excess calcium precipitate.

The wine must now be passed through a carbon or asbestos filter to dispose not only of the sediment, but all the additives used to activate precipitation. At this point, the wine should be brilliant and transparent and with no sediment in suspension. This is phase five.

Phase six takes on the problem of the tartaric acids, which would react to turn the wine cloudy over a period. This phase, with fine wines for aging, takes several months in the cask; but, in this process, it is done by refrigerating the wine for five or six days at a temperature between $-4°$ and $-7°$ C., according to the alcoholic content of the wine. This is essential for white wines but not for reds, because whites are often delicate, but even more because people put them into their domestic refrigerators to chill them. A wine that has already been refrigerated and has precipitated its acids will remain clear after being chilled in the refrigerator: if not, it may precipitate again. It is the cold that makes a wine, red or white, precipitate; this explains why in cold climates there is more sediment and greater need for careful handling and cellaring of wine.

Phase seven. During this refrigeration period, a further clarification of the wine may be done with casein, followed by a further filtration to remove the casein, the sediment, and the precipitated tartaric acids. During refrigeration, inert carbon dioxide or nitrogen may be added to reduce the oxygen suspended in the wine, since this is always harmful.

Phase eight is the finishing-touches phase, in which citric acid may be added to improve the acidity of the wine, enhance its flavor, and improve its aging qualities. Vitamin C may be added for the sole purpose of reducing the oxygen in the wine; but since vitamin C's period of activity is very brief, it must be added as close as possible, in time, to the actual bottling.

Phase nine, which is carried out not more than a few hours before the final bottling and immediately after the adding of vitamin C, is the last sterile filtering, through cellulose and asbestos sheets, which removes all sediment and any micro-organisms that might still be in suspension in the wine. This is called the biological stabilization of the wine.

The tenth and last phase is the bottling. The whole bottling system will have been sterilized as well as the bottles, the corks, and the stainless-steel pipes through which the wine passes to the bottles.

This ten-phase cycle of treatment is expensive and takes over thirty working days. After completing the first three phases, producers would not necessarily go ahead immediately, but would allow the wine to rest some months. Needless to say, for inexpensive wines to be sold locally, some of these processes are abbreviated and some are omitted or done simultaneously, to reduce costs. In the case of red wines, irrespective of quality, some phases can be curtailed or omitted; especially, the refrigeration and repeated filtrations can be reduced. Many wineries proudly boast that they never use a filter for red wines; others, that at most they use a paper filter.

Phase nine, of biologically sterile stabilization, can also be done with anti-fermentation additives, which halt all further biological action and are widely used in all Europe save Italy,† or by pasteurization or by the hot-bottling process.

A word about pasteurization and hot bottling; this is a subject

† See footnote p. 12.

that arouses heated arguments among wine lovers and requires some explanation:

First, perhaps it should be said that neither method is used with the finest wines, red, white, or rosé, all of which should have sufficient alcoholic strength and other qualities to stand up on their own. However, either system may be used with secondary, inexpensive wines—usually whites and sweet whites—which are intrinsically unstable; also with wines that come from poor crops or from second pressings of the grapes; or with a wine that, during the course of processing, has started to oxidize and must be stabilized quickly. Wines in these categories are usually sold without a vintage year and often with a metal twist-off cap or a soft-drink crown cap rather than a cork, but some quality white wines are hot-bottled and corked, and this leaves the buyer in a quandary.

Pasteurization is not much used, since it is a clumsy method which requires that the bottles be filled under sterile conditions and then heated in a sort of steam double boiler. The alcoholic and sugar content and the amount of oxygen in suspension in the wine must all be taken into account when deciding on the temperature and number of minutes that are required to halt any further activity of the yeasts and other micro-organisms: on the average, the treatment lasts up to two hours at between 45 ° and 55° C. It was, in the past, the difficulty of reaching the time-temperature ratio as well as the physical problem of heating all the bottles equally that often was the cause of the infamous "cooked" taste of pasteurization: the enologists played safe and gave the wine that extra five minutes of heat.

Hot-bottling is different and, due to its and enologists' greater technological efficiency nowadays, somehow seems to avoid the "cooked" taste completely; perhaps this is because the wine passes over plates heated 50–70° C. for only a few seconds. In all events, it is difficult, if not impossible, to detect from the taste whether a wine has been hot-bottled.

In both systems, the yeasts and other no-longer-useful micro-organisms are inactivated, thus preventing further growth in the wine, which would turn it cloudy. The flexibility of the wine is, without doubt, reduced. Its bouquet, after an initial four-month halt, will return and improve but will never be great. That is to say, it will not age usefully beyond two or three years, after which it will begin a gentle decline. But, on the positive side, it will take on a false maturity that otherwise it would never have reached, a smoothness not to be expected from a newborn wine and one that is welcomed by drinkers.

Rather than accuse these two systems of "killing" wines (a common charge), they should be applauded for saving wines with too many inherent defects and making them much better than they ever deserved to be. Pasteurization and hot-bottling are essentially processes for stabilizing capricious white wines and the most modest of wines; they should in no circumstances be used on red wines of quality. It should be added in favor of these systems that the medicinal qualities and chemical and alcoholic content remain unaffected, while the taste is often improved.

It is my view that if heat treatment has been given to a wine, it should be clearly marked on the bottle, not because the wine will be any less wholesome or in any way defective, but because it will not improve in any worthwhile way if kept for, say, three years in a cellar, and if you and I are so unfortunate as to cellar a pasteurized wine thinking it is not pasteurized, we are wasting our time and cellar space and tying up money at a dead loss. Heat-treated wines should be recognized for what they are: they should be inexpensive and should be drunk, without solemnity, as "beverage" wines, as the British call them. Such wines should not only have it clearly marked on the label that they have been hot-bottled, but the date this process was done. A vintage date, in fact, is important for a hot-bottled wine, since one can easily be deceived and keep it too long.

Technically speaking, pasteurization affects only the microorganisms of the wine: these take no part in the aging process, which is essentially chemical, though there is a school of thought which believes that the residual "flor" serves a purpose in the aging process. It is not the pasteurization in itself that inhibits the aging of a wine, but the fact that a wine incapable of aging (due to its inherent defects and lacks) in any event or with any processing, has been pasteurized to bring it to the apex of its quality; and that apex, more often than not, is not very high. Logically if you hot-bottle a skittish claret or Chianti, you have not done it any harm, but you would no more do it than you would boil a T-bone steak if you were not constrained to do so.

Sulphur is often used in phase one to stabilize the grape juice, but this vanishes during the fermentation and filtration. Sulphur is still used also in later phases to prevent oxidation and unwanted fermentation, but with all the other weapons that the modern enologist has in his armory, it has become far less important than in the past, when it was used in massive doses. It could often be stronger than the natural bouquet of the wine, particularly a white wine, when poured into a glass, thus making chilling necessary to mask the smell, and often a dose of magnesia, later, to stabilize the stomach, since the sulphur had upset the pepsin secretions. However, the quantities of sulphur permitted by Italian law are half those permitted and too often still used by other European countries. There is a strong school of thought in Italy that the maximum quantities of sulphur should be agreed upon on a European level.

But a lot of this may turn out to be ancient history; even the theory that hot-bottled wine lasts only three years may be wrong. I have never come across a hot-bottled wine that had oxidized, but this is perhaps because I have never come across a four-year-old one. But I do not think that the enologists *really know* that it lasts only three years. I think they say it to play safe, just as an engineer, when he builds a bridge, will put up a notice saying, for example, WARNING: MAXIMUM WEIGHT 10-TON TRUCKS, when his bridge has been built to carry up to fifty tons.

The technological breakthrough in this oxidation problem may already have been found; it may lie in phase seven of the processing. This phase deals with the refrigeration of the wine and the forcing of just sufficient inert carbon dioxide into the wine to drive out the oxygen. If this is as successful as some enologists hope, other processes, such as the addition of vitamin C, citric acid, etc. will be abolished: perhaps other phases will become superfluous. Or it may be that, with this new system, instead of hot-bottling, warm-bottling at 45° C. or less is all that is necessary; that is to say, sufficient heat to prevent proliferation of micro-organisms would be given, rather than that required to deactivate them completely.

Spumante, or *mousseux,* wines have a very special production system, which resembles no other in the whole wine field. The sweet Moscato grapes are pressed lightly and the juice is passed to a special vat, where a preliminary clarification is made by a pump producing centrifugal pressure; this done, there is little or no likelihood of the wine fermenting, at least till hot weather comes around again. It is then filtered and passed to vats in a cold cellar, where it passes the winter undisturbed. With the spring, it is again filtered and passed to *cuves closes,* which are vacuum-tight vats with a surrounding envelope that can be heated or chilled. First the vat is heated and the grape juice, with the aid of cultivated yeasts, starts to ferment; fermentation is halted at a point leaving the correct amount of sugar in the wine; and the chilling process is put into action. This stabilizes the wine and completes any precipitation that has not occurred during the winter rest. It also assures that precipitation will not recur when the spumante is put in a home refrigerator or meets intense cold in any other form. It is then tested for quality and pressure (it should have around four atmospheres): at this stage, minor adjustments can be made before it is passed, still under vacuum conditions, through a filter to another vat from where, sparkling, clear, and under four atmospheres of pressure, it proceeds to the bottle.

This complex and difficult procedure from fermentation to

bottling, which retains the flavor of the wine and its fresh aroma, takes all of a month. Since a bottle of spumante costs less than a dollar f.o.b. winery, it cannot be said to be expensive. It is not everybody's cup of tea, with its 5 per cent sugar content, but it is appreciated by millions and millions of people. It is, however, a most valuable drink for making cocktails and fruit cups, in which the sweetness can be attenuated by the addition of other elements, such as bitters or lemon juice.

For more classic drinkers, *méthode-champenoise brut* spumantes are made in Italy in considerable quantities, but rather like the aged wines of Chianti, they are not made merely for the sake of lucre; at least, the profit must be minimal, especially with the bruts of the big vermouth companies, which surely make them for prestige reasons and because they like the stuff anyhow.

These bruts are made with finest Pinot grapes, the correct champagne system, and normally three years of aging, which is more than is usually given in France, while the price in the wine store in Rome, say, is three dollars.

I have listened to a variety of criticisms of Italian bruts: some say the bubbles are bigger than champagne's, others that they are smaller, it being implicit that neither larger nor smaller bubbles are in any way acceptable. Bubbles apart, there is a profound difference that seems to pass unnoticed: it is that champagne is made from a bitter grape but, with sugar and the genius of the French enologists, a wonderful, incredibly dry champagne is produced. The Italian bruts are made from the same Pinot, but ones that have come to fruition in a kinder climate: the grapes are naturally richer in sugar and offer a rounder and less acid drink than the highly strung thoroughbred champagne.

An unusual wine-making method is that used for making vin santo sweet dessert wines, which have about 16 per cent alcohol. A strong white wine, usually a passito, made from semi-dried grapes, is poured into a cask, along with sediment and wine from the previous year, and it is allowed to ferment, repose, and referment, just as it wishes, for two, three, four, or even five years. It bubbles in summer and sleeps in winter. Such wines may be fortified and stabilized with distilled wine, particularly if they must travel overseas.

CHAPTER FIVE
The Social Significance of Wine

I have often wondered if the Greek, the Jew, the Arab, and the Latin of the famous Salerno medical school that flourished in late-medieval times had not got onto something scientifically sound with regard to wine and one's health. There are often, in Italy, medical conventions at which the therapeutical value of wine is discussed, but the press reports are usually brief, though all conclude that wine taken regularly and in reasonable quantities, except in specific cases, is a very good thing.

Recently, investigating more profoundly on this subject, I have confirmed the view that wine, like milk and certain mineral waters such as Fiuggi, Montecatini, and Vichy, has mineral salts that are very important to the human organism. Pasteurized milk, of course, is the greatest health-giving liquid, though somewhat heavy in fats; mineral waters do miracles in tidying up one's internal functions, removing fats, flushing livers, and all sorts of useful tasks. But wine?

To start with, wine has a fair percentage of vitamin B_{12}, more than in the original grape juice, due to the fermentation; only liver contains a higher percentage. The whole B group of vitamins is represented quite well, though vitamins A, D, E, and K are completely absent.

Then there is a broad range of essential minerals and salts: calcium, potassium, magnesia, manganese, silica, iodine, zinc, fluor, and sodium, all of which the body can make good use of. There are also iron and copper, but these are often removed for stabilization reasons.

The most important medicinal characteristic of wine is its anti-cholesterol effect: it not only breaks down fat during digestion (Lambrusco is particularly noted for this, but all wines do it to a greater or lesser degree), but also breaks down fatty substances that get into the blood stream better than orange juice or artichokes, which are recognized as being among the best agents for this task. It is said that the water-alcohol formula of wine is more effective for this purpose than the water-glucose suspension of orange juice or the water suspension of the artichoke.

Wine passes into the blood in from thirty to a hundred minutes and creates no difficulty in digestion; rather, digestion of food consumed at the same time is vastly facilitated, particularly the fats, thus reducing the risks of thrombosis; also, the wine tends to dilate the arteries.

Another informal service that wine does is to encourage the innumerable glandular secretions of the human body, in the stomach, the pancreas, and other organs, thus contributing to a harmonious and efficient working of the system. The wine's bouquet, alone, stimulates all sorts of digestive juices.

Wine is also said to be a valuable aid for the prevention of lung congestion and inflammation and is also a help in cases of tuberculosis, bronchitis, common colds, and influenza. It is said to be useful in counteracting poor blood circulation and that sparkling wines in particular are excellent for stimulating a tired nervous system.

The doctors insist that it is not the simple alcohol that does all this, but that it is the wine because it is wine and has certain properties. They point out, for example, that grapeskins contain tannic and other acids, which kill the bacteria they come across in the human body—even typhus and lesser bugs. Drinking wine, they state, is also a protection from infection caused by poor hygiene in the kitchen—from unwashed fruit and salads and from raw seafood that is not absolutely fresh. All wines have the quality of attacking bacteria, but good, strong, medium-aged red wines are the best, they say.

Wine is recommended for those suffering from heart trouble, but not for those who have an ulcer, gout, liver or kidney complaints, or any mental disturbance.

The French Medical Academy (always the French to the fore!) pronounced that a liter of wine a day provides man with all the necessary salts he needs: this daily quota should be increased to 1½–1¾ liters a day for those who do heavy work in the open air. This latter figure would not be enough for Mr. Bertall's bear-hugging model, but it should provide a sufficient intake of alcohol for most people, without too great a recourse to apéritifs, beer, or whisky between meals.

The French and the Italians consume an average of 110 to 120 liters per head every year, a figure that includes every newborn babe in its calculation, which means that a goodly proportion of Italians and Frenchmen do their best to follow the advice of the French Medical Academy. But the Americans and the British, who drink only about ten liters per head per year, should seriously consider taking their share of the burden of drinking the world's wine instead of leaving the task to the Italians and the French, remembering all the time that it is very good for their health.

I have recounted the medical standpoint on wine and I would like to add a human one: wine is a great soother of our tribulations and the most courteous offering to a friend since the Indians offered tobacco. The sharing of a bottle of wine is as good as any pipe of peace; it calms acerbities, arouses good nature and intellectual activity, and, at a suitable time, ensures tranquil sleep. And returning for a moment to the medical theme, there are few drinks more suitable and acceptable for the convalescent, since wine is not only alcoholically relatively bland, but sufficiently strong to raise the spirits and give that extra energy and determination for physical recovery which is often half the battle. Over the decades—perhaps the centuries—strong red wine used to be recommended for anemics, the idea being that red wine made red blood. This is probably an old wives' tale, but it worked pragmatically. One can only assume that the strong red wine produced that sense of well-being required to overcome the apathy, lack of appetite, and weariness of the anemic and and to start him back on the road to health. Italian doctors all agree that wine is part of the cure for many illnesses and that it is an ideal tonic for convalescents.

There is something magic about wine. One looks at it in the glass and it has a beautiful color, whether it be straw yellow or a deep gold or a rich ruby or a pale pink. It is a pleasure just to look at the color. Then one notices the aroma. Each wine has a different aroma: some have a delicate perfume of flowers, others a richer one of freshly gathered fruit, others a powerful male smell of wine, and others of the hot earth from which they come. Here one's imagination can travel from Alpine valleys to wild Sardinian countryside.

Some South Tyrol wines are so perfumed with mountain flowers that they take me to Nepal and Tibet, the rooftops of the world; thus I never have need to go there in reality. I know it all. Drink a strong, black Oliena from the mountains of Sardinia: immediately, you feel the wildness of man and nature, a certain fear of bandits hiding behind boulders; drink again, and a barred-and-bolted cottage door is opened and one is invited into the warmth and safety of human friendship.

One could write poetry about the bouquets of wine and the memories they conjure up and the dreams they arouse. Many poets have done so, but I am not a poet, so I shall proceed, prosaically, with something practical: how to judge wine.

Wine tasting is a highly subjective affair, or it is a highly professional one. Plainly its purpose is to taste wines and draw some aesthetic and practical conclusions. Taste involves flavor (sweet, sour, etc.), temperature (icy, cool, tepid, etc.), and texture (astringent, smooth, rough, etc.). But there is more to wine tasting: we include a critique of the clarity, the color, and the bouquet, as well as the taste of the wine.

The professionals in the game are able to taste up to sixty different wines at a session. If they swallowed a mouthful of each, they would not remain sober. Since they are at work, must make notes and take decisions, they must stay sober. Accordingly they use spittoons and buckets of sawdust. They are, unfortunately, at work, doing a difficult job, but this does not seem to me a good reason for saying—as they do—that the way they taste wine is the best and only way. It is the best and only way for a person who, at a sitting, must taste sixty wines for commercial purposes.

The professionals prefer midmorning sessions to give themselves time to taste a large number of wines. Small amateur groups of wine lovers, with a small number of wines to taste—say, a half dozen—need not start till a more civilized forty-five minutes before lunch.

Two profoundly different attitudes to wine tasting exist. The professionals, to my mind, are investigating something that is their specialty. For production and commercial purposes, for estimating the value of a wine in cash terms, for reckoning how long it must stay in the cellar before marketing, for deciding on the sales-talk description of the wine to be marketed, the taste-and-spit method is more than adequate. Everything, they say, can be learned about a wine from its appearance and bouquet (i.e. eye, nose, and mouth tests)—its elegance, its strength, its body, its future possibilities—particularly if you have a long and broad experience in the field, and a memory like a computer's. But if you are an amateur—just a lover of wine, rather than a purveyor —there is a desire to go deeper. Spitting out is no better than *coitus interruptus:* of course, one can learn all about the wine with the professionals' system, but the wine's soul is only revealed with perfect consummation. One cannot but feel that a warm, loving wine resents being spat into a pail of sawdust before it has had the chance to express its full affection and to have left a long, lingering memory and a hankering for more. Experts all acknowledge that a "farewell," if long and lingering, is a sign of a good wine, but for health and professional reasons, they are constrained to deny themselves this satisfying experience at wine tastings. The rider to all this is that, the drinking way, you cannot tackle sixty wines at a session; you can tackle only, say, six. But whoever in the world wanted to taste and spit out sixty wines at a sitting without being paid to do it? There can be very little pleasure in it.

There are various styles of tasting sessions: the professional, the mass (from fifty to three hundred persons), and the group session (from ten to fifty). Leaving the professionals to their inelegant expectoration, the mass session inevitably turns into a cheerful cocktail party after the first half hour, and its purpose can only be to introduce some new wines to a broad group of people. The ambience is suited only to introducing regular-quality wines, rather than special or aged wines. For these latter, one needs the small group of enthusiasts, particularly as these wines will have cost quite a lot. With, say, half a dozen bottles, with up to fifteen tastes a bottle, one can safely run a tasting for a dozen people.

With fine and noble wines, which tend, within limits, to be erratic and experience major changes in their characteristics as they age, it can still be said, as the experts say, that a wine tasting is "good for this bottle and this time only," but not for all bottles of the same house and vintage. It is much less true for the general run of quality wines, which nowadays are much more stable than in the past.

With wine tastings, one must decide whether one is dealing with high-quality table wines or great, matured wines: and in the latter case, whether these are still relatively young or fully mature. In the case of young pret-à-porter quality wines, one can reach a final decision and, if the price is right, the matter ends there. You might say the same of mature noble wines, though a greater knowledge of wine is required and the price will be vastly higher, though here further aging may have to be taken into consideration. More than anything, it is the adjudicating of young fine wines that is difficult. At, say, three years of age, a wine is still sharp and rough, but what will it be like at six years old? It is anybody's guess, and the expert, with a long experience of that particular wine and its habits, is likely to be nearest to being right. Yet it is at this stage that great wines are bought for cellaring before they get too expensive.

I say that the man with long experience in that particular wine is most likely to be right not for platitudinous reasons (he will be as wrong as the next man if you take him away from his specialty), but because he has a far vaster range of terms of reference. He has disciplined his senses and records them better than the majority of us—but even he is an amateur in comparison with the blind who read braille through their fingers or the deaf who lip-read.

Science, in the past few years, has reached the conclusion that we do not see with our eyes. Two people confronted with something neither has ever seen before will either scarcely see it at all or see it differently, because they have no terms of reference. The argument—and it is most plausible—is that light and shadow, picked up through our eyes, are run through our private mental computers till they hit something out of past experience that looks the same, and this information is passed to the brain. The brain may reject the information, saying it just cannot be so and ask for a rerun. One's past experience is what has been fed into the computer; it is the only term of reference the computer has. The expert wine taster will have stored away in his computer much more than the amateur and has a greater chance of coming up with the right answer. The amateur, with his lesser data storage, might hit lucky, but the odds are against him.

Suppose a man and his wife simultaneously see a man entering their golf club. The husband will note that the golfer is carrying brand-new clubs, that he must be a new member since he doesn't know him, and that perhaps he is the new local bank manager, since he doesn't look a very athletic type. His wife will note that he is wearing a hand-knitted sweater, then that he is wearing also a wedding ring, and will conclude that his wife has sent him to take off a little surplus weight. Each has used a different data-processing machine, and a different and subjective answer has been supplied from the same image.

In the same sense that we do not actually see with our eyes, I suspect that we do not smell with our nose or taste with our palate and taste buds. I think that also here we have data-processing machinery at work. If we have not fed our private computer with information, it cannot give any back.

Suppose a French wine expert says a wine has a perfume of violets. Suppose that one guest at the wine tasting has never smelled a violet in his or her life. Suppose that violets smell different in Southern California, Scotland, and New South Wales (because they are different varieties) from where three other guests have come and where they have smelled violets and mentally docketed that experience, and that violets, in the experience of the French wine expert, are those sold in the flower market at Nice. The various data-processing computers are going to come up with doubts and rejections when they sniff the wine allegedly with the smell of violets, since what the French expert says does not fit their personal experience. However, the human computer will accept the data for further reference, docketing two different smells in the "violets" file.

In this sense, then, wine tasting is a highly subjective affair, but that is no reason for not doing it: drinking is also a highly subjective affair, and the variations and nuances experienced are its fascination. It can't be helped if there is not a hundred-per-cent consensus; after all, who wants a hundred-per-cent consensus?

One distinguished wine writer, in a book about wine tasting, wrote to the effect that there are important variations in the wines produced in temperate zones and fewer variations in the wines of hotter climes such as North Africa, South Africa, South Australia and Southern California. The reliability of climate makes for more uniform and less interesting vintages, even if they are of high quality; wines without surprises, he goes on, wines that rarely reach great peaks. His implication is that such wines do not make for a very interesting wine tasting. I cannot speak for them with any authority, but what astonishes me is that the writer does not mention Italian wines, though he appears to be quite at home with Yugoslav vintages! I am surprised that he does not find enough difference of climate in Italy, where vines are grown at over four thousand feet up in the Aosta Valley, on the rolling moors of Piedmont, high up in the South Tyrol, at over two thousand feet in the Valtelline, and almost as much in the Tuscan Hills and the Sardinian mountains, and even halfway up Vesuvius and Mount Etna, for Italy to merit a little paragraph. After all, Italian wines are better known than Yugoslav wines, and there are rather more of them.

The professional art of wine tasting and the ability to give justly the points for clarity, bouquet, and taste is beyond the reach of most of us. But that does not mean we should write ourselves completely out of the game, even if we are chain smokers. Certainly the majority of professional wine tasters are non-smokers, but let us take courage in the fact that one of the top sherry tasters is recorded to have had a cigarette between his lips most of his waking hours. However, one should not smoke during wine tastings, if only not to upset one's fellow tasters.

The Italian view of this subject is that one should, before trying a wine, prepare one's mouth, and I say, also one's stomach: to me, almost any wine tastes tart on an empty stomach, whereas after even a bite of bread, it becomes itself again. A biscuit and a little water to calm the stomach and clear the palate is the first step; then, to awaken the taste buds, a walnut or a hazelnut or two, but if these are out of season, a bite of a cheese that is not too strong in character will do very well.

Choose a good, clear, transparent glass, preferably with a stem and a rounded bowl that tends a little inward at the lip. Fill it less than half full and look at it. The whole setup should be attractive, the color of the wine particularly. Lift the glass to the light to see if the wine has any unusual reflections: often, for example, you will find green tints in white wines and orange reflections in reds. You might make a mental, or even written, note as to whether you think the wine is bright, sparkling, or only "very clear"; or whether, on the other hand, it is filmy, opalescent, or downright cloudy. Then proceed to judge its color, for example as transparent white—paper-white, as they say—straw-colored, golden yellow, or amber; or, in the case of reds, tawny, ruby, or garnet. On the basis of these conclusions, decide if the wine is elegant-looking or of a satisfactorily good appearance, or whether, conversely, it is shoddy or even slovenly.

Next swirl the wine in the glass gently to see if it leaves a generous amount of viscous "tears" on the sides. If the tears are thin and watery, the wine is likely to be a modest one, but if they cling to the glass, there are excellent prospects of a good wine to come. Fortified wines and spirits also have tears. As far as Italian wines are concerned, tears are always good news, though in the case of certain fine French wines, it is said that they are not necessary for a fine wine, though no Italian enologist would agree. This gentle swirling also helps release the aromatic qualities of the wine, and here one should, as elegantly as possible, savor the perfume, breathing in deeply. At this point the experts leave the amateurs and go beyond simple judgments such as that the wine has a perfumed bouquet or a grapy one or a fruity one and to identify the perfume as reminiscent of raspberries, peaches, hazelnuts, violets, cherries, or tar; this discernment, with practice, comes also to amateurs, though, to my mind, it is always highly subjective.

Having done eye and nose tests and found them encouraging, the next step suggests itself. Take a first sip, and not too small a one. Allow the wine to roll over your tongue down to the taste buds at its root and to rise to the walls of the mouth. As this thoughtful process goes on, a wine will demonstrate its pedigree and its true nature. A poor wine, beyond the obvious taste it has, will offer nothing more. A fine wine offers all sorts of nuances and sidelights to its character and will also, in the mouth, offer new highlights to its bouquet, especially if you open your mouth and breathe in a little air. At this point the professional wine taster knows everything about a wine that he needs to know; he spits it out. You drink it. Here you decide first some relatively easy matters: Is the wine sweet, semi-sweet, or dry? Is it still, or sparkling? You might make a guess as to whether it is a wine weak in alcohol or otherwise, but this is often deceptive. The important decisions are whether it is a wine that will go on aging well or whether it is best to drink it straightaway.

The twelve points for taste include a judgment on the wine's body, its refinement, and its general quality. Then the conclusion can be, let us say, that the wine is complete, full-bodied, strong, powerful, vigorous, stern, austere, rounded, well balanced, harmonious, fine, delicate, velvety, elegant, lively, alert, prickly, animated, nervous, or just palatable; on the other hand, it might be heavy, woody, coarse, thick, uncouth, bodiless, empty, dumb, anemic, thin, nerveless, decrepit, unbalanced, unharmonious, toneless, sickly, bitter, sour, or plain vinegar.

As you allow a wine to rest in your mouth, it also tells its tale: the land it has come from, who were its parents, and how it was looked after till you drank it. Not only is the taste in the mouth; as the wine goes down the throat, there is with some wines an aftertaste, which may differ most pleasantly and appreciably from the foretaste. It is only at this stage that a wine can be fully judged for its all-over texture and personality because the better the wine the longer its savor will remain alive in the various sense organs that have been in action, and in your memory.

If you are proposing to try several wines either at a tasting or at dinner, there are a few standards of precedence to be followed, but since they sometimes conflict, you must reach your own compromise. They are: young before old, white before rosé, rosé before red, dry before sweet, lighter before stronger, delicate before robust. If you have two wines, a young one of a sturdy variety and an older one of a more delicate nature, it would be wrong to put them in order of age; if you have a dry white of character, it may well be tasted after a dry red. The principle of serving wines precisely in accordance with their vintage dates—the oldest last—was and perhaps is still current. But even vintage wines should be ruled by the principle of lighter-before-stronger and delicate-before-robust, otherwise the palate, having accustomed itself to the more generous wine, is no longer able to appreciate the more subtle one.

A red wine normally goes after a dry or an abboccato white, except when the white is a sweet dessert wine or a much stronger one than the red. One might have a rosé or light red, for example, with hors d'oeuvres and a plate of spaghetti, and drink a Sardinian white Vernaccia with a roast chicken as the next course, since the Vernaccia is much stronger both in alcohol and character.

Needless to say, the habit of apéritifs, dry martinis, and scotch and soda before a meal is basically destructive of the fine wines to follow, but it is a habit we are not likely to kick without orders from the doctor. According to logic, the best preprandial drink would be a light, sparkling white wine, say a Prosecco, a brut champenoise spumante, champagne, or even an Asti Spumante, which is not, in fact, sweeter than a lot of apéritifs; or, as a personal preference, a dry Dorato di Sorso—a white wine from Sardinia with pink highlights that is cultivated near the sea and has a special charm. This might sound a little grand, especially for those who live in high customs- and excise-duty areas, but in Italy, sparkling and charmat-method spumantes are not expensive and even champenoise-method bruts are well within the range of reason.

On the subject of taste, I have something of a grouse against wine producers, or at least as far as their labeling is concerned, though it is not leveled only at Italian producers. In Italy it is usually considered that a wine with 1 per cent of sugar left in it counts as *secco* (dry), with 1–2½ per cent of sugar as *abboccato* (slightly sweet), with 3 per cent as *amabile* (medium sweet), and with 3–6 per cent as *dolce* (sweet). But quite often the producer makes the same wine as a dry and as a sweet and uses the same label for both, which produces confusion and often bad temper. My contention is that the Common Market should insist that the sugar-residue percentage be clearly stated so that one does not buy a sweet wine to eat with one's steak.

It would be no help at all for table-wine producers to use the champagne terminology of dryness and sweetness (which is also used by the Italian producers of spumante), as this is even more misleading for the simple soul. *Brut,* for example, means 1½ per cent sugar residue; thus—stretching a point—can be called "dry." *Extra Sec* means 1½–2½ per cent sugar; thus, instead of being extra dry, is in fact abboccato, or slightly sweet. *Sec* is 2½–5 per cent sugar; thus, rather than being dry, is amabile, or medium sweet. *Demi-sec* is 5–8 per cent sugar and is, instead of being half dry, sweet. *Doux* (sweet) is 8–15 per cent sugar and, I should think, is undrinkable by anybody over the age of twelve.

Let us hope, therefore, that the Common Market will decide that not only the percentage of residual sugar should be shown on every label, but that, in the case of hot-bottled wines, this should be stated clearly, along with the date of processing. It might also be nice to know at what low temperature a wine is likely to start precipitating again. If it has been refrigerated, one is fairly safe: if it has been produced "naturally," a spell of very cold weather can start up the process.

If we are to give credence to Marxist-Leninist imperatives and, for once, perhaps we should, wine bibbing, though a bourgeois habit in most countries, in a wave-of-the-future sense is the right of the militant masses. France and Italy have always thought likewise and fought tooth and nail against taxation of wine in any form that threatens to deny the worker his liter. The Soviet Union, in a new-found historical perspective, has seen that with wine it takes much more dedicated drinking time to become an alcoholic (*pace* the devoted winos of New York) than with vodka or other potato-or-grain-alcohol products.

This of course is true, and it brings new hope to learn this news from *Pravda*. This approval of wine from the Marxist-Leninist standpoint is of profound social and intellectual importance: in the early 1950s there was an anti-wine campaign in Italy from Communist quarters that might have had a destructive effect on the rebirth of the industry after the war, had not the Italians liked wine as much as they do. This turning point in the drinking history of modern times will mean that even the left-wing intelligentsia may drink wine with ideological confidence, instead of estate-bottled vodka, which risks leaving them in the dangerous position of being thought revisionists.

Many highly contemporary people have abjured hard liquor in favor of wine, but for health reasons rather than ideological ones. The health reason in question is one that is never touched on in those medical conventions held in delectable spa towns. It is that if you smoke hashish and drink gin, your insurance company will not give you a long expectation of life and will consequently raise your premium. If you are a hard-drug addict and an alcoholic on hard liquor, you won't get past the first year's payment anyhow. With wine, you will—so they say. Though let it not be said that I encourage the drinking of wine to cut the dangers of dope: the dangers of an unwise intake of drugs are enough, without adding those of an unwise intake of alcohol; and vice versa.

Wine drinking is, on the whole, a mealtime habit and not, therefore, conducive to alcoholism, since one of the signs of alcoholism is the ability to live with little or no solid nourishment; wine, instead, stimulates the appetite. Though one could take a shot of brandy or rum at seven o'clock in the morning, the thought of a glass of Sherry or Chianti is somehow not attractive. Perhaps the Communists will be marketing a new breakfast wine, but this surely will be for home consumption. I foresee its having little success abroad. Champagne at 10 o'clock in the morning is another matter!

As the doctors say, regular drinking of modest quantities of wine will do you no harm and quite a lot of good. The major problem in the world is to keep wine at a price that makes daily drinking possible. The danger is not from the finest wines, which sell at fancy, speculative prices; these make up only a minuscule part of the world's wine production. The danger lies with governments that like to tax wine as though it were a luxury, when only that minuscule part of it is a luxury.

At present, Italian producers are concerned that wines may be triply hit by taxes; not only are there value-added tax and local taxes, but a joint European tax on wine is threatened. Though wine is not a luxury, it is not a prime necessity, like bread. It is one of the items that, in difficult times, gets removed from the shopping list or a cheaper brand is bought.

Wine is not a commodity that can be maneuvered by economic pressures, such as, say, gin. You can stop a nation by taxes, guidelines, and propaganda, from drinking gin for ten years to overcome a difficult period; you can then permit production again, and all is well. There arise no problems in getting the production going again. But you cannot do this with wine, at least not easily, as was discovered in California during Prohibition, because the specialized workers leave the land to find other occupations, never to return, while the vineyards age and die.

Those who work in the vineyards and the cellars of Italy recently had a 30 per cent across-the-board pay hike,* but this does not make them rich. But perhaps it will suffice to encourage them to stay rather than to make for the cities. This is very im-

* This pay hike, along with the 10 percent shortfall in the 1972 crop, is pushing up prices.

portant, as wine requires a far higher quota of human effort than any industrial product.

Already over a decade ago, there was a great exodus of farmers and farm hands from Tuscany and the Italian countryside generally. Foreigners bought up hundreds of abandoned farms, vineyards, and cottages, but so did hundreds of Sicilians, who brought also their skills in cultivating the vine. The Sicilians now have the reputation of being the best *innestini* of Italy; that is to say, the men who graft shoots onto a growing vine.

Despite the reduction in the number of workers in the vineyards and a reduction of acreage, there is still, in good years, more wine available than can be easily consumed; the prices are, consequently—except in a few rare cases—highly competitive. The present Barone Bettino Ricasoli has said that the profit margins on wines are such as not to permit extensive publicity: all are looking to the government for a well-funded all-over wine publicity campaign.

The Italians have, in the past decade or so, acquired an automatic mistrust of any wine that advertises itself heavily. And this has led to the exaggerated reaction of so many Italians of going to the local farmer and buying homemade wine out of a plastic bucket. There is, of course, a *via media,* but this requires some intelligent, discriminating effort on the part of the wine lover and his importer or wine merchant.

The medium and small producers in Italy, rather than those large firms that mostly buy and bottle, have studied the DOC rules and, without great enthusiasm, gone along with them. The lack of enthusiasm is due to the fact that to meet the stringent conditions laid down by the Common Market, you have to invest heavily, restructure your operation, and perhaps replant your vineyards, and with no guarantee that at the end of all this you will sell your wine for more than you were selling it before. At the time of writing, thousands of producers have done, patiently and painstakingly, all that was asked of them by the technocrats in Brussels and are now waiting to see what it was all about.

It cannot be said that nothing has happened: the quality of the wines has improved, prices have gone up a bit, and sales to the rest of Europe have increased appreciably. American, British, and French importers are making contacts and signing contracts. But to date there is no jubilation, no success story or talk of getting a return on capital invested within the foreseeable future. According to the FAO projections, all should be well, but much still remains to be seen; meanwhile wine prices are still low, and those of aged wines (except for a few famous houses) are proportionately even lower, since prices have not risen in proportion to costs. This situation has probably arisen due to a shortfall in the expected annual rise in Italy's gross national product caused by industrial unrest and political uncertainty: consequently the domestic market has not taken up the slack of the increased production as the estimated economic trends had prophesied. The snag with wine is that once you have sunk your capital in vineyards you must go ahead and make the wine and sell it for what you can get for it, even the minimum for making industrial alcohol; with gin or beer, you just cut back production when your market research bids caution.

Producing fine wine is still very much a gentlemen's profession. Peasants and small landowners make wine for family consumption and perhaps a little for sale locally or to a co-operative. Larger landowners can make meaningful quantities of wine. These larger landowners are often members of families that, despite expropriation of slices of their territory, death duties, and the ravages of the centuries, have always owned land, usually much more than they do today; these are the territorial aristocracy, the *marchesi,* the *baroni,* and the *conti.* The marquises, in olden times, were responsible for the defense of the marches, or frontiers, of their state, while the counts and barons were responsible for in-depth defense and internal security. They did not live at court, but on their lands, which they personally supervised and worked. Today they are no longer responsible for defense, but they continue to work their lands.

As you look through the names of recommended producers, you will note a remarkable number with titles of nobility; there may be many more—I am sure there are—but in republican Italy many peers do not use their titles, particularly in business. I have therefore given the names of the producers, with or without title, just as I have found them.

In many cases, farming is not a full-time occupation: the landowners are often in business or politics, or work in the professions. Many Italians, on retirement, take to viticulture. The making of wine, then, is a passion that may or may not be profitable, like raising prize cattle. It is also not necessarily a year-round job, particularly if on a small scale and not involving the production of sparkling wines. Only the selling of wine can drag itself out through the twelve months. But one should not assume that wine making is amateurish: today nobody can make it without the professional services of a qualified enologist.

The whole DOC-VQPRD concept, invaluable as it is in regulating and guaranteeing quality, in many cases has little intrinsic meaning. I recall that, in 1969, the sales of Barolo wine were halted by government order. Chaos, of course, reigned. Needless to say, the newspapers started screaming that Barolo was made with NATO surplus ammunition, boots, banana skins, and methylated spirits. It was a saying that the Bourbons never forgot anything and never learned anything, but this is much more apt a criticism of some sectors of the press. In any event, what had actually happened was that some functionary, who plainly knew nothing about wine, had noted that Barolo had a DOC appellation dating from June 1966 and that, three years later, the producers were still marketing non-DOC Barolo; i.e. Barolo made before the presidential decree for Barolo's denomination was signed. It took the Barolo producers quite a time to explain the principles of maturing in the barrel and refining in the bottle that had caused their apparent flouting of the law, but finally they got the seals taken off their cellars and warehouses, and returned to business.

The DOC system is good, but it is not definitive. There are plenty of wineries that have always worked on altogether higher levels than those required by the law: wineries that own better land, have more skilled employees and enologists, cooler cellars, and better vats, casks, and equipment, and mature their wines longer than the law specifically demands. And there are wineries that, due to their traditional modes of production, cannot insert themselves into the DOC orbit, and others that do not wish to vitiate their reputations by joining their neighbors, and prefer to stand alone.

My regional chapters, followed by listings of producers, are an effort to direct the reader's attention to the broad range of DOC wines and some non-DOC ones and onto a limited range of producers of high reputation; though in some cases they have been listed as almost the only producers of any note at all. I should perhaps make quite clear that though many producers know that I am writing this book—many have most kindly supplied me with information and publications—none knows whether he will finish up on the list: this has been made up by myself and improved upon by one or two persons who are equally disinterested as far as the wine trade is concerned.

The introduction to the various regions also aims to give the reader a feeling for the area, an idea of what to expect, so that he or she can—from my judgment, whether enthusiastic or measured in its words—orientate an approach to Italian wines that can reach a happy conclusion with less chance of disappointment.

My aim has been to put the wines into new and obvious mnemonic groups and to put the best into high relief at the same time, though covering the full range of DOC and DOC-ing (soon to be recognized under DOC legislation) wines, ignoring or soft-pedaling secondary products.

In the past, most books on Italian wines covered such an enormous range (and usually in alphabetical order) that the really important wines of Italy got lost in a mass of names of local wines that were literally unfindable and probably not worth finding. One book comes to mind that has over seven hundred named varieties, many with red, white, sweet, dry, and sparkling subvarieties. I have only admiration for the writer and his liver: I would be a client of Alcoholics Anonymous if I had attempted such a tasting feat. Such an incoherent mass of information inevitably results in the reader's mentally docketing Albana, Alcamo, and Aprilia together, for example, and on the same level, or just deciding that the whole business is much too complicated.

My other complaint about books on Italian wines is that they are joyless: rarely have I been caught by a wine writer's enthusiasm and immediately telephoned my supplier for a wine I have never tasted before. An Italian journalist wrote recently to the effect that tourism, from an official point of view, is no longer something to do with people who visited Italy to enjoy a vacation; it is a complete academic science, with its own pedantic scholarship constructed on a bureaucratic infrastructure. He ironically suggested that you will soon be able to take a Ph.D. in tourism without enjoying yourself at all. This could happen to wines too. Just as with tourism, where authorities and federations cannot say that town A is better than town B or that hotel X is better than hotel Y without all the others complaining bitterly, so wine authorities must build an all-inclusive, lowest-common-denominator panorama that ignores the exceptional or, rather, puts the exceptional on the same level as all the others.

As any reader of this book will quickly note (especially those who have read earlier books on Italian wines), except in a limited number of well-established areas such as parts of Piedmont, the Valtelline, and Tuscany, the wine scene of Italy is in rapid evolution: the large number of types of wine available ten years ago has been decimated. Vineyards have been replaced and whole new areas are gaining reputations they never had before, particularly in the South.

In a changing scene, I turn to my favorite Florentine Renaissance writer, Francesco Guicciardini, to see what he has to say. Incidentally he was a contemporary of Machiavelli and much more intelligent. In his advice to his grandchildren he wrote: "Doing everything with absolute precision is desirable, but it is very difficult. In fact, it is a mistake to spend too much time making fine distinctions, because the circumstances may well change while you are still aiming at perfection and you will find that you have wasted your time. It is almost impossible to do anything which has not some infelicity or confusion. Therefore, my advice is to accept things for what they are and take for good that which is least bad."

This book, then, whatever its defects, is an effort to photograph a slowly moving target, a changing scene. In all probability, the picture will be altered as time goes on, though I have attempted, where possible, to project likely eventualities.

Over the past year, I have tried to get the view of the Italian producers and enologists as to where they think Italian wines stand in the international field and have been surprised to receive much the same answer from all quarters. It is a very simple one: the consensus says that Italy has only a few wines, produced by a handful or two of producers, that can be put into the same category as the most famous French wines. After all, nobody is going to argue, persuasively or plausibly, that a wine that costs, in Italy, the equivalent of five dollars is as good as a French one that sells for five times as much: you would be accusing intelligent people of being ignoramuses. But when it comes to high-quality table wines, all the Italian experts, without reservation, say that their products are far and away the best buy. I here only repeat the opinions of others, but they are men who, in many cases, have studied enology in France or at least have made many wine-tasting tours and are familiar with the wines of France.

The issue nowadays is not so much what is best, or which country produces the best, but that people (and the Italian people, above all, since they are the obvious and immediate consumer market for Italian wines of quality) learn to recognize good wine from wherever it may come, so that those who put their hearts into making it are rewarded rather than those for whom it is a great commercial operation. With the trials and tribulations of producing wine from planting the vine to selling the bottle years later, without an intelligent, discriminating public the smaller and better producers could lose heart and leave wine production to industrial manufacturers—a sad day for all of us.

In conclusion, I would say that the difference between a good wine and an outstanding one is, *at source,* usually a matter of less than a dollar a bottle, in which case, the outstanding wine would be a well-aged one.

This gap, which is not great even in Italy, becomes proportionately less as the wine is crated, shipped, passed through customs, and again stored in a cellar in a foreign land, since all these latter costs are the same for all wines.

It is therefore good sense not only to buy wines marked *classico, riserva, superiore, vecchio, auslese,* DOC, and the like, which are guarantees of quality, but to buy from the distinguished smaller producers, who still attach their personal honor and reputation to the wine they market.

Such wines are more than worth searching out, not only for the pleasure they can bring but because, due to the abundance of wine offered on the market today, they—and particularly the aged reds—are still being sold at prices that, to my mind, are much lower than they should be and often have no reference to the real cost of production and maturing.

Part Two

The order in which the various wines are placed in the ensuing chapters is not the order of their importance but, rather, the order of their mention in the texts of the regional chapters, to help the reader find them.

After the individual descriptions of the various wines in the regional chapters, there is a list of producers of repute. The order of the names in these lists is casual and has no reference to any intended preference for one winery over another. When preferences exist, they are mentioned in the text. Below each name, in parentheses, is the town and province where the winery or its offices are sited. If Azienda Vinicola (i.e. wine company) is included in the address, there is good reason to believe that a letter will reach the destination.

Where there is an entry (headed "Additional Description") to the right of the name and address of the producer, this is an indication of the producer's best product, the name of his winery, or the trademark to look for when purchasing, since the producer's name may be on the bottle's label in small print.

CHAPTER SIX

Piedmont

The northwestern corner of Italy, the part that Julius Caesar called Cisalpine Gaul, is a gold mine of fine wines. There are five distinct zones of varying importance. The largest is south of Turin, central Piedmont, where the great Barolos, Barbarescos, Grigno-linos, and Dolcettos are produced, on rolling hills and moors. The second zone is the Novara Hills, to the northeast of Turin, which is the home of Gattinara, Ghemme, and other Nebbiolo-based wines. The third is the Aosta Valley, which in Alpine conditions produces Nebbiolos that, due to the climate, are very different from those of the other two zones. The fourth zone is the Oltrepò Pavese, which means the hills on the south side of the River Po, where most of the fine Pinot grapes are grown; this, geographically, is part of Piedmont's rolling hills but adminis-tratively part of Lombardy. Last and least is the coastal strip of Liguria, which produces less important wines in small quantities every year. But let us start in the north and work down.

The Aosta Valley was a Roman military colony, Augusta Pre-toria, in ancient times and it dominated the St. Bernard Pass into

France. The name of the major city, Aosta, is a simple corruption of the name of the Roman colony, Augusta; first the "u" got dropped, then a vowel changed over the centuries. After the collapse of the Roman defenses and the arrival of the Dark Ages, the valley was overrun by barbarian Burgundians, who finally civilized themselves but never got around to speaking Italian.

These hundred thousand French-speaking Aostans, however, have demonstrated a quite remarkable tenacity in cultivating their vines on terraces high in the valley without mechanization and in ungenerous, rocky soil, often between four and six thousand feet up. At such altitudes it is a battle against the snow, which often falls after the vines have started budding in the spring, and often the harvest is brought in when snow is already lying on the ground.

Working under such conditions cannot be fun, especially as the price of the resultant wine is not sufficiently high to sweeten the task. In fact, the Aostans were beginning to leave the land after the war to work in the nearby cotton and synthetic-fiber factories; but, with the opening of the motorway tunnels through the Alps to France and a consequent huge growth of tourism and through traffic, a new burst of energy, encouraged by regional authorities and by regional pride, was found to keep the vineyards alive and producing; so there was still the right, ethereally Alpine wine to go with the famous fondue of Fontina cheese produced in the valley, a dish that can be improved only with paper-thin slices of white Alba truffles, when it becomes one of the greatest gastronomic delights of the world.

The Donnaz is the best-known wine and is produced in modest quantities from the Nebbiolo grape at reasonable altitudes around the town of Aosta. The Chambave sweet malmsey, from the same area, is available but in rather lesser quantities. The Enfer, made from the Petit Rouge grape, comes from higher up the valley, while the Blanc de Morgex is grown at over four thousand feet, producing a light, golden 10 per cent wine, with a bouquet of Alpine flowers. All these wines are grown on pergolas and have a high fixed acidity, which means that they will age. Needless to say, the quantities produced the higher one goes, get smaller. Among the famous wines is the Malvasia de Nus— Nus being a small town and the wine being made by the parish priest. The quantities are quite uncommercial.

Carema, which is produced on the border between the Aosta Valley and Piedmont and also at twenty-five hundred feet in the hills, is the last but quantitatively and qualitatively not the least of the valley's wines: it is an austere red, 130,000 liters of which are put on the market annually. This is no great quantity, but it is much more than the the others.

Although the Gattinara and Ghemme wines of the Novara Hills have always had a high reputation, it is the DOC zoning that has brought lesser known or almost forgotten wines of this area to the fore: Boca, Fara, Sizzano, and Lessona. These wines are all Nebbiolo-based wines with varying quantities of Bonarda, which softens the youthful harshness of the Nebbiolo. Even here, the production figures are not great: of Gattinara only a little over 200,000 liters is produced each year; 71,000 of Ghemme; 126,000 of Sizzano; 60,000 of Fara; 14,000 of Boca, and even less of Lessona. There is a certain amount of wine that sells under the name Spanna (the local name for the Nebbiolo grape), which, like Lessona, is not a DOC category, but is usually as sturdy as the others.

Curiously Ghemme was imported into the United States with some success back in 1864 by an Italian called Giovanni Frazza. There is considerable correspondence between him and the Ghemme wine producers in which he writes that the Americans like a "good rich wine" and that the doctors were prescribing Ghemme for their convalescent patients and that "comparative analyses of Ghemme, Bordeaux, Chateaux and Laffitte" (sic!) had been made in New York with a favorable result for Ghemme.

Ghemme has had, throughout history, a reputation for "bringing back youth and resuscitating the dead"; but it was not able to heal the loss of faith of the Novara Hills producers, pushed to the wall by the competition of the big commercial companies, chiefly of the Veneto. The DOC zoning came along in time to give them back their prestige and a hope for a better future. They are all "big" wines and noted for their fine bouquet, and it would be a great loss if they were again to lose courage.

The major wine-producing area of Piedmont is to the south of Turin: its chief product is Barbera, usually a stern masculine wine, though at times one finds it sweet and even effervescent. This is the *vin du pays,* which is produced in ideal conditions only around Asti and Alba, where it reaches a remarkably high quality and DOC qualifications.

The great wines of the area are the Barolo, the Barbaresco, and the Grignolino, though there is less and less real Grignolino available every year, due to some genetic trouble with the vine. These three wines, as made by the best producers, are Italy's challenge to the rest of the world's fine wines. They are followed by the Dolcetto, which is a fine dry Nebbiolo, the Nebbiolo d' Alba, and the Freisa d'Asti and Chieri. The last two are also made as slightly sweet wines that, however, go pleasantly with spiced and highly flavored meat dishes.

Here the production is on a larger scale. Four million bottles of Barolo a year, but only 130,000 of Barbaresco and far less of Grignolino. Surprisingly, there are 17 million liters of appellation Barbera made each year, but considering how little of it one sees around outside of Piedmont, one must conclude that the Piedmontese drink it as enthusiastically now as they did a century ago, when Monsieur Oudard of Rheims invented it: needless to say, it costs half the price of a Barolo or Barbaresco when young, but a Barbera, from a distinguished producer, becomes a formidable rival to the others with age, and a great dinner wine. Another fine wine that is now being "discovered" is the Dolcetto: it costs only a little more than a Barbera, but ages even better. It has never gained the public reputation it merits, nor, consequently, the prices it deserves. People say the name Dolcetto is wrong and that it sounds like a sweet wine when, in fact, it is a robust dry wine of great character. All these wines are best drunk at a warm room temperature, if they have reached four or five years of age.

Piedmont, it is often forgotten, has white wines too. The Cortese white has a taut, disciplined personality that does not seem to accept being treated lightly or frivolously, whereas the Moscato asks only that of life and to be drunk with high spirits as Asti Spumante.

Carlo Gancia, who learned how to make champagne in Rheims, went to work on the Moscato grape when he came back to Piedmont, but turning Moscato into champagne was not as easy as he had expected. The Moscato grape is far richer in sugar than champagne's Pinot: the Piedmont Moscato did not require the customary addition of heavily chaptalized wine after the *dégorgement* (i.e. the removal of the sedimented wine from the neck of the bottle). It took ten years of experiments, with bottles exploding daily, to reach a final, satisfactory solution. Carlo Gancia then imported Pinot vines and, with far less trouble, made a regular dry champagne. Until 1918, both the Moscato and the Pinot méthode-champenoise wines were called champagne, when the French producers remonstrated. The Asti Spumante is a remarkably fine and delicate drink if you like 5 per cent sugar content; the Pinot bruts are a remarkably fine drink with no qualifications or reservations. Both are quite inexpensive.

Piedmont does not have a Mediterranean climate, even though it is protected from the worst north winds by the Alps. The Dukes of Savoy once ruled over Nice, on the French Riviera, and Chambéry, in French Savoy, which they ceded to France in 1860. After the fall of Napoleon and the regaining of the lands he had taken, the Savoys had shifted the capital from Chambéry to Turin. Though there is nothing specifically French about Piedmont proper (excluding the French-speaking Aosta Valley), it is the least Italian of the regions. Once one gets into the countryside, there is an overwhelming sense of the nineteenth century in the air; it is slow, steady, quiet, and uneffusive—characteristics not admired in the rest of Italy. Except for the Ringsberg Castle Wine Museum, at Caldaro, in the Alto Adige, the only two collections of old-world wine-making machinery are in Piedmont: one, the Enological History Museum, beautifully set up by the Martini and Rossi Company at Pessione, and the other, mostly outdoors, the Bersano Collection at the Arturo Bersano winery at Nizza Monferrato. Piedmont also has one of Italy's three major enological experimental institutes, at Asti; the others are at Treviso and Trento.

The Piedmontese may be accused of being old world—even fuddy-duddies—by a contemporary Italy, for which everything has to be "young" to be acceptable. True there is nothing very "young" about an austere Barolo. The Piedmontese, however, are smarter than their detractors, because not only have they had an enormous vermouth industry for a hundred years but, in the past decade or so, they have been inventing "young" drinks— Americanos and all sorts of bitter-sweet apéritifs—that are much more avant-garde and progressive than well-aged, dry, full-bodied, harmonious Barolo with a delicate bouquet of violets, a slightly bitter aftertaste, and 13% alcohol.

AOSTA WINES

DONNAZ

Donnaz red has come from the hillsides halfway up the Aosta Valley, just below the city of Aosta, and around the towns of Peroulaz, Pont-St.-Martin, and Donnaz, for the past thousand years.

It is produced chiefly from the famous Nebbiolo grape, which makes almost all the great Piedmont and Valtelline wines: in the Aosta Valley, which is French speaking, it is called Picoutener. The yield per acre is among the lowest in Italy, and this is not surprising, considering the ungenerous nature of the landscape and the two-thousand-foot altitude of the vineyards.

The Donnaz, as with any Nebbiolo, requires aging in the wood, and in this case two years in oak or chestnut casks is obligatory, followed by one in the bottle. It is then a light-garnet color, smooth and with a good but not heavy body, a light bouquet, a satisfying aftertaste, and at least 11.5 per cent alcohol, though this often runs to 12 per cent. Traditionally, Donnaz has been considered an aphrodisiac.

Producers
FRATELLI GHIGLIERI
    (Aosta)
LUIGI FERRANDO
    (Ivrea, Aosta)

Additional Description
also BLANC DE MORGEX

CAREMA

The rocky hillsides, up to twenty-five-hundred feet high, to the north of Turin, in Ivrea province, offer Carema wine, produced from the Nebbiolo wine in the commune of Carema.

Carema is well documented back to the sixteenth century and was drunk at the tables of the Dukes of Savoy. The production is small, but of high quality. It is a clear, ruby-red wine, with a smooth, full-bodied, dry taste, a fine bouquet, and an alcoholic content of at least 12 per cent. These characteristics are shown after four years of aging: two in the wood and two in the bottle. Experts recommend that this wine be opened several hours before drinking.

Producers
LUIGI FERRANDO
 (Ivrea, Aosta)
CANTINA PRODUTTORI NEBBIOLO DI CAREMA
 (Carema, Turin)

PASSITO DI CHAMBAVE

This is a strong (15 per cent) dessert wine made from semi-dried muscat grapes in the vicinity of Chambave, high in the Aosta Valley. When young it is sweet, but with long aging in the wood it becomes velvety and dry.

Producer
EZIO VOYAT
 (Chambave, Aosta)

ENFER D'ARVIERS

An intense red wine with a strong Alpine perfume and a rich and full flavor and aftertaste. It is made from the Petit Rouge grape some dozen miles beyond Aosta, at over two thousand feet above sea level. Improves with bottle age.

Producer
FRATELLI GHIGLIERI
(Aosta)

NOVARA HILLS WINES

GATTINARA

Gattinara is produced in relatively small quantities from the Nebbiolo vine (locally called Spanna) on the hillsides of the little town of Gattinara, in north Piedmont toward Lake Maggiore. Its fame goes back to the Middle Ages, and today it is often considered among the very finest of Italian wines.

It must be at least four years old before being sold, two years of which have to be spent in oak or chestnut barrels. The color is a garnet red, tending to orange; it is round, smooth, full-bodied, and has a fine perfume and a minimum alcoholic strength of 12 per cent which, in practice, is often between 12.5 per cent and 13.5 per cent. It is a taut, elegant, and aristocratic wine that ages very well and has justly earned its reputation.

Producers
GIANCARLO TRAVAGLINI
    (Gattinara, Vercelli)
CONTE DON UGO RAVIZZA
    (Gattinara, Vercelli)
ANTONIO VALLANA
    (Maggiora, Novara)

Producers
LIVIO NERVI
    (Gattinara, Vercelli)
LUIGI CALDI
    (Borgomanero, Novara)
VITTORIO CALIGARIO
    (Gattinara, Vercelli)
MARIO ANTONIOLO
    (Gattinara, Vercelli)
CONSORZIO VINICOLO DI GATTINARA
    (Gattinara, Vercelli)

GHEMME

Ghemme comes from a small growing area immediately south of that of Sizzano. It has been described as a cure for all physical and moral ailments; this is perhaps an exaggerated claim, but regular and sufficient doses should make most ailments, moral or physical, tolerable and maybe a pleasure.

Ghemme is made from at least 60 per cent of Nebbiolo grapes (called Spanna locally), with an admixture of Vespolina and Bonarda. As with Barolo and Sizzano, Ghemme is harsh and tart when young, but with four years of aging—three in the wood —it becomes velvety and harmonious and acquires a pleasing tart aftertaste and a delicate aroma. The alcoholic content is at least 12 per cent and often 13 per cent. It is a deep-red wine with a lighter, brick-colored tint with aging.

Producers
GUIDO PONTI
    (Ghemme, Novara)
GIUSEPPE SEBASTIANI
    (Ghemme, Novara)

DINO UGLIONI
(Ghemme, Novara)
CANTINA SOCIALE DI SIZZANO E GHEMME
(Ghemme, Novara)

BOCA

Boca is the most northerly of the Gattinara-Sizzano-Fara group of Novara Hills wines and comes from an equally small growing area, mostly at over fifteen hundred feet. As with the others, it is a mixture of Nebbiolo (Spanna) and Bonarda and Vespolina grapes, in this case 45–75 per cent of Nebbiolo.

It is a wine for aging, and by law it must have two years in the wood and one in the bottle before being marketed. It begins its public life a ruby red and tends to a soft brick color with the years, when it becomes dry and harmonious and gains an unusual aftertaste of pomegranate. As with the other members of this family, there is a very distinctive bouquet and a good 12 per cent alcohol. A wine worthy of extra bottle age.

Producers
CANTINA SOCIALE DI FARA
(Fara, Novara)
ERMANNO CONTI
(Maggiora, Novara)

FARA

The Fara is one of the small group of the Novara Hills wines and comes from immediately to the south of Sizzano, around the towns of Fara Novarese and Briona.

Although all these Novara Hills wines are basically Nebbiolo wines, with an addition of Bonarda and Vespolina, the proportions of the mixture differ. Ghemme has 60–80 per cent of Nebbiolo, Boca 45–70 per cent, Sizzano 40–60 per cent, and Fara 30–50 per cent. Fara, like the others, requires three years' aging—two in the wood to remove its youthful asperity and one in the bottle. It is then a ruby-red, dry, harmonious, and full-bodied wine with a delicate bouquet and an alcoholic content of 12–13 per cent. Being a cousin of the famous Gattinara, it can take some bottle age.

Producer
CANTINA SOCIALE DEI COLLI NOVARESI
    (Fara Novarese, Novara)

SIZZANO

Sizzano is a name out of the past: it was famous in the days of the Risorgimento, when Piedmont's prime minister, Camillo Cavour, used to send crates of it to his diplomats abroad.

The Sizzano delimited area is very small, and consequently, so is the production. It would seem that very few bottles succeed in getting past Turin without being opened.

With the new DOC legislation, this wine's name surfaces again on a national level; perhaps the production will increase too.

In any event, as a wine, it is in the Gattinara family, made mostly from the same vine that gives us the famous Barolo and fine Lombardy Valtelline wines, the Nebbiolo, which in this province of Novara is more commonly called Spanna. This word Spanna often turns up on labels and can be taken as a good augury in all circumstances, even though the wine may be a non-appellation one.

As with the Barolo, Sizzano is a harsh wine when young: it requires at least two years in the wood and one in the bottle before being marketed, and it welcomes a few more. Ruby red and rough when young, it turns darker with age, when it becomes a dry, harmonious, and full-bodied wine, noted for its delicate aroma and satisfying aftertaste. It has between 12 per cent and 12.5 per cent alcohol.

Producers

FRANCESCO FONTANA
(Sizzano, Novara)
GUIDO PONTI
(Ghemme, Novara)
CANTINA SOCIALE DI SIZZANO E GHEMME
(Ghemme, Novara)

LESSONA

The production of Lessona is very small. Like Gattinara, and with the same Nebbiolo grape, it comes from the Novara Hills and counts as one of Italy's best wines. It matures in three years, after which it can age for another two decades, turning from a garnet red to orange. It is dry, vigorous, smooth, and generous.

Producer
AZIENDA VINICOLA SELLA
    (Lessona, Vercelli)

BONARDA

This is a high-quality table wine made from the Bonarda grape and grown in the Novara Hills. It is a ruby red with a lively personality, medium body, a pleasing aroma, and between 11.5 per cent and 12 per cent alcohol. It is usually drunk relatively young and cool.

Producer
CANTINA SOCIALE DEI COLLI NOVARESI
    (Fara Novarese, Novara)

CENTRAL PIEDMONT WINES

BAROLO

Produced from the Nebbiolo vine in an area between Cuneo and Alba in the Langhe (clay-soil moors) of south Piedmont, Barolo is considered among the very finest of Italian wines. It is harsh and unattractive till its fourth year, when it becomes a clear, garnet-red wine with orange tints, dry, full-bodied, austere, yet harmonious and smooth. It has a strong and individual bouquet and at least 13 per cent alcohol: a vintage Barolo can often have as much as 14–15 per cent. If it is aged for four years, it may be labeled riserva; if for five years, riserva speciale. It reaches a ripe old age in the bottle.

Producers	Additional Description
MARCHESE PAOLO CORDERO DI MONTEZEMOLO (La Morra, Cuneo)	
GIULIO MASCARELLO (Barolo, Cuneo)	
MARCHESE MAURIZIO FRACASSI DI TORRE ROSSANO (La Morra, Cuneo)	

Producers	*Additional Description*
ALFREDO PRUNOTTO (Alba, Cuneo)	CRU BUSSIA
FRATELLI ODDERO (La Morra, Cuneo)	
RENATO RATTI (La Morra, Cuneo)	ABBAZIA DELL'ANNUNZIATA
FRANCESCO RINALDI (Alba, Cuneo)	
GIUSEPPE CONTRATTO (Canelli, Asti)	
RICCARDO CERETTO (Alba, Cuneo)	ZONCHETTA
PIO CESARE (Alba, Cuneo)	
EREDI DI LUIGI EINAUDI (Dogliani, Cuneo)	
ANGELO GERMANO (Barolo, Cuneo)	
GIUSEPPE MARCARINI (La Morra, Cuneo)	VIGNETI BRUNATE
ARTURO BERSANO (Nizza Monferrato, Asti)	CONTI DELLA CREMOSINA
ISTITUTO AGRARIO ENOLOGICO (Alba)	

BARBARESCO

Barbaresco wine comes from the same Nebbiolo grape as the Barolo but from around the town of Barbaresco, close by. The difference between the two wines is that the Barbaresco is less austere and alcoholic but more delicate and softer. It ages well and should not be drunk under three years; in fact, by law it must be given one year in the wood and one in the bottle. If the aging is for three years, the wine may be labeled riserva; if for four years, riserva speciale.

It is a deep ruby red, turning to garnet with orange tints with age. It is dry, full-bodied, robust, yet harmonious and with a delicate aroma. Minimum alcoholic content is 12.5 per cent.

Producers	*Additional Description*
PARROCO DI NEIVE	
(Neive, Piedmont)	
ANGELO GAJA	
(Barbaresco, Cuneo)	
ALFREDO PRUNOTTO	
(Alba, Cuneo)	
GIUSEPPE CONTRATTO	
(Canelli, Asti)	
FRATELLI ODDERO	
(La Morra, Cuneo)	
PIO CESARE	
(Alba, Cuneo)	
RICCARDO CERETTO	MONTEFICO DI OVELLO
(Alba, Cuneo)	
BRUNO GIACOSA	
(Neive, Piedmont)	
FRANCESCO RINALDO	
(Alba, Cunco)	
FONTANAFREDDA	
(Serralunga di Alba, Cuneo)	
CANTINA SOCIALE DI BARBARESCO	
(Barbaresco, Cuneo)	
FRATELLI MINUTO	
(Barbaresco, Cuneo)	

GRIGNOLINO D'ASTI

The Grignolino wine is often considered by connoisseurs to be the finest in Piedmont. Of recent years, due to a vine malady, it is becoming rarer. Grignolino, made from the Grignolino grape, is not the usual robust wine of Piedmont, but light-bodied, dry, with a slightly sharp aftertaste, a delicate bouquet, and a soft, autumnal color. It is not a wine for great aging in the bottle: it is usually ready for drinking in its third year and should be drunk inside the next five. Its alcoholic content runs between 11 per cent and 13 per cent.

Producers
GIORGIO CARNEVALE
    (Cerro Tanaro, Asti)
BRUNO GIACOSA
    (Neive, Piedmont)
NOVELLONE BERRUTI VIGLIANI
    (Portocomaro, Asti)
PAOLO BIGGIO
    (Migliandolo, Asti)
CANTINA SOCIALE GOVONE
    (Govone, Piedmont)

DOLCETTO

Made from the Dolcetto grape, this wine is a strong, stern, and well-balanced dry red wine, despite its name which hints at sweetness. It is grown fairly widely in southern Piedmont and its area has not yet been delimited by law. It normally requires two years of aging, when it has a remarkable strength of character. However, it is not noted for being a great long liver like Barolo, and is usually drunk in its first decade. This, however, does not detract from Dolcetto's importance as a very fine wine, with up to 13 per cent alcohol. Its DOC areas are likely to include the Langhe (the Moors), Ovada, Alba, Dogliani, and Asti.

Producers	*Additional Description*
ALFREDO PRUNOTTO	CRU CAGNASSI DI RODELLO
(Alba, Cuneo)	
GIACOMO CONTERNO	
(Monforte d'Alba, Cuneo)	
EREDI DI LUIGI EINAUDI	
(Dogliani, Cuneo)	
PIO CESARE	
(Alba, Cuneo)	
GIUSEPPE ROCCA	
(Barbaresco, Cuneo)	
RICCARDO CERETTO	
(Alba, Cuneo)	
BRUNO GIACOSA	
(Neive, Piedmont)	
MARIO SAVIGLIANO	
(Diana d'Alba, Cuneo)	
EGISTO SCAGLIONE	
(Valdivilla di San Stefano, Cuneo)	

BARBERA D'ASTI
BARBERA DI MONFERRATO
BARBERA DI ALBA

The Barbera vine is not only one of the basic producers of wine in southern Piedmont, but it has stretched its tendrils as far as southern Italy and the islands. Along with Barolo's Nebbiolo vine, it was chosen as the best to perfect in the great leap ahead in wine technology of the past century.

When young, it is either harsh and bitter or semi-sweet and *frizzante*. When produced as a dry, still wine, which is customary from the better wineries, with age it becomes a formidable rival to the Barolo, though it does not live as long. The semi-sweet and frizzante varieties are not particularly interesting.

Of the three DOC zones for Piedmont Barbera, two are almost identical geographically (Monferrato and Asti), around the town of Asti, while the third (Alba) is immediately to the west of the famous truffle-market town of Alba.

The Monferrato Barbera, by DOC law, must be obtained from the Barbera di Monferrato grape, but up to 25 per cent of Grignolino, Dolcetto, or Freisa may be added. The Barbera d'Asti must be 100 per cent Barbera. The Alba and Asti varieties are a deep ruby red, fading to an amberish garnet with age; the Monferrato is a bright ruby red fading to amber. All three must be matured for three years, and they are at their optimum from the fourth or fifth year: all must have a minimum alcoholic content of 12–12.5 per cent, though you will find Barberas with 13–15 per cent, which are called superiore. The Asti Barbera tends to be more alcoholic than the others and to age better.

Producers	*Additional Description*
PARROCO DI NEIVE	
(Neive, Piedmont)	
ALFREDO PRUNOTTO	CRU PIAN ROMUALDO
(Alba, Cuneo)	MONFORTE
GIORGIO CARNEVALE	VECCHIO DELLA ROCCHETTA
(Cerro Tanaro, Asti)	
MARCHESE ADORNO CATTANEO	CASTELLO DI GABIANO
(Gabiano, Monferrato)	
EREDI DI LUIGI EINAUDI	
(Dogliani, Cuneo)	

Producers	*Additional Description*
FRATELLI ODDERO	
(La Morra, Cuneo)	
FRATELLI ALBERTI	
(Canelli, Asti)	
ARTURO BERSANO	CREMOSINA
(Nizza Monferrato, Asti)	
PIO CESARE	
(Alba, Cuneo)	
RICCARDO CERETTO	
(Alba, Cuneo)	
FRATELLI COLOMBI	
(Nizza Monferrato, Asti)	
CANTINA SOCIALE GOVONE	
(Govone, Piedmont)	
CANTINA SOCIALE CASTIGLION	
FALLETTO	
(Castiglion Falletto, Piedmont)	
CARLO BALDOVIO	
(Costigliole, Asti)	
CANTINA SOCIALE DI CANELLI	
(Canelli, Asti)	
FONTANAFREDDA	
(Serralunga di Alba, Cuneo)	

GAVI CORTESE

The Gavi Cortese is the most distinguished dry white table wine of Piedmont. It comes from the Cortese grape, cultivated halfway between Alessandria and Genoa. It appreciates moderate aging, when it takes on a very dry bouquet, greenish tints, and an elegant finish.

Producers	Additional Description
VITTORIO SOLDATI	LA SCOLCA
(Rovereto di Gavi Ligure, Alessandria)	
MARIA FUGAZZA BUSCH	
(Monterotondo, Alessandria)	

NEBBIOLO D'ALBA

The Nebbiolo d'Alba is produced on the hills north of Cuneo, in southern Piedmont, not far from the French border. It has much the same characteristics as the Barolo, though sometimes it has a sweetish undertone. For the rest, it is a ruby-red wine with up to 13 per cent alcohol. It ages very well; at five it is well matured; at nine it is even better.

Producers	Additional Description
ARTURO BERSANO	CONTI DELLA CREMOSINA
(Nizza Monferrato, Asti)	
PIO CESARE	
(Alba, Cuneo)	
ALFREDO PRUNOTTO	CRU BRIE ROSSINO
(Alba, Cuneo)	
RICCARDO CERETTO	
(Alba, Cuneo)	
CANTINA SOCIALE VEZZA D'ALBA	
(Vezza d'Alba, Cuneo)	

FREISA D'ASTI
FREISA DI CHIERI
FREISA DELLE LANGHE

These wines are produced as dry matured wines and as amabile (slightly sweet) ones. They both come from the hills just outside Turin to the southeast and are made from the Freisa grape. The Freisa is best known as Freisa di Chieri.

It is ruby red, rough, and sharp when young, smooth and round after two years' aging. It is considered an excellent table wine; the sweeter variety, being very full-bodied and not aggressively sweet, also makes a pleasing table wine suited to certain highly spiced dishes: chicken livers, pâtés, etc. The dry has about 12 per cent alcohol; the amabile a little less.

Producers
ARTURO BERSANO
(Monferrato, Asti)
MELCHIORRE BALBIANO
(Andezeno, Turin)
ALFREDO PRUNOTTO
(Alba, Cuneo)
GIORGIO CARNEVALE
(Cerro Tanaro, Asti)

BRACHETTO D'ACQUI

Brachetto d'Acqui is a sparkling wine, made both sweet and dry, that is a festive drink rather than a table wine. The town of Acqui is in the Asti Spumante zone, which does not lack enological experts in this particular field of sparkling wines. The Brachetto, instead of being champagnelike, is a light ruby red tending to rosé, but it has a persistent natural small-bubble effervescence. The wine is smooth, mellow, and ingratiating, with a delicate bouquet and 11.5 per cent alcohol, sometimes 12.5 per cent. It is much praised by the medical profession for its curative qualities, particularly in convalescence.

Producers

ABBAZIA DI SAN GAUDENZO
 (Santo Stefano Belbo, Cuneo)
GIORGIO CARNEVALE
 (Cerro Tanaro, Asti)

ERBALUCE DI CALUSO

For as long as history records, the Erbaluce vine, producing white grapes, has been cultivated over a small strip of rocky hillside north of Turin, with its main production center at Caluso. This straw-colored wine has a dry, fresh taste, a delicate bouquet, and between 11 per cent and 12 per cent alcohol. Up to four years of maturing is recommended.

A *passito* and a *passito liquoroso,* which are sweet dessert wines, are made from the same grapes, by a careful selection of the grapes and the semi-drying process, which leaves a heavy sugar content in the grapes. To this wine, up to 5 per cent of Bonarda may be added, after which it must be aged five years. These two dessert wines are sweet, full-bodied, and velvety, with at least 13.5 per cent alcohol.

Producers

ISTITUTO PROFESSIONALE DI STATO PER
 L'AGRICULTURA "CARLO UBERTINI"
 (Caluso, Turin)
MARIA BOUX PASSERA
 (Caluso, Turin)

MALVASIA DI CASORZO D'ASTI

This is a malmsey produced in the land of Barbera and Asti Spumante; that is to say, in the Asti province of Piedmont. It is ruby red to cherry-colored (according to how long the wine is left to color with the grapeskins), amabile or sweet, with a delicate aroma, a lively taste, and at least 10.5 per cent alcohol. It is a sparkling wine, produced either by fermentation in the bottle (champenoise system) or, more commonly, by the charmat method, in large vats.

Producer
CANTINA SOCIALE DI CASORZO
    (Casorzo)

RUBINO DI CANTAVENNA

This is a wine without a history, having been institutionalized only in 1949 with the formation of the wine producers' co-operative of Cantavenna, in the town of Gabiano, on the hills south of the River Po and adjacent to great vine-growing areas.

The wine is basically a Barbera, with an admixture of up to 25 per cent of either Grignolino or Freisa or some of each, but since Grignolino is a rarity, the admixture is most certainly Freisa. It must be matured for fifteen months before being put on sale. The result is a wine lighter in color and alcoholic content than a Barbera d'Asti but otherwise similar in color, balance, and body.

Producer
CANTINA SOCIALE DI CANTAVENNA
    (Cantavenna, Alessandria)

ASTI SPUMANTE (or ASTI)
MOSCATO NATURALE D'ASTI
MOSCATO D'ASTI SPUMANTE (or MOSCATO D'ASTI)

The sparkling, champagnelike wines of Asti are made by the cuve-close, or charmat, system (called *autoclave* in Italian), which means they are made in bulk in sealed vats and not fermented in the bottle. They are made with Moscato grapes, which come from the same Piedmont zone that produces the great, robust red wines such as Barolo, Barbaresco, and Barbera.

These famous sparkling wines have similar characteristics and a pale golden color. The Asti Spumante is a little more amber with a semi-sweet and fresh taste. The Moscatos are a trifle sweeter and have a delicate and fragrant bouquet. They all have a long-lasting bubbling froth on being opened. The Moscatos are usually served cold, the Asti Spumante very cold.

The Contratto Company continues to make small quantities of Asti with the méthode champenoise; i.e. in the bottle.

There are brut spumantes and brut champenoise-method wines, but these are usually made with Pinot grapes and have been listed separately on pages 150–51.

Producers

FRANCESCO CINZANO
  (Turin)

GIUSEPPE CONTRATTO
  (Canelli, Asti)

GIORGIO CARNEVALE
  (Cerro Tanaro, Asti)

FRATELLI GANCIA
  (Canelli, Asti)

ORESTE GARAVELLI
  (Asti)

Producers

FONTANAFREDDA
   (Alba)
MARTINI E ROSSI
   (Turin)
OTTAVIO RICCADONNA
   (Canelli, Asti)
CANTINA SOCIALE DI CANELLI
   (Canelli, Asti)

VERMOUTH

This is the traditional Turin production, known throughout the world chiefly as "Martini." However, there are wide variations of wines and infusions made by half a dozen and more major producers. Turin vermouth was first produced by Benedetto Carpano in 1786, to be followed by the Cora brothers; both names are still to the fore in this sector. In the main, there is the sweet white, the less-sweet red, and the dry white. There are also bitter vermouths, which have had quinine added to the infusion of herbs and spices. The various ingredients of these infusions are tightly kept trade secrets. Most of the wine from which vermouths are made comes from Locorotondo and Martina Franca in Puglia and Alcamo in Sicily.

Producers

GIUSEPPE CARPANO
   (Turin)
FRANCESCO CINZANO
   (Turin)
G. & L. CORA
   (Turin)

Producers
FRATELLI GANCIA
    (Canelli, Asti)
MARTINI E ROSSI
    (Turin)
OTTAVIO RICCADONNA
    (Canelli, Asti)
G. CONTRATTO
    (Canelli, Asti)

SPUMANTE BRUT

The first méthode-champenoise spumantes were made in Italy a hundred and twenty-five years ago; if you visit any of the companies now making them, you will find the same enormous cellars as in France, piled high with bottles—resting—and tens of thousands of bottles on racks, which are continually twisted and given a *frisson* to encourage the precipitation of the sediment to the neck of the bottle. When this process is completed, the neck of the bottle is frozen and the *dégorgement* of sediment carried out. The bottle is then topped up with wine—sometimes an older and sweetened wine—and stored away for a year at least, sometimes three. These Piedmont champenoise bruts are made from selected Pinot grapes, and the resultant wine is of the highest quality.

Producers	*Additional Description*
GIUSEPPE CONTRATTO	SABAUDA IMPERIALE
(Canelli, Asti)	BRUT
	BACCO D'ORO
FRATELLI GANCIA	GRAND CREMANT
(Canelli, Asti)	CARLO GANCIA BRUT

Producers	*Additional Description*
LUIGI CALISSANO (Alba, Cuneo)	DUCA D'ALBA
MARTINI E ROSSI (Turin)	MONTELERA
CINZANO (Turin)	BRUT

CHAPTER SEVEN

LOMBARDY

Lombardy

In Lombardy we have three distinct and completely diverse wine-producing areas. First, the Oltrepò Pavese, the zone previously mentioned as being an extension of the rolling hills of Piedmont, which is called "Vecchio Piemonte" (Old Piedmont) because it belonged to the old kingdom under the ruling house of Savoy, when Milan was dominated by the Austrians: to this day it retains the Piedmontese traditions and style of life. This area has, for the past century, been the chief supplier of Milan with good Barbera and Bonarda, either straight or with mixtures of other wines. You will find unusual names for wines, such as Barbacarlo (Uncle Charles), Buttafuoco (spitfire), Sangue di Giuda (blood of Judas), and Balestriere (crossbowman), that are old favorites in Milan. You will also find the excellent Frecciarossa (red arrow) wines of Giorgio Odero, who is equally unorthodox in naming his wines: St. George rosé, Grand Cru red, and La Vigne blanche; these latter have earned an international reputation, particularly the Grand Cru, which is a Barbera aged for four years in the wood and, if nursed for an equal time in the bottle, counts itself among the finest wines of Italy and gives proof that the Barbera grape is to be taken very seriously as a producer of fine wine.

There are other, small productions of wine around Casteggio: the Clastidium Gran Riserva, a strong, sweet white wine made from black Pinot grapes; and the Clastidio white, made from Rhine and Italian Riesling, and the red from Barbera. There are also the Canneto Amaro and Montenapoleone, reds with a Barbera base. The ancient Roman town of Casteggio (Clastidium) is the center of considerable activity. Not only does the zone have a natural "vocation," as they say, for wine production—that is, the lay of the land is right, the soil is right, and the skills and investment capital are there—but it is developing fast. The Pinot vines, brought there by Carlo Gancia in the nineteenth century, are very happy and contributing large quantities of grapes for the making of méthode-champenoise brut at the Santa Maria della Versa Co-operative, and Pinot grapes are also being sold in large quantities to the bigger producers of Piedmont. This zone will naturally look toward Milan and Turin for its market, rather than worry about selling in Chicago or Edinburgh, since its development is step by step with the growth of the former two cities. Perhaps only Giorgio Odero will be interested in extending his reputation to foreign climes.

It is said that the DOC regulations are to be reviewed and altered to include the various traditional Oltrepò four-wine conglomerates. As the law stands now, it is very difficult to say which wines fit precisely into which category: these problems will no doubt sort themselves out in time, either by the law being rewritten or the producers either altering the make-up of their wines or—one can never tell—going on just as they have in the past, selling their wines to the people who have always trusted their good name and don't fuss too much about whether a wine is DOC or non-DOC as long as it is good wine. Here, as in other parts of Italy such as the Alto Adige and Friuli, it is more important to know the names of the producers than to understand the DOC categories.

The Gutturnio DOC zone, which has a similar vocation but not as great a reputation for its wines as the Oltrepò, lies a little to the east in the same range of hills. However, administratively it comes in the Emilia-Romagna region and will be written about in that section.

The Oltrepò is still evolving, but the Valtelline, with its capital at Sondrio, is completely established and with a reputation as solid as a rock, its zones clearly assigned and its wines well known long before DOC regulations were ever thought up.

Grown at around two thousand feet up in the foothills of the Alps, the Valtelline reds, though obtained from the famous Nebbiolo grape, are lighter than a Barolo and have a mountain bouquet. Like the Barolo, they welcome aging and turn into the most elegant of wines.

The Valtelline DOC wines traditionally have been bottled under the names Sassella, Grumello, Inferno, Valgella, Villa Perla, Fracia, and Sforzato di Spina, which are household words in Italy and also in Switzerland, where large quantities are exported.

The first four wines require that Nebbiolo constitute 95 per cent. Of these, usually the Sassella gets the pick of the bunch, though there is a Castel Chiuro made by Nino Negri that probably gets the pick of the pick of the bunch and the best barrel to rest in. These vines are produced in ideal conditions of sun and clay soil on the north bank of the river Adda (the Adda flows east–west) in strictly limited areas east and west of Sondrio.

This Valtelline zone has been distinguished for its wines since ancient Roman times, and its popularity today is such that the Valtelline superiore wines are being produced at close to the maximum rate allowed by the law; that is to say, the prices are well sustained and likely to rise more sharply than those of other zones, which still have some delimited land left to plant and exploit.

The third zone is that of Brescia, the western banks of Lake Garda, and the Mantua Hills. Here we move to an altogether different style of wine; mostly light, young, fresh ones with the stress on rosés—lunchtime wines par excellence. The best-known Brescia wines are the Botticino, Cellatica, and Franciacorta, though it would not be true to say that they are well known even nationally, and certainly not internationally. Of all three collectively, only a million liters of DOC quality are produced yearly, and this seems to be consumed entirely locally. This production is little in comparison with the 3.5 million liters of DOC Garda wines produced on the Lombardy side of the lake and not counting the similar wines coming from the Mantua Hills.

With the Garda wines we are no longer in the world of wines that inspire the composition and singing of drinking ballads, as Barbera does, nor among those which inspire respect, like Barolo. The Garda wines do not impose themselves: they are light-hearted, unobtrusive, and light in alcohol; they are an excellent introduction to wine for those who have not acquired a taste for the finer breeds.

The new DOC zone of the Mantua Hills, south of Lake Garda, has no well-known producers; it probably has supplied, in the past, the wineries and bottling plants around Lake Garda. Now, as is intended by the DOC system, such lesser wines can no longer supply more famous wineries, due to the zoning discipline. We shall, no doubt, hear more of Mantua wines in the future, bottled and marketed under their own flag.

OLTREPÒ PAVESE (River Po-Pavia Wines)

Oltrepò Pavese literally means "on the other side of the river Po, in the Pavia area." This is hilly land that in fact has little to do with the river Po or the famously foggy and flat valley of the Po, but much to do with Piedmont; it is little more than an extension into Lombardy of the famous Piedmont wine-producing hills.

The notable increase of this area's wine production is mostly postwar and parallel with the growth of Milan as an industrial city, which it supplies with good and not expensive wines. The wines—Bonarda, Barbera, Riesling, Cortese, Frecciarossa, Moscato, and Pinot (with the exception of the Barbera and Bonarda) —are on the light side. But if a bottle announces only that it contains Oltrepò Pavese, it will be mostly Barbera, about which many drinking songs have been written over the decades in Milan. Most of the producers mentioned in this list produce several Oltrepò wines; they are, however, mentioned under the category for which they are best reputed.

BARBERA dell'Oltrepò Pavese

This is made chiefly of Barbera grapes with a small permitted percentage of Vespolina and Croatina Uva Rara. It is a good, masculine table wine, rich in tannin, a pleasing ruby red, and with an unsubtle but honest aroma. It is a full-bodied wine with an alcoholic content of between 11.5 per cent and 12 per cent.

Producers

LUIGI VALENTI
(Vallescoropasso, Pavia)
CONSORZIO VINI TIPICI OLTREPÒ PAVESE
(Pavia)
MARIO BRANDOLINI
(San Damiano al Colle, Pavia)
GIORGIO ODERO
(Casteggio, Pavia)

BONARDA dell'Oltrepò Pavese

A pleasing table wine (11 per cent), smooth, full-bodied, dry, fresh, and lightly tannic. It has a rich ruby color and an intense, vinous aroma.

Producers

CONSORZIO VINI TIPICI OLTREPÒ PAVESE
(Pavia)
MAGA LINO
(Broni, Pavia)
EDMONDO TRONCONI
(Rovescala, Pavia)

RIESLING dell'Oltrepò Pavese

A straw-yellow-colored wine, with greenish tints and a pleasant, fresh bouquet. It is dry, fairly full-bodied, and with 11 per cent alcohol.

Producers
CANTINA SOCIALE SANTA MARIA DI VERSA
    (Santa Maria di Versa, Pavia)
DUCA ANTONIO DENARI
    (Santa Maria di Versa, Pavia)

CORTESE dell'Oltrepò Pavese
A pale, straw-colored table wine, dry, and pleasing to nose and palate. Minimum alcohol 11 per cent.

Producer
AZIENDA BARUFFALDI
    (Casteggio, Pavia)

MOSCATO dell'Oltrepò Pavese

A dark-golden wine with an intense aroma, sweet and with a light, 10.5 per cent alcohol. This wine is chiefly used for making spumante.

Producer
CANTINA SOCIALE SANTA MARIA DI VERSA
    (Santa Maria di Versa, Pavia)

PINOT dell'Oltrepò Pavese

The DOC regulations for this Pinot seem very broad-minded, but this is explained easily, because the wine is mostly used for producing spumante. By law, the wine may be straw-colored with green tints, rosé, or red; however, in all cases, it must be dry, fresh, and pleasing, with 11 per cent alcohol.

Producer
CANTINA SOCIALE SANTA MARIA DI VERSA
　(Santa Maria di Versa, Pavia)

FRECCIAROSSA

This is a proprietary brand name, well known for many decades, that may or may not fit into the Oltrepò Pavese category, since the white (La Vigne blanche) is a mélange of Pinot Nero and Riesling, half and half, while the rosé (St. George) and red (Grand Cru) are from the Barbera and Croatina Uva Rara vines. The Grand Cru is matured for four years in the cask, without any DOC regulation to insist on this. All offer a generous 12–12.5 per cent alcohol.

Producer
GIORGIO ODERO
　(Casteggio, Pavia)

VALTELLINE WINES

The Valtelline wines are among the most interesting of Italy. They are cultivated in the valley of the river Adda, which flows through Lake Como, in Lombardy, and center on the town of Sondrio.

History reports wine making in this area back to the fifth century A.D. Today the wines are made with a variety of the Nebbiolo called the Chiavennasca, the Nebbiolo being the famous vine used to obtain Barolo and other fine wines in Piedmont. Due, however, to differences of soil, climate, and above all, altitude (the Adda Valley is about two thousand feet above sea level), there are many differences in the wines; but also there are many similarities.

The Valtelline wines all age well, and in fact require a minimum in-the-wood maturing. The law insists on one year for simple Valtellina and two years for Valtellina superiore: in the latter case, one year also in the bottle. However, the Valtelline wines that have made their reputations are aged more than this before being marketed, and they are sold under zonal or proprietary names that are far better known than the generic term Valtellina or Valtellina superiore.

Special mention must be made of Grumello, Inferno, Sassella, and Valgella, which are recognized by law and which must have 95 per cent of Nebbiolo grape. The Sforzato (Sfurzat) di Spina is a sweet wine, made with semi-dried grapes, that reaches 14.5 per cent alcohol. Castel Chiuro is a superior aged wine made only by the Nino Negri winery and, whatever its percentage of Nebbiolo, it seems to me by far the best wine of the Valtelline. The Enologica Valtellinese produces a "Paradiso," which is well aged before being marketed and can be considered in the Castel Chiuro special category. The producers of this area are all of very high reputation and mostly cover the full range of the Valtellino superiore wines, so I will, in this case, just list their names without making any specific recommendations as to which wine they are reckoned to be particularly noted for making.

Producers

ENOLOGICA VALTELLINESE
   (Sondrio)

GUIDO BETTINI
   (Teglio, Sondrio)

GIOVANNI TONA
   (Villa di Tirano, Sondrio)

NINO NEGRI
   (Chiuro, Sondrio)

CANTINA COOPERATIVA
   (Villa di Tirano, Sondrio)

FRATELLI POLATTI
   (Sondrio)

RAINOLDI E FIGLIO
   (Chiuro, Sondrio)

A. PELIZZATTI
   (Sondrio)

FRANCO BALGERA
   (Chiuro, Sondrio)

BRESCIA WINES

BOTTICINO

The Botticino and the Cellatica come from Lombardy, between lakes Iseo and Garda. They are very similar, with Botticino being the more robust. The Botticino is a multiple wine, taking its components from adjacent regions, though they are, of course, grown within the DOC zone; Barbera (30–40 per cent), from Piedmont; Schiava and Marzemino (35–55 per cent), from the Trentino-Alto Adige; and Sangiovese (10–20 per cent) from Tuscany. The addition of 15 per cent of wines from other areas is permitted.

The result is a ruby-red wine when young that turns to a rich garnet with age. It is warm, full-bodied, and fairly tannic, as might be expected from such a mixture of grapes. It ages well, becoming nicely balanced, with an intense bouquet and elegant finish. The minimum alcoholic content is 12 per cent.

Producer
PIETRO BRACCHI
(Botticino, Brescia)

CELLATICA

The Cellatica red wine has been produced on the hillsides just north of Brescia, around the town of Cellatica, since Renaissance times, which seems valid proof of the popularity of the wine.

The only change in the formula over the centuries is that originally the wine was entirely from the Schiava grape, but now some Barbera and Marzemino have been added. This mixture offers a well-balanced, full-bodied ruby-red wine that ages usefully. It has a dry, lively taste and a slightly tart aftertaste. The alcoholic content is at least 11.5 per cent. This closely resembles the Botticino; however, the production is appreciably larger, though in neither case is it big. There are 500,000 liters of Cellatica made annually, against 155,000 of Botticino.

Producer
COOPERATIVA VINIVITICOLA CELLATICA "GASSAGO"
    (Cellatica, Brescia)

FRANCIACORTA PINOT
FRANCIACORTA ROSSO

Franciacorta is produced in a small area between Brescia and Lake Iseo. There are many theories about the derivation of the name, some of which go back to the fifteenth century; the most likely is that the name is a corruption of the name of the nearby town of Cortefranca, or vice-versa.

The white is drunk young, when it is dry, fresh, and lively. It is a pale-straw-colored wine with greenish reflections; it has a pleasing aroma and between 11.5 per cent and 12 per cent alcohol.

The red, obtained from a mixture of Cabernet Franc, Barbera, Nebbiolo, and Merlot, ages well, when it loses its violet lights for a deep red. With bottle age, it becomes a distinguished but not a heavy wine.

Producers   *Additional Description*

GUIDO BERLUCCHI   CASTEL BORGONATO
    (Borgonato di Corte franca, Brescia)
GIACOMO RAGNOLI
    (Brescia)

LAKE GARDA WINES

LUGANA

Lugana comes from a small area south of Sirmione. Excavations show that the vine was cultivated here even in the Bronze Age. The vine grown there now is the famous Trebbiano, which is used for the Soave wines of Verona and widely throughout all of central Italy. This Lugana variety is particularly noted for its maturing qualities: at three or four years of age, it acquires a warm amber color. However, when young it is a straw-white wine with greenish tints; light, fresh, and delicate, with at least 11.5 and often 12 or 13 per cent alcohol.

Producers

GIULIO AMBROSI
 (Rivoltella del Garda, Brescia)

LAMBERTI
 (Lazise del Garda, Verona)

LODOVICO MONTRESOR
 (Peschiera, Brescia)

SENATO FRATELLI
 (Peschiera, Brescia)

RIVIERA DEL GARDA (Chiaretto)

Riviera del Garda wines have been highly prized for many a decade, the chiaretto (rosé), in particular, being widely known and respected. These Garda wines are cultivated on the west side of the lake and also on the south, overlapping the Lugana zone.

Chiaretto is often incorrectly translated as claret and the two wines compared, to the detriment of chiaretto, which is essentially a light wine, a luncheon wine, not to be aged usefully beyond a few years. The only thing claret and chiaretto have in common is that they are both multiple wines. In the case of the latter, the wines used are Gropello (50–60 per cent), Sangiovese (10–25 per cent), Barbera (10–20 per cent), and Marzemino (5–15 per cent). The chiaretto is a handsome rosé with deeper, ruby lights, rich and warm, with a slightly sharp aftertaste, a delicate bouquet, and a light 11–11.5 per cent alcohol. There is a Riviera del Garda red made from the same grapes, which, if aged for a year and reaching 12 per cent alcohol, may be called superiore.

Producers

AZIENDA AGRICOLA BERTANZI
    (Moniga, Brescia)
FABIO BOTTARELLI E FIGLIO
    (Picedo, Brescia)
ALBERICI PALAZZI
    (Picedo di Polpenazze, Brescia)
LAMBERTI
    (Lazise del Garda, Verona)

TOCAI DI SAN MARTINO DELLA BATTAGLIA

Tocai is a Friuli-Venezia Giulia wine, but sometime in the early part of this century someone found that it was equally at home in the Lugana DOC zone, at the south end of Lake Garda.

Tocai, at any time or in any place, is a most satisfactory wine and one with a particularly attractive personality. It is round and warm, yet with a characteristic tartness that is not easily forgotten. It also ages more than most whites, when it loses its lemonish color and turns golden. It always has a good 12 per cent alcohol.

Producer
CONTE CAMILLIO PELLIZZARI
    (Desenzano, Brescia)

COLLI MORENICI MANTOVANI DEL GARDA
(Mantua Hills wine)

This delimited DOC zone is on the hills between Lake Garda and Mantua; it is a new zone, and its wines, to date, have made no impression on the Italian market.

Producer
CANTINA SOCIALE DI MONZAMBANO
    (Monzambano, Mantua)

CHAPTER EIGHT

Liguria

Liguria is said to have sixty-four different varieties of wine, almost all produced in very small quantities and consumed by the Ligurians privately and with no assistance required from outsiders. Only two are widely known and available.

Liguria is a strip of land, more commonly known as the Italian Riviera, stretching from Monte Carlo to San Remo, to Genoa, and to just after Portofino. Behind this narrow coastal strip of flat land, hills rise and lead back to the great wine-producing lands of Piedmont. On the hills overlooking the sea, the farmers have for centuries built terraces on which to grow vines and fruit and olive trees. In this post-World War II period the value of land has rocketed up both on the coast and in the hills. The towns have doubled and tripled in size, and new trunk roads and *autostrade* have been built, also eating up agricultural land. This evolution led farmers to change profession and become townsmen, abandoning the struggle of eking a living out of their little patches of terraced land, which could not even be mechanized. Those who stayed also changed profession: they took to growing flowers and employing Sicilians and Calabrians, whose love of the soil was more deeply rooted. The production of wine has dropped year by year, and greater quantities have been imported into the region to meet the needs of an ever-growing population that, in summer months, runs to hundreds of thousands more, due to the vacationers and those passing from the French Riviera to all parts of Italy and beyond.

There is little doubt that a lot of wine labeled as Ligurian wine is flying under false colors, though this is not to say that the wine is in any way bad; quite otherwise; it is good. The criticism is that it is not from Liguria. However, this credibility gap will shortly be closed by the two major wines—Rossese di Dolceacqua and the Cinqueterre—getting their DOC recognition. Wines with a long history, such as Polcevera, and Cornata, are, unless somebody resuscitates them, already part of past history. There is, however, still some Vermentino available.* This is from a vine of the same name that over a century ago was transferred to Sardinia, to the Gallura, where it is now producing considerable quantities of exceptionally high-quality wine. As with the wines of Capri and Ischia, which are equally redolent of sunshine and sea breezes, the Liguria wines are light and fresh of taste, but one should drink with prudence, as they all have a larger alcoholic content than one initially thinks, and can make driving, let us say, a trifle hazardous.

ROSSESE DI DOLCEACQUA (or DOLCEACQUA)

The Dolceacqua, or Rossese, comes from the hills behind the Italian Riviera from Alassio to San Remo and to the French border. The town of Dolceacqua lies behind Bordighera and Ventimiglia. It is made from the Rossese grape to about 70 per cent. The wine is a dry red of around 13 per cent alcohol that ap-

* Cantina Crespi (Imperia)

preciates a few years of bottle age. It also appreciates being opened half an hour before serving: in all, an elegant wine.

Producer	*Additional Description*
CANTINA CRESPI	TERRE BIANCHE
(Imperia)	COSTE DI BUSSANA
	(Vermentino)

BIANCO DELLE CINQUETERRE
SCIACCHETRÀ

The Cinqueterre (the five lands) are on the south end of the Ligurian Riviera, after Genoa and Chiavari and before La Spezia. Here, on precipitous hillsides, they grow the Vernaccia grape and make a white wine that ages very nicely and also a sweet wine, the Sciacchetrà, from the same grape. This latter is a passito, made from semi-dried grapes, whereby it reaches a good 16 per cent and a deep amber color. This wine, however, is becoming rare. The dry is a golden straw color with a high perfume and between 12 and 13 per cent alcohol.

Producers	*Additional Description*
ASALDO	SCIACCHETRÀ
(San Pier d'Arena, Genoa)	
GIULIANO CROVARA	
(Monarola, Liguria)	

CHAPTER NINE

TRENTINO-ALTO ADIGE (South Tyrol)

Alto Adige Wines

Trentino-Alto Adige

The Trentino-Alto Adige wine-producing region spreads from south of Trento right up the Adige Valley to Bolzano, Merano, and Bressanone, to the Austrian frontier. Of all the wine-growing areas of Italy, it resembles most of all the Valtelline in that it is a zone producing a very high percentage of quality wines—the more distinguished wineries producing 80 to 100 per cent DOC wines and at prices that are well-sustained due to demand being greater than supply.

The zone is dual, as one can see from its name: Trentino-Alto Adige. The Trentino is the area around Trento, in the south; the Alto Adige is the narrowing valley to the north, toward Austria. The former is Italian-speaking and more French in its style of wines; the latter mostly German-speaking, often called the South Tyrol, and inevitably more German in its choice of wines, though it has plenty of full-bodied reds.

Archaeology has shown that the vine was cultivated and wine made in prehistoric times by Etruscans in the valley; the Romans used the area as a source of supply for their Spanish legions garrisoned north of the Alps—a supply vocation that the Trentino-Alto Adige retains to this day, not for Spanish troops but a large body of customers.

After the fall of the Roman Empire, the zone continued to supply the barbarian Lombards of Bavaria. With the Middle Ages and the Christianization of Germany, the German bishops staked their claims in the Tyrol to assure supplies of good wine.

The Trentino today produces 6 million liters of DOC wine: 2.5 million of Merlot, 1.3 of white Pinot, .9 of Cabernet, and lesser quantities of Lagrein, Riesling, Marzemino, and Traminer. There are four major producers, the C.A.V.I.T. co-operative, which, to my mind, is among the very best in Italy; the Conti Bossi Fedrigotti winery; that of the Endrizzi Brothers; and the Ferrari Company, producer of 150,000 bottles of brut spumante each year by the méthode champenoise, using black Pinot and Chardonnay grapes grown at between fifteen hundred and two thousand feet in the hills near Trento. Giulio Ferrari is the only estate-bottled champenoise brut made in Italy: the other producers buy their grapes and process them. The founder of the firm, in the 1890s, studied in France, first at the Enological Institute of Montpellier and then in the champagne industry. He returned to Trento, bringing with him Pinot vines, and reproduced the ambient conditions and processing methods. The brut, nowadays, is marketed after four years in the bottle; the riserva after six.

There are now ten DOC Trentino wines: Cabernet, Lagrein, Marzemino, Merlot, black Pinot, white Pinot, Riesling, Traminer, Moscato, and Vin Santo. At the time of writing, there are only two DOC wines for the Alto Adige: Caldaro and Merano Hills; but another seven are on the way: Santa Maddalena, Terlano, white Pinot, Italic Riesling, Rhine Riesling, Sauvignon, and Sylvaner. These two lists, however, do not fit the facts too well, since there are, for example, Lagreins and black Pinots (the magnificent Blauburgunder) and Gewürztraminer produced in the northern province, but listed only in the south. And there are traditional wines such as Grauvernatsch (Schiava grigia), San Giustina (red Vernaccia), Casteller (Schiava, Merlot, and

Lagrein), Sorni (a Müller-Thurgau of grafted Riesling and Sylvaner) that do not seem to fit in anywhere. And perhaps not surprisingly, the Bossi Fedrigotti Fojaneghe, made like a claret (including the immersion of the grapeskins during fermentation, which improves the bouquet at the expense of the alcoholic content) from Cabernet Franc, Cabernet Sauvignon, and Merlot, and matured for two years in 200-liter casks and for three in the bottle, does not fit in either; this wine, needless to say, does not lack either aficionados or purchasers for the fifty thousand bottles produced each year.

The difficulty of growing vines on hillside terraces, often at considerable heights, requires that what is produced be of high quality and command good prices: in fact, the f.o.b. winery price in the Trentino-Alto Adige does not drop much below one dollar for a bottle of young but matured wine (some areas of Italy can offer wine at a quarter of that price in bulk). All the reds —Caldaro, Teroldego, black Pinots, Sornis, Marzeminos, Merlots and Santa Maddalenas—appreciate being offered some bottle age, and so do the German-style whites—the Rieslings and the Sylvaners.

In the Alto Adige, after an initial resistance to the DOC principle, years ago the producers began the structural alterations necessary to their vineyards and the varieties grown; this investment of work and money has not yet come fully to fruition. However, one can say quite safely that the Alto Adige—and the Trentino too—will spread the very high reputation already gained in Switzerland, Germany, and Austria much farther abroad.

Throughout the whole area you will come across a wide use of the German language and Gothic lettering on the labels of the bottles, which are often of the "hock" variety. You will also find the use of German wine terminology, such as *auslese,* meaning "choice" or "select."

TRENTINO WINES

The following wines are made in Trento province; that is, in the lower part of the Adige Valley. These, if anything, tend to have more body but less bouquet than the wines from higher up, around Bolzano. Piling all these completely different wines into one DOC category seems to have little meaning, but let it be: the wines are all of high quality, well known and produced by wineries that merit the reputations they have earned over the decades.

CABERNET TRENTINO

The Cabernet lives up to the reputation of a distinguished name, offering a smooth, full, pleasantly tannic red wine that ages very well indeed, when it takes on orangy tints. Minimum alcoholic content 11 per cent, but this usually runs to 12 per cent from the better wineries.

Producers
C.A.V.I.T. CO-OPERATIVE
(Ravina, Trento)
GIUSEPPE BONVECCHIO
(Trento)

Producers

CANTINA SOCIALE DI ISERA
(Isera, Trento)
FRATELLI ENDRIZZI
(San Michele all'Adige, Trento)
CONTE FEDERIGO BOSSI FEDRIGOTTI
(Rovereto, Trento)
MARCHESE ANSELMO GUERRIERI GONZAGA
(San Leonardo D'Avio, Trento)
BOSCHI E GAMBERONI
(Volano, Trento)
ISTITUTO SAN MICHELE ALL'ADIGE
(San Michele all'Adige, Trento)

LAGREIN TRENTINO (and Alto Adige)

Lagrein is something of a specialty wine, unusual in personality.
It is made from the Lagrein grape near the little town of Gries.
Most of the wine is produced as a rosé, when it is often called
Lagreinkretzer. It is dry, full, yet delicate, with a minimum of
11 per cent alcohol, which, from the best houses, is usually 12
per cent; a wine worth cellaring.

Producers

CANTINA SOCIALE DI GRIES
(Gries, Bolzano)
J. HOFSTATTER
(Termeno, Bolzano)
KLOSTERKELLEREI
(Muri-Gries, Bolzano)

Producers
BARONE DE CLES
(Mezzolombardo, Trento)
FIORINDO DELANA
(Trento)
CONTE FEDERIGO BOSSI FEDRIGOTTI
(Rovereto, Trento)

MARZEMINO TRENTINO

This is a traditional wine of the Trento area that only two decades ago was usually made slightly sweet to meet the then-current taste. Nowadays it is being treated as a fine, dry red wine and aged in the wood to offer a full-bodied, slightly tannic, but well-balanced wine of between 11 and 12 per cent alcohol.

Producers
C.A.V.I.T. CO-OPERATIVE
(Ravina, Trento)
FRATELLI ENDRIZZI
(San Michele all'Adige, Trento)
CANTINA SOCIALE DI ISERA
(Isera, Trento)
CONTE FEDERIGO BOSSI FEDRIGOTTI
(Rovereto, Trento)
ISTITUTO AGRARIO SAN MICHELE ALL'ADIGE
(San Michele all'Adige, Trento)

MERLOT TRENTINO

The Merlot vine has, more than any other foreign resident vine, acclimatized itself in Italy to perfection and has been most generous in its gratitude for the sunshine and hospitality received. This ruby-red dry wine can become, with a few years' aging, a most distinguished guest at table.

Producers

CONTE FEDERIGO BOSSI FEDRIGOTTI
    (Rovereto, Trento)
BARONE DE CLES
    (Mezzolombardo, Trento)
C.A.V.I.T. CO-OPERATIVE
    (Ravina, Trento)
CANTINA SOCIALE DI ISERA
    (Isera, Trento)
VITTORIO FORADORI
    (Mezzolombardo, Trento)

PINOT NERO TRENTINO (and Alto Adige)

Pinot Nero, which is the black Pinot grape famous for producing Burgundy, is much at home in the Trentino-Alto Adige: the wine it produces is often called Borgogna Nera or Blauburgunder. This big wine, with its generous 13 per cent alcohol, is a wine for cask and bottle age. It first matures into a harmonious, full-bodied dry wine and then refines in the bottle, gaining a delicate aroma and an elegant finish.

Producers

ISTITUTO SAN MICHELE ALL'ADIGE
(San Michele all'Adige, Trento)

RUDOLF CARLI
(Nalles, Bolzano)

K. VON ELZENBAUM
(Termeno, Bolzano)

CANTINA SOCIALE DI TERMENO
(Termeno, Bolzano)

J. HOFSTATTER
(Termeno, Bolzano)

J. NIEDERMAYR
(Girlan, Bolzano)

PINOT TRENTINO

The white Pinot is called Weissburgunder or Borgogna bianca in this region. The bulk is sold as table wine locally, but the choicest bunches are processed for bottling either as a fine and remarkably strong white table wine or as sparkling brut spumante (cf. SPUMANTE BRUT), both of which have high reputations, particularly the latter. As a still wine it is straw yellow, fresh, yet round even when young, and with a pleasingly tart aftertaste.

Producers

ISTITUTO SAN MICHELE ALL'ADIGE
(San Michele all'Adige, Trento)

CANTINA SOCIALE SAN MICHELE
(San Michele, Bolzano)

RIESLING TRENTINO

The Trentino Riesling, produced from the Rhine Riesling vine, offers a much heavier wine than its German cousin. It is a straw yellow tending to green, with all of 12 per cent alcohol. When chilled, it retains many of the northern characteristics of bouquet.

Producers

C.A.V.I.T. CO-OPERATIVE
   (Ravina, Trento)
FRATELLI ENDRIZZI
   (San Michele all'Adige, Trento)
ISTITUTO SAN MICHELE ALL'ADIGE
   (San Michele all'Adige, Trento)

TRAMINER AROMATICO TRENTINO (and Alto Adige)

A golden-yellow dry wine produced around the town of Tramin (Termeno), just south of Bolzano. It is a sturdy wine that will take a decade of bottle age if nursed. It is especially noted for its bouquet and its dry-dry aftertaste.

Producers

K. VON ELZENBAUM
   (Termeno, Bolzano)
J. HOFSTATTER
   (Termeno, Bolzano)
G. KETTMEIR
   (Bolzano)

Producers

CANTINA SOCIALE DI TERMENO
   (Termeno, Bolzano)
ABBAZIA DI NOVACELLA
   (Bressanone, Bolzano)
CONTI BOSSI FEDRIGOTTI
   (Rovereto, Trento)
ISTITUTO SAN MICHELE ALL'ADIGE
   (San Michele all'Adige, Trento)

MOSCATO TRENTINO

This white dessert wine is produced to the east of the city of Trento. Like most of the wines of the Adige Valley, it has a high bouquet; it is also sweet and alcoholic and suitable for those with an incurable sweet tooth.

Producers

CONTI BOSSI FEDRIGOTTI
   (Rovereto, Trento)
FRATELLI ENDRIZZI
   (San Michele all'Adige, Trento)
ISTITUTO SAN MICHELE ALL'ADIGE
   (San Michele all'Adige, Trento)

VIN SANTO TRENTINO

A rich and luxuriant amber-colored wine that is aged for as long as five years. It is very sweet and strong in alcohol (16 per cent);

connoisseurs of Vin Santo put it among the very best of all Italy.

Producers
FRATELLI MARCHETTI
    (Arco, Trento)
C.A.V.I.T. CO-OPERATIVE
    (Ravina, Trento)

TEROLDEGO ROTALIANO

This fine red wine comes from halfway between Trento and Bolzano in the Adige Valley and from the Teroldego vine. It is a big and lusty wine rather than a refined and elegant one, but no less enjoyable for that; it reaches maturity at two years and goes on improving in the bottle. At two years of age it may be labeled as superiore, when it is ruby red and beginning to turn a brick color; it has a striking aroma, is harmonious and full and pleasantly tannic, and has a highly personal and heady aftertaste.

Producers
BARONE DE CLES
    (Mezzolombardo, Trento)
CANTINA COOPERATIVA MEZZOLOMBARDO
    (Mezzolombardo, Trento)
CONSORZIO DEL TEROLDEGO ROTALIANO
    (Mezzocorona, Trento)
CONTE FEDERIGO BOSSI FEDRIGOTTI
    (Rovereto, Trento)
ISTITUTO AGRARIO SAN MICHELE ALL'ADIGE
    (San Michele all'Adige, Trento)

SORNI

This wine is close to the Riesling Trentino but does not seem to be DOC-ing, despite its local fame. It is made with Müller-Thurgau Riesling-Sylvaner, and Nosiola grapes to produce a light white table wine with greenish tints and between 11 and 11.5 per cent alcohol. It is produced just north of Trento.

There is a red Sorni, made mostly of the popular Schiava grape, that produces a full-bodied wine much appreciated in Germany.

Producer
CANTINA SOCIALE LAVIS SORNI
   (Sorni, Trento)

SPUMANTE BRUT

The "champagnes" of the Trentino are well recognized at home and abroad for their quality. Only the best Pinot grapes are used and either the méthode champenoise or the charmat for processing. The wine is "paper white"—almost colorless, and transparent—and is made brut, reserve, dry, semi-dry, etc. Particularly notable is the Ferrari spumante, which is fermented in the bottle and aged four or five years.

Producers
GIULIO FERRARI
   (Trento)
C.A.V.I.T. CO-OPERATIVE
   (Ravina, Trento)

ALTO ADIGE WINES

CALDARO-KALTERER
LAGO DI CALDARO-KALTERERSEE

In the South Tyrol, by Bolzano, on the road from Trento to the Brenner Pass, the tiny Lake of Caldaro is to be found. The delectable mountain valley produces some of Italy's best wines; its exports to Switzerland and Germany are very large.

The Caldaro-Kalterer wine is the most abundant but not necessarily the best: it has many hard rivals. The name requires, for those who know no German, a word of explanation: Bolzano province is mostly German-speaking, and consequently labels are often either bilingual or in German only. Kalterer is the German adjectival form of Caldaro, and Kalterersee means Lake Caldaro: Caldaro is Kaltern. Also Bolzano is Bozen, Bressanone is Brixen, Appaiano is Eppan, Nalles is Nals, Termeno is Tramin, Novacella is Neustift, Cornaiano is Girlan, and Egna is Neumarkt.

The main producing area is the classic zone around the lake, stretching toward Bolzano and also downriver. The ordinary zone is not just an extension of this area but, due to the configuration of the mountainous country, is made up of seven small enclaves up and down the river from Caldaro. The vines are grown at an altitude of between one thousand and two thousand feet.

If the grapes of the classic zone's production are selected so as to give a wine with an alcoholic content of more than 10.5 per cent (usually a good Caldaro reaches 12 per cent), it may be called superiore. In the case of ordinary-zone wine reaching eleven per cent, it may be called *scelto* or *auslese,* which means select.

The three types of grapes used to obtain Caldaro are all varieties of the Schiava vine. The main characteristics of the Caldaro-Kalterer are: a ruby-red wine tending to garnet, a smooth, round taste with an overtone of almonds, and a pleasing vinous aroma. The superiore and scelto (auslese) repay maturing in the bottle.

Producers

J. HOFSTATTER
   (Termeno, Bolzano)

CANTINA SOCIALE SAN MICHELE APPIANO
   (San Michele Appiano, Bolzano)

RUDOLF CARLI
   (Nalles, Bolzano)

JOSEF BRIGL
   (Cornaiano, Bolzano)

G. KETTMEIR
   (Bolzano)

CANTINA SOCIALE DI TERMENO
   (Termeno, Bolzano)

MERANESE DI COLLINA (Merano Hills)

This is a little-known table wine, made chiefly by the co-operative of Merano, which lies near the Austrian border. The grape used is the familiar Schiava, which produces a most pleasing ruby-red wine, round and with 11 per cent alcohol. If produced in the Tyrol province, which is a classic zone, it may be called Burgravio or

Burggrafler. You may find wine labeled Küchelburger, which means that it is a superior wine from the Merano region.

Producers

CANTINA SOCIALE DI MERANO
(Merano)

G. KETTMEIR
(Bolzano)

SANTA MADDALENA-ST. MAGDALENA

The Santa Maddalena is made from a variety of Schiava grown on the hillsides directly to the north of Bolzano and the Isarco River. Once bottled, the best quality can be called Santa Maddalena Classico or Magdalener Klassischer Ursprungsgebiet. This is a formidable wine when aged for a while in the wood and several years in the bottle, when its delicate mountain perfume is enhanced and accentuated, its ruby red pales to brick, and it takes on an ethereal character not easily forgotten.

Producers

G. KETTMEIR
(Bolzano)

KELLEREI-GENOSSENSCHAFT ST. MAGDALENA
(Bolzano)

JOSEF BRIGL
(Cornaiano, Bolzano)

J. HOFSTATTER
(Termeno, Bolzano)

TERLANO

The various white wines known as Terlano or Terlaner (the German adjectival form), according to Italian or German usage, come from the hills around the town of Terlano (Terlan), which lies to the north of Bolzano, toward Merano (Meran). Traditionally the Terlano is a composite wine, made up of 50 per cent white Pinot and the other 50 per cent of Italic Riesling, Rhine Riesling, Sauvignon, and Sylvaner. These various wines now are being approved individually by the DOC regulations. The original Terlano is a very clear, straw-colored wine tending to green, dry, slightly tart, yet fairly full. It has a fresh and persistent aroma and between 11.5 and 12.5 per cent alcohol. It is often used as an apéritif. All the Terlano wines are noted for improving in the bottle.

Producers

J. HOFSTATTER
(Termeno, Bolzano)
CANTINA SOCIALE DI TERLANO
(Terlano, Bolzano)

TERLANO PINOT BIANCO

The white Pinot is often labeled, in the Alto Adige, as Weiss-burgunder. Equally well known is the Pinot Grigio, often sold under the name Ruländer and called Sonnengold in Bolzano; surprisingly, this wine is not among those so far on the list for DOC-ing. But there seems to be some confusion between these two vines and wines, which perhaps in time will be sorted out by the DOC regulations. Meanwhile the Pinot white burgundy remains a golden wine with greenish tints, dry, and with a mountain-fresh bouquet and at least 11.5 per cent alcohol.

Producers
RUDOLF CARLI
    (Nalles, Bolzano)
J. HOFSTATTER
    (Termeno, Bolzano)
G. KETTMEIR
    (Bolzano)
CANTINA SOCIALE DI SAN MICHELE APPIANO
    (San Michele Appiano, Bolzano)
CANTINA SOCIALE DI TERLANO
    (Terlano, Bolzano)

TERLANO RIESLING ITALICO

Italic Riesling is known best as one of the components used to make the regular, traditional Terlaner. It is better known locally in the Alto Adige as a carafe wine, and perhaps it has more future than past. In any event, its characteristics are: dry, lively

yet well balanced, light golden in color, and a minimum alcoholic
content of 10.5 per cent.

Producers

CANTINA SOCIALE DI TERLANO
      (Terlano, Bolzano)

RUDOLF CARLI
      (Nalles, Bolzano)

J. HOFSTATTER
      (Termeno, Bolzano)

BARONE DI PAULI
      (Caldaro, Bolzano)

A. CRASTEN
      (Schloss Rametz, Merano)

TERLANO RIESLING RENANO (Rhine Riesling)

The Rhine Riesling is a distinguished wine, as much as its
Alsatian forebears, which it resembles in its broad characteristics.
It is a delicate, fragrant wine, golden with greenish undertones,
full-bodied, dry, and with a good 12 per cent alcohol.

Producers

A. CRASTEN
      (Schloss Rametz, Merano)

CANTINA SOCIALE DI TERLANO
      (Terlano, Bolzano)

RUDOLF CARLI
      (Nalles, Bolzano)

J. HOFSTATTER
      (Termeno, Bolzano)

BARONE DI PAULI
      (Caldaro, Bolzano)

G. KETTMEIR
      (Bolzano)

TERLANO SAUVIGNON

The Sauvignon, which in the past was only an ingredient of the Terlano, is now modestly standing on its own feet. It is to become a DOC wine in due course, and more of the vines are being planted. Having acclimatized itself admirably to the mountain air of the Alto Adige, the Sauvignon offers a natural 12 per cent wine with a notable fragrance, full flavor, and considerable body.

Producers

G. KETTMEIER
    (Bolzano)
CANTINA SOCIALE DI TERLANO
    (Terlano, Bolzano)

TERLANO SYLVANER

This German vine is cultivated in the hills around Bressanone (Brixen), which run to well over two thousand feet above sea level, on the route to the Brenner Pass. In this mountain scenery it produces a most taut, dry wine with a full bouquet and as much as 12 per cent alcohol.

Producers

ABBAZIA DI NOVACELLA
    (Bressanone, Bolzano)
JOSEF BRIGL
    (Cornaiano, Bolzano)
CANTINA SOCIALE DI CHIUSA
    (Chiusa, Bressanone)
FRATELLI ENDRIZZI
    (San Michele all'Adige, Trento)

GRAUVERNATSCH

A much appreciated local wine that does not seem to be listed for DOC-ing. It is made from the gray Schiava grape and is a dry, strong 12.5 per cent red wine that, like the Lambrusco, goes well with sausages and other fat-laden foods.

Producers
RUDOLF CARLI
    (Nalles, Bolzano)
ABBAZIA DI NOVACELLA
    (Novacella, Bressanone)
CANTINA SOCIALE DI CORNAIANO
    (Cornaiano, Bolzano)
CANTINA SOCIALE DI SAN MICHELE APPIANO
    (San Michele Appiano, Bolzano)

CHAPTER TEN

VENETO

River Piave Wines

Veneto

The Veneto is an agricultural region par excellence; its wine production is very large—850 million liters annually, twice that of Tuscany. However, when it comes to DOC wine, Tuscany runs slightly ahead of the Veneto, with 107 million liters against 91 million. The production figures of the major Veneto DOC wines are still large: for example, there are 40 million liters of Soave and 14 million liters of Bardolino, in comparison with a modest 4 million liters of Piedmont Barolo or the 7 million liters of the whole Trentino-Alto Adige. These quantities inevitably mean a heavy commercial production and that the prospective purchaser must proceed with caution. DOC is a preliminary safeguard; superiore and riserva are a second line of defense, classico is a third, while knowing the names of the more distinguished producers from whom to buy Veneto wines makes for further in-depth protection.

Not all the vines are grown in the hills: valley bottoms and plains produce secondary wines. The good producers process their hill grapes apart, since these have a higher acidity and will make a better wine, particularly for aging. They often make further

divisions of these grapes, especially in the Valpolicella area, which
has its Recioto made from the top grapes on each vine, bunches
that have received the most sunshine and consequently have the
most sugar to form a stronger wine.

The Veneto divides up into three separate growing zones. The
most famous of these is, of course, the Verona-wines area, from
which come the Valpolicella, the Bardolino, and the Soave wines.
The second includes the hills running down toward Padua and
Venice from Verona and Vicenza—the Euganean Hills—which
is a little-known zone. The third is that of Treviso and Conegliano,
which is an explosion of very fine table wines—reds, whites, and
sparklers—and one, the Venegazzù, that can face any rivalry or
comparison.

The Veneto has had its wine-producing vocation for two and
a half millennia, according to archaeologists who dug up Etruscan
wine jars with grape seeds in them. Even during the Dark Ages,
wine making continued, and as soon as civilization returned,
with the Renaissance, it become compulsory. During the long
period when the Veneto was under the Austro-Hungarian Empire,
it was a major exporter to Vienna; it still retains a bit of interest
in that direction.

The Bardolino, from the hillsides overlooking Lake Garda, is,
like a young Chianti or Beaujolais, an excellent all-purpose
luncheon wine. Bardolino from exceptional years ages up to five
years, but this is of abstract interest, because Bardolino's major
charm lies in its freshness and youth. If one wants a more mature
Verona wine, one moves easily a few miles east to enjoy a
Valpolicella, which, oddly, is produced from the same grapes,
yet produces a very different wine. For myself, I prefer the
Valpolicella from the Valpantena; its components are slightly
different, it has more body and ability to age, and it is also
usually half a percentage point stronger.

The second zone includes the Gambellara wines, which are
not exactly earth-shattering. And then there are the Breganze
wines, an isolated group of six wines that has a history of only two

decades; that is, from when a co-operative was formed. This is an area with a natural vocation and with excellent prospects for the future, especially if the growers can raise cheap capital to mature their black Pinots and Cabernets in the wood.

The DOC white of Custoza is something of a mystery—at least to me and the many people I have asked. I have never managed to trace it, and I have truly tried. However, to avoid disappointment, there is a Costozza wine (could it be that the DOC people have made two typographical errors?) that is very good indeed and has a history going back five hundred years and comes from close to where the DOC Custoza should come from, if it existed. The Costozza wines are from the Berici Hills, south of Vicenza. The production of Riesling, Cabernet, and Pinot rosé is very limited—only 100,000 bottles a year. Price levels 50 per cent above most other wines of the region are maintained. The Counts of Schio at their Costozza winery at Lungara, Vicenza, pride themselves on their modern equipment, estate bottling, and traditional methods, and regret only that the demand is such that they cannot age as much wine in their *caves* as they would like to.

Farther east, toward Padua, we find a first-class co-operative—Cantina Sociale dei Colli Euganei—which currently makes half a million bottles of wine per annum at modest prices and is increasing its capacity. We find also the famous Luxardo company, which took over a dying rosolio-cum-cherry-syrup business back in 1821 and, setting up in Yugoslavia, then part of the Austro-Hungarian Empire, invented Maraschino, which was more to modern taste and has remained so. Having left Yugoslavia after World War II, they settled in the Paduan Hills as a good place to grow their twenty thousand cherry trees and their vines. They now produce both red and white DOC wines of considerable distinction, though these are, as yet, little known, at least on a national level.

The Treviso DOC-ing wines, which come from the hills to the north and northeast of Venice, include the white Conegliano and

Valdobbiadenes, Merlots and Cabernets, and, above all, Tocai di Lison. But, in truth, there are also available many other fine wines that are not DOC-ing: white Pinot, Riesling, Sauvignon, Ramandolo, and, I repeat, Venegazzù, which is a mixture of Cabernet Franc, Cabernet Sauvignon, Merlot Malbec, and Petit Verdot. And there are other, similar mixes made by other, if less famous, producers.

The white Conegliano and Valdobbiadene are mostly sparklers and mostly *abboccato*. However, there are dry ones and especially those from the classic area of Cartizze. These are fresh, light, and fitting as apéritifs or at table; they are also remarkably inexpensive, considering the quality, the bouquet, and the pleasure they offer. The brut, however, costs around two dollars f.o.b. winery, double the abboccato's price.

To the south, around the town of Treviso, we find the reds: the Cabernets, the Merlots, and the Rabosos, as well as the well-known white Tocai; these are generically called "the wines of the river Piave." Since there are a lot of red-wine vines cultivated on the plains here, it is sage to purchase DOC wines from noted producers, as DOC regulations preclude the use of such grapes; reputable producers age their reds from two to four years, and you don't do that with a grape grown on the plains.

An organization called Cantina Club, of Treviso, opened the door to wines that I should probably never have found myself. Whoever the organizers of this club are, they plainly love good wine and have searched out the best, without reference to or consideration of DOC rulings. Several of their choices are of mixed Cabernet-Merlot wines, which are not likely to be approved as DOC. But, in any case, the regulations for this zone and the make-up of the various wines have not, at the time of writing, been laid down. It seems unlikely that the producers who, at present, make delicately balanced mixtures of Cabernet and Merlot in the Bordeaux spirit will happily settle for selling straight Cabernets and straight Merlots.

The most surprising wine of this area is the Raboso; it comes from the grape of the same name. It is very tannic, robust, strong, (13 per cent), yet well balanced when aged a little; and it has a bouquet that arouses—almost attacks—all the components of one's senses of taste and smell simultaneously, in a way that it is difficult to believe possible.

Of the two whites produced next to the Raboso zone, the Verduzzo is a pleasing but not outstanding wine, while the Tocai (here called Tocai di Lison) can be a delight: it is a rich, full-bodied wine with an intense bouquet and a very mature, almost tart aftertaste.

Already we begin to have one foot in the Veneto and one in Friuli-Venezia Giulia. The big Santa Margherita di Portogruaro and the Conte Antonio Verga Falzacappa wineries make wines from both regions, and the Grave del Friuli DOC zone is a borderline case which, in part, is called Grave del Piave.

VERONA WINES

VALPOLICELLA
VALPOLICELLA VALPANTENA
VALPOLICELLA RECIOTO AMARONE
RECIOTO DELLA VALPOLICELLA

Valpolicella is the Verona wine par excellence and, with Bardolino and Soave, is among the best known of Italian wines at home and abroad. It has several close relatives: the Valpolicella Valpantena and the Valpolicella Recioto Amarone, which might be considered respectively a classic-classic zone and a reserve wine; there are also sweet Recioto della Valpolicella and a sparkling variety. All these are red wines.

The growing area is immediately to the north of Verona, stretching toward Lake Garda for the classic zone and to the east for the simple Valpolicella denomination. The vines used are the Corvina, the Rondinella, and the Molinara, though Barbera and Sangiovese may be added.

The Valpantena is directly north of Verona and has the reputation of producing the best grapes and consequently the best wine, which is marketed under the label Valpolicella Valpantena. This Valpantena is not part of the classic zone, despite its superior wines.

The Valpolicella, both classic and simple categories, are produced in two forms: ready-to-drink and those for aging. The former, like young Chiantis, are subjected to the governo process, which speeds their maturity and gives a fresh, slightly *pétillant* (prickly) wine. The Valpolicella for aging is made from selected grapes and can be called superiore when aged for a year or so, though the precise time has not been laid down by law. This wine should be a medium ruby red, darkening with age; it is dry, but with the slightest touch of sweetness, very smooth and full-bodied, with an elegant finish that is accentuated with the Valpantena. Both have a most pleasing almondy aroma and at least 12 per cent alcohol.

In the case of the Recioto, only superiore grapes are used. After being semi-dried to increase the sugar and alcohol ratio, they are made into a deep-garnet wine that is warm, smooth, and slightly sweet. This sugar can be burned up completely to produce a wine, Amarone, with similar characteristics but dry. This same sugar can be used to make a natural sparkling wine, which is marketed as Recioto Spumante Naturale.

Producers

G. B. BERTANI
    (Verona)

FRATELLI BOLLA
    (Soave, Verona)

GIUSEPPE QUINTARELLI
    (Ciriè di Negrar, Verona)

CANTINA SOCIALE DI NEGRAR
    (Negrar, Verona)

FRATELLI BOSCAINI
    (Marano di Valpolicella, Verona)

CANTINA SOCIALE DI ILLASI
    (Illasi, Verona)

AZIENDA AGRICOLA SANTA SOFIA
    (Valpolicella, Verona)

GIACOMO MONTRESOR
    (Parona, Verona)

BARDOLINO

Bardolino is a wine with a reputation that has spread far from the delightful hillsides overlooking Lake Garda, from where it comes. The classic Bardolino area is in the immediate vicinity of the lakeside towns of Garda, Lazise, and Bardolino, while the simple Bardolino denomination includes vines grown on a rather broader area, extending chiefly to the north.

Bardolino when young is a fresh, pétillant wine, rosé or cherry-colored, that with aging becomes garnet. Bardolino is included in the grouping commonly called Verona wines, which includes Soave and Valpolicella. It is made up of grapes from the following vines: Cortina (50–65 per cent), Rondinella (10–30 per cent), Molinara (10–20 per cent) and Nigrara (10 per cent). It is noted for its fresh fragrance, and if matured for a year it may be called superiore, though Bardolino is not a long-lived wine. It does, however, appreciate and even repay aging up to three or four years. A wine of character.

Producers

COMM. BELLORA DI NAIANO
(Cavaion, Verona)

LAMBERTI
(Lazise, Verona)

FRATELLI BOLLA
(Soave, Verona)

FRATELLI POGGI
(Affi, Verona)

A. & G. PIERGRIFFI
(Bardolino, Verona)

GUERRIERI-RIZZARDI
(Bardolino, Verona)

STERZI
(San Martino Ba, Verona)

SOAVE
RECIOTO DI SOAVE

Soave is one of the well-known trio of Verona wines, a white that can document its history back to the thirteenth century. It is produced east of Verona, north of the little town of San Bonifacio. It has a small classic zone inside the delimited zone. Soave superiore and Soave classico superiore mean that the grapes have been selected to give an alcoholic content of 11.5 per cent rather than the normal 10.5, and that the wines are likely to improve appreciably with bottle age.

All the varieties of Soave and Recioto di Soave are made from the same vines: Garganega (70–90 per cent) and Trebbiano di Soave (10–30 per cent). In view of the very large production of Soave, the classico and classico superiore should be purchased; and in fact it is these which have made Soave's reputation as a first-class table wine that is a brilliantly clear, straw-colored liquid with a tendency to green, dry, medium-bodied, slightly tart yet harmonious, and with a delicate aroma. Serve cool, but not icy as so many people do nowadays.

The Recioto di Soave is a strong dessert wine, not overly sweet, in fact, it has a slightly bitter aftertaste. It is golden in color and has an intense perfume and 14 per cent alcohol from the better producers. A sparkling wine is made from the Recioto, but this is not widely known outside the region.

Producers

G. B. BERTANI
    (Verona)
FRATELLI BOLLA
    (Pedemonte di San Pietro, Verona)

Producers

CANTINA SOCIALE DI SOAVE
  (Soave, Verona)
CANTINA SOCIALE DI ILLASI
  (Illasi, Verona)
LAMBERTI
  (Lazise sul Garda, Verona)

PADUA HILLS WINES

COLLI EUGANEI (Euganean Hills)

The white, the dessert white, and the sparkling white of the Euganean Hills, south of Padua, between Abano Terme and Este, have been well known for many a decade and, along with the Conegliano wines from behind Treviso, have supplied Venice with its daily wine.

It is good wine-producing land; the vine was first planted there some three thousand years ago, so archaeologists say. There is also documentation to the effect that the poet Petrarch built a cottage at Arquà in 1370 that was surrounded by an olive grove and a vineyard.

Today among the offerings there are a Merlot and a sparkling Merlot, neither of which can go far back in history.

The whites are a mixture of Garganega, Serprina, Tocia, and Sauvignon grapes; the reds are Merlot with a small proportion of Cabernet or Barbera.

The Euganean Hills white is a golden wine, dryish but tending to abboccato, smooth, full, and with a pleasing aroma. If it has 12 per cent alcohol and a year's aging, it may be called superiore.

The Euganean Hills red is a rich ruby, dryish, yet, like the white, tending to abboccato; for the rest, it is a good, honest, and well balanced table wine. If the alcohol content rises to 12 per cent and the wine is matured in the wood for a year, it may be called superiore.

There is a sweet Moscato also made, which comes from the more famous Piedmontese vine that produces the spumante. Here, too, it is used to make sparkling wines with considerable success; particularly, the Cantina Sociale co-operative pride themselves on the success they have had with this golden spumante, which they are also making fully dry.

Producers	*Additional Description*
CANTINA SOCIALE COOPERATIVA	SANT'ELMO red
DEI COLLI EUGANEI "VÒ EUGANEI"	MONTE VEDA white
(Padua)	
LUXARDO	
(Torreglia, Padua)	
ROMEO ZACCARIA	
(Tencarola, Padua)	

GAMBELLARA

The Gambellara zone lies between Vicenza and Verona in the Veneto and adjacent to the Soave zone, which is a sound augury for good wine. The vines used for the Gambellara are the Garganega with up to 20 per cent of Soave Trebbiano—the Soave formula.

This wine is processed in five different ways, from still wine through to spumante and vin santo, by a wine growers' co-operative. While private firms tend to specialize, the co-operatives usually aim to cover with their production what was previously done by their various associates as private producers and, in any case, to cover all the requirements of their area. One has the feeling that sometimes they overstretch their facilities.

Most of the Gambellara wine, however, is white table wine: a golden wine, dry, delicately tart yet balanced; and smooth, with 11 per cent alcohol.

The Recioto di Gambellara can be either a still or a sparkling wine: most is the latter. This is a golden liquid, produced from selected grapes, that is sweetish and with 12 per cent alcohol.

Vin Santo di Gambellara is a deep amber wine with a strong, sweet aroma, velvety, and with at least 14 per cent alcohol. This wine, made from semi-dried grapes, must be aged for at least two years in the wood before being marketed.

Producer

CANTINA SOCIALE DI GAMBELLARA
    (Gambellara, Vicenza)

BREGANZE WINES

Breganze is in the Veneto, north of Vicenza and between Lake Garda and Bassano del Grappa; its wine-producing zone has been noted for a hundred and fifty years, chiefly for its Tocai whites and Merlot reds, though there have been many changes and experiments made by the over a thousand smallholders who produce grapes there.

Since 1950, when a wine producers' co-operative was founded, the innumerable wines previously made have been reduced to a standard six, which is still a lot for a small zone and normally frowned on by the DOC authorities. However, it seems that the co-operative persuaded the authorities that all of its offerings were worthy of recognition. They are as follows:

BREGANZE BIANCO

A straw-colored, dry, fresh wine, full-bodied and well balanced, with a delicate and persistent aroma. Alcohol 11–12 per cent.

Made from 85 per cent Tocai and 15 per cent Pinot, Riesling or Sauvignon.

BREGANZE ROSSO

A ruby-red, dry, round wine, slightly tannic, harmonious, and with a pleasing bouquet. Alcohol content 11 per cent. Made of 85 per cent Merlot and 15 per cent other grapes.

BREGANZE CABERNET

This is a dark-ruby table wine, which may be made broadly from either Cabernet Franc or Cabernet Sauvignon or a mixture of the two; if made from selected grapes to give a minimum alcoholic content of 12 per cent it may be called superiore. It is a fairly tannic, full-bodied wine, dry and with a strong vinous bouquet.

BREGANZE PINOT NERO

Ruby red with brick-colored tints, this Pinot Noir is a dry, robust, and fairly tannic wine when young. With the use of selected grapes and a consequently higher alcoholic content, 12 per cent, this wine may be called superiore and is worth a few years of bottle age.

BREGANZE PINOT BIANCO

This has a light straw color, a velvet-smooth taste, a lively aroma, and 11.5 per cent alcohol. If the alcoholic content reaches 12 per cent, it may be called superiore.

BREGANZE VESPAIOLO

This has a deep golden color, a full flavor, a strong vinous aroma, and 11.5 per cent alcohol. Again, with this wine, as with the others, if the alcoholic content reaches 12 per cent, it may be called superiore.

These Breganze wines are just beginning to make their presence felt on the Italian market as quality table wines. There seems no reason why they should not, with time, make a reputation.

BIANCO DI CUSTOZA

This DOC white wine is alleged to come from between Verona and Lake Garda, next to the Bardolino zone. It is alleged to be made from the Tuscan Trebbiano, Garganega, Friuli Tocai, Cortese, Tuscan Malvasia, and Italico grapes. I have never found it.*

* At proofreading time, I have come across an advertisement for this wine, made by the Cantina Sociale Veronese del Garda (Castelnuovo, Verone), describing the wine as coming from the Custoza Hills and having two years of aging.

VENETIAN WINES

PROSECCO DI CONEGLIANO-VALDOBBIADENE CARTIZZE

The Prosecco zone is north of Treviso, in the Veneto, toward Belluno. It has been famous for its white wines since the Middle Ages, when peasants were fined if they did not plant a certain number of vines each year.

The difference in the denominations, however, is not as great as the difference in the types of wines produced. These run from dry to amabile to sweet, and from still through sparkling to spumante. The Cartizze superiore, from a small zone near Conegliano, is considered the best and the driest and is alcoholically strongest. Unless otherwise specified, it can be assumed that these wines are abboccato (very slightly sweet) and that the spumante is processed by the charmat method.

The main characteristics of all these wines, whatever their processing, are straw color, brilliant clarity, a pronounced yet very fresh bouquet of grapes, and between 11 and 12 per cent alcohol. These are very-high-quality wines and popular for celebrations and receptions as well as at table.

Producers   *Additional Description*

CARPENE MALVOLTI
    (Conegliano, Treviso)
DE BERNARD
    (Conegliano, Treviso)

Producers	*Additional Description*
VALDO VINI SUPERIORI	BRUT
(Valdobbiadene, Treviso)	
CANTINA SOCIALE DI VALDOBBIADENE	
(San Giovanni Battista, Treviso)	
CANTINA SOCIALE DI SOLIGO	
(Soligo, Treviso)	
PINO ZARDETTO	STILL
(Conegliano, Treviso)	

TOCAI DI LISON

A certain amount of Tocai is produced in Venice Province, in the hills of Valdobbiadene, and around Lison, which is toward the east and Trieste. It is not considered as outstanding a Tocai as that of Friuli, farther to the east, but it is a very good table wine, much appreciated throughout Italy. It is a straw-colored wine with greenish tints, dry, full-bodied, and with at least 12 per cent alcohol.

Producer

TENUTA SANTA MARGHERITA
(Fossalta di Portogruaro, Treviso)

PRAMAGGIORE CABERNET
PRAMAGGIORE MERLOT

Pramaggiore is in the best vine-growing zone of the Treviso area; the town is well known for the annual wine fair, at which wines from all over Italy are tasted by a panel of experts, and suitable prizes, medals, and other honors are given. From a logical point of view, Pramaggiore Cabernet and Pramaggiore Merlot should be excellent, but I have never found any. I suspect, since this is a new DOC zone, that in the past the wines have been chiefly sold under the Piave label, but plainly we shall hear more of Pramaggiore in the future.

VENEGAZZÙ

The bottles bearing this label are among the most outstanding wines of Italy. The red is obtained from Sauvignon, Malbec, and Merlot grapes, and the white from Riesling and Pinot, all of which are grown in the Treviso area. The remarkably high quality that the raw materials of the wine of the Treviso-Piave area exhibit is surpassed only by the production methods of the Conte Loredan winery at Venegazzù. The red, and the red Riserva di Casa, both age magnificently; they are rare, full-bodied, thoroughbred wines, and it is said that, over and above being aged in oak casks, there are other secrets in the making of this remarkable wine. The white is a fresh, dry wine, with an intense fragrance; it enjoys some bottle age. Neither the red nor the white is DOC, since the grapes used do not fit the category.

Producer
CONTE PIERO LOREDAN
    (Venegazzù del Montello, Treviso)

Additional Description
RESERVA DI CASA

RIVER PIAVE WINES

CABERNET DEL PIAVE
TOCAI DEL PIAVE
VERDUZZO DEL PIAVE

The town of San Donà di Piave, to the northeast of Venice, is the center of the production of Cabernet, Tocai, and Verduzzo, wines that have not yet been approved for DOC listing, nor have any regulations been laid down. However, there are other Piave wines, such as the Rubino and the Raboso, and a Merlot too, for that matter, which are equally worthy of note. The traditional Rubino and Raboso are particularly interesting wines because of their virile nature. Until such time as DOC rules exist, the best I can do is to give the names of the best producers of the area.

Producers

Cabernet del Piave

LUCIANO CANELLA
(San Donà di Piave, Venezia)
CANTINA SOCIALE
(San Donà di Piave, Venezia)
ANTONIO VERGA FALZACAPPA
(San Vendeniano, Treviso)

Producers

Tocai del Piave

LUCIANO CANELLA
(San Donà di Piave, Venezia)
CANTINA SOCIALE
(San Donà di Piave, Venezia)
BIANCHI DI KUNKLER
(Mogliano Veneto, Treviso)

Verduzzo del Piave

LUCIANO CANELLA
(San Donà di Piave, Venezia)
ANTONIO VERGA FALZACAPPA
(San Vendeniano, Treviso)
CANTINA SOCIALE
(San Donà di Piave, Venezia)

Merlot del Piave

BARONE CIANI BASSETTI
(Roncade, Treviso)
CANTINA CLUB
(Treviso)
ANTONIO VERGA FALZACAPPA
(San Vendeniano, Treviso)

Rubino del Piave

TENUTA SANTA MARGHERITA DI PORTOGRUARO
(Portogruaro, Treviso)

Producers

Raboso del Piave

AZIENDA AGRICOLA ITALO MACCARI
(Conegliano, Treviso)
CANTINA SOCIALE COOPERATIVA
(Ponte di Piave, Treviso)

CHAPTER ELEVEN

FRIULI-VENEZIA GIULIA

Friuli-Venezia Giulia

Friuli-Venezia Giulia is something of a never-never land to Italians and visitors alike. Most of the cities were founded in Roman times, before the Romans added Dalmatia to the Empire: it was a frontierland. It was devastated by Attila the Hun and later passed under the domination of the Byzantine Empire. It was constantly being invaded and destroyed by Franks, Lombards, and Hungarians until it was incorporated into the Venetian Republic, around A.D. 1000, for which it served as a buffer state. Along with the Veneto and much of Yugoslavia, it became part of the Austro-Hungarian Empire, Trieste being Vienna's outlet to the Mediterranean. Friuli was badly devastated by World War I, after which it became Italian territory; again, during World War II, it was a battleground, after which a large slice of Venezia Giulia was ceded to Yugoslavia, and the region became a militarized frontierland once more, though relations between Italy and Yugoslavia are essentially cordial.

Needless to say, the vineyards were destroyed twice in fifty years; it takes a long time—at least seven to ten years—to reestablish vineyards and sell their produce, but they have been reestablished twice.

Friuli-Venezia Giulia has a vocation for producing wine, but no great vocation for public relations with the rest of Italy. Any wine-loving Italian knows and trusts implicitly names such as Angoris, D'Attimis Maniago, and Collavini and will buy anything they care to put on the Italian market, but there their knowledge stops. Isola Augusta, however, is a new name for top-quality Tocai and Merlot, well worth remembering.

A good friend of mine, who hails from Monfalcone, near Trieste, tells me that the people of his area do their utmost to drink all the wine produced, that the smallholding farmers (and they are legion) can get permission to turn their outbuildings into hostelries for fifteen days and serve wine, bread, and salami between five and nine o'clock in the evening. This they do when the wine is mature, and the locals, and even the dockyard and factory hands from nearby towns who arrive by car, work hard every evening to finish the cru before the fifteen days are up: when, hopefully, another small wine producer will make the happy announcement that his wine is ready. One might assume that the small producer in this way makes a quicker and slightly larger return for his home production than if he sold it in bulk. But, perhaps more importantly, he has had the pleasure of seeing people enjoying his wine. Real wine producers are like actors; they just could not go on without compliments. Their wine's virtues are their virtues, and vice-versa.

The never-never land of Friuli-Venezia Giulia is an ethnic situation too, in the same way as is the French-speaking Val d'Aosta and the German-speaking Alto Adige. Here we find that half the smallholders who produce wine have Slavic names such as Gradmir, Rosic, Komjanc, Komic, and Princic.

The wine production is not very large, but it is not small either: it adds up to 1.9 million liters, divided in a ratio of 15:4 whites to reds. In fact, the statistics are incomplete. Only Gorizia wines are fully tabled. This is perhaps because the dozens and dozens of smallholders with Slavic names don't fill in forms for the Ministry for Agriculture, considering it a waste of time to register the production of, say, twelve hundred liters of Pinot Noir and twenty-five hundred of Traminer. Better drink it and forget it; if you sold it to a bottling plant, you would certainly pay taxes.

The major wine-producing area is between Gorizia, on the Yugoslav frontier, and Udine, particularly for reds, and farther to the south and west for the whites; but this is a tendency rather than a rule. Each of the three DOC areas produces a range of whites and two or three reds (Merlot, Cabernet, and black Pinot) and sometimes the Refosco, a maverick wine of virile characteristics. It cannot be said that there is a really profound difference in the styles of the wines produced in the different DOC zones, as there is between the Soave, Bardolino, and Valpolicella zones, for example. And there are no figures available for Verduzzo production, the pleasing white wine from which the more famous Ramandolo dessert wine is made, but I suspect that it is produced in largish quantities.

Beyond the exports to northern Europe, the heavy domestic drinking, and the modest sales to the rest of Italy, I have every reason to believe, though I have no proof, that what is left is sold to the pursers and chief stewards of the merchant ships that dock at Trieste and Monfalcone, ports that, despite the closure of the Suez Canal, still have heavy maritime traffic.

The most famous wine of Friuli scarcely exists. It is the Picolit, which, particularly in the nineteenth century, was considered a very great dessert wine and was as renowned as much in Paris as in Vienna. However, it caught a genetic disease called floral abortion and stopped producing. Experts from Treviso's enological institute have produced hybrids, and a bottle of young Picolit today can cost fifteen dollars in Rome . . . and still be a disappointment. However, nobody wants this historic wine to die, and perhaps a solution will be found.

The other most famous wine, which is in excellent health, is the Tocai, a dry, round, strong wine with good acidity, both for taste and moderate aging; this wine has nothing to do with the Hungarian Tokay, though the name is said to have derived from a village called Tocai that existed in Austro-Hungarian days. (The Italian wine that most resembles the historic Tokay of Hungary is said to be the Sardinian Nasco.)

A new DOC zone is being recognized for the hills along the coastal strip behind the island of Grado. This is to be called "Littorale Friulana-Aquileia," Aquileia being the ruins of a large Roman frontier fortress-town founded in 183 B.C. by some legionaries under Publius Scipio. At the time of writing, no details are available, but this zone is most likely to be a producer of Tocai, Sauvignon, Riesling, and Verduzzo.

COLLIO GORIZIANO
(Gorizia Hills Wines)

The Friuli-Venezia Giulia area has been noted for its wine back to the second century A.D. In the past century, its vineyards and cellars have been destroyed and drunk dry twice by the armies of various nations, but, each time, they have been replaced and replenished.

The harsh landscape and ungenerous soil of the foothills of the Alps, on the present Yugoslav border, produces a generous, soft wine with considerable body. The DOC category here is particularly broad-minded inasmuch as it includes eleven different wines. The locals do their best to drink the lot, but fortunately do not succeed.

Any wine that sails under the flag of Collio Goriziano or just Collio must be a straw-colored white that is dry, lively, full-bodied, suitably tannic, and with a minimum of 11 per cent alcohol. It must be made from the yellow Ribolla (45–55 per cent), Malvasia or Istrian malmsey (20–25 per cent), and Tocai (15–25 per cent). It is the Ribolla that is documented back to the second century A.D.

The other ten DOC wines are straight wine, which must be clearly marked Collio or Collio Goriziano followed by the name of one of the following vines: Riesling Italico, Tocai, Malvasia, Pinot Bianco, Pinot Grigio, Sauvignon, Traminer, Merlot, Cabernet Franc, and Pinot Nero—seven whites and three reds, all with an alcoholic content of over 12 per cent. All come into the category of being dry, well-balanced table wines of very high quality; the Merlot and the Tocai in particular have gained a reputation throughout northern and central Italy.

COLLIO (Goriziano)

Producer
CONTE MICHELE FORMENTINI
(San Floriano, Gorizia)

COLLIO RIESLING ITALICO

A pale golden-yellow wine, dry, full-bodied, and harmonious, with a fresh bouquet and a pleasing finish.

Producers
ANGORIS SACTA
(Cormons, Gorizia)
D'ATTIMIS MANIAGO
(Cormons, Gorizia)

COLLIO TOCAI

A full wine with a lemonish color, a delicate bouquet, dry, and with a sharp aftertaste.

Producers
LIVIO FELLUGA
(Brazzano di Cormons, Gorizia)
MARCO FELLUGA
(Gradisca d'Isonzo, Cormons)
ERCOLE PIGHIN
(Pordenone)
BARONI CODELLI
(Mossa, Gorizia)
ANGORIS SACTA
(Cormons, Gorizia)

COLLIO MALVASIA

A straw-colored, dry, velvety wine with the typically warm Malvasia bouquet.

Producer
BARONI CODELLI
(Mossa, Gorizia)

COLLIO PINOT BIANCO

A straw-colored dry wine with considerable body and delicate bouquet.

Producers
MARCO FELLUGA
(Gradisca d'Isonzo, Gorizia)
ISTITUTO "CERRUTI"
(Capriva del Friuli, Gorizia)
D'ATTIMIS MANIAGO
(Cormons, Gorizia)

COLLIO PINOT GRIGIO

A golden-yellow wine, dry and distinctly astringent, with an intense vinous aroma.

Producers
MARCO FELLUGA
(Gradisca d'Isonzo, Gorizia)
ERCOLE PIGHIN
(Pordenone)
BARONI CODELLI
(Mossa, Gorizia)
SIGISMONDO ATTEMIS
(Lucinico, Gorizia)
CONTE MICHELE FORMENTINI
(San Floriano, Gorizia)

COLLIO SAUVIGNON

A dark straw-colored wine with a notable bouquet and at least 12.5 per cent alcohol. Negligible quantities available.

Producers
ERCOLE PIGHIN
(Pordenone)
CONTE MICHELE FORMENTINI
(San Floriano, Gorizia)

COLLIO TRAMINER

Golden yellow, robust, and full-bodied, with a fine bouquet, particularly with bottle age, of which this wine will take quite a lot. Only 25,000 liters produced in all.

Producers
GRADMIR GRADNIK
(Gradisca, Gorizia)
ANGORIS SACTA
(Cormons, Gorizia)

COLLIO MERLOT

A ruby-red wine, sharp and tannic when young, even prickly, that matures well into a fine, well-balanced wine.

Producer
MARCO FELLUGA
(Gradisca d'Isonzo, Gorizia)

COLLIO CABERNET FRANC

A strong, dry, ruby-red table wine, very smooth but with a sharp-ish aftertaste and a generally pleasing finish with maturing. Minimum alcoholic content 12.5 per cent.

Producers
LIVIO FELLUGA
    (Brazzano di Cormons, Gorizia)
MARCO FELLUGA
    (Gradisca d'Isonzo, Gorizia)
GRADMIR GRADNIK
    (Cormons, Gorizia)
CONTE MICHELE FORMENTINI
    (San Floriano, Gorizia)

COLLIO PINOT NERO

The Burgundy grape here produces a very sturdy, full-bodied wine, though the quantities are modest. It is a ruby red when young and with a strong vinous fragrance that softens with a little bottle age.

Producers
ISTITUTO "CERRUTI"
    (Capriva del Friuli, Gorizia)
LIVIO FELLUGA
    (Brazzano di Cormons Gorizia)

COLLI ORIENTALI DEL FRIULI (Eastern Friuli Hills Wines)

The Eastern Friuli Hills are an extension of the Gorizian Hills, but closer to Udine. This area also has a long history of vine growing and wine producing, but the major producers are few and each of them makes several types of wine. Therefore, in the list of wineries, though a producer is recorded for a specific wine for which he is noted, it should not be assumed that this is all he makes. My recommendation, therefore, is a guide to what might be considered the names most worth remembering.

TOCAI

See COLLIO TOCAI

Producers
LIVIO FELLUGA
    (Brazzano di Cormons, Gorizia)
FRATELLI PIGHIN
    (Risano, Udine)

VERDUZZO (Ramandolo)

A golden table wine, full-bodied, slightly tannic, and with a vinous aroma that is more marked in the amabile wine made from the same grape and called Ramandolo.

Producers
LIVIO FELLUGA
    (Brazzano di Cormons, Gorizia)
CONTE GIANFRANCO D'ATTIMIS MANIAGO
    (Buttrio, Udine)

RIBOLLA

A historic and traditional wine; it is a straw yellow with greenish tints, dry, fresh, and with a persistent aroma. Alcoholic content 12 per cent.

Producer
M. E. COLLAVANI
    (Corno di Rosazzo, Udine)

PINOT BIANCO

See COLLIO PINOT BIANCO

Producer
LIVIO FELLUGA
    (Brazzano di Cormons, Gorizia)

PINOT GRIGIO

See COLLIO PINOT GRIGIO

Producer
LIVIO FELLUGA
    (Brazzano di Cormons, Gorizia)

SAUVIGNON

See COLLIO SAUVIGNON

Producer
CONTE GIANFRANCO D'ATTIMIS MANIAGO
    (Buttrio, Udine)

RIESLING RENANO (Rhine Riesling)

A golden-yellow wine, dry, well balanced, and with a minimum
alcoholic content of 12 per cent.

Producer
LIVIO FELLUGA
    (Brazzano di Cormons, Gorizia)

PICOLIT

A golden dessert wine, amabile or sweet, full-bodied, warm, well
balanced, and with a good 15 per cent alcohol. Now rare.

Producers
LIVIO FELLUGA
    (Brazzano di Cormons, Gorizia)
FRATELLI PERINI
    (Savorgnano del Torre, Povoletto, Udine)
CONTE PERUSINI DI ROCCABERNARDA
    Ipplis, Udine)

CABERNET

See COLLIO CABERNET

Producers
CANTINA SOCIALE DI LATISANA
    (Latisana, Friuli)
LUIGI VALLE
    (Buttrio, Udine)

MERLOT

See COLLIO MERLOT

Producers
CONTE GIANFRANCO D'ATTIMIS MANIAGO
    (Buttrio, Udine)
FRATELLI PIGHIN
    (Risano, Udine)
CANTINA SOCIALE DI CERVIGNANO
    (Cervignano, Udine)

PINOT NERO

See COLLIO PINOT NERO

Producers
VOLPE PASINI
    (Togliano di Cividale, Udine)
GIOVANNI MONAI
    (Nimis, Udine)

REFOSCO

An intense, purplish wine, full-bodied and with a strong vinous aroma and tannic aftertaste. Needs bottle age.

Producer
GIOVANNI MONAI
    (Nimis, Udine)

GRAVE DEL FRIULI (Western Friuli Hills Wines)

These are the same vines as before, but grown on the gravel soil of western Friuli.

Producers

CANTINA SOCIALE DI CASARSA
   (Pordenone)

FRIULVINI
   (Porcia di Pordenone, Friuli)

CANTINA SOCIALE COOPERITIVA TREVISO
   (Ponte di Piave, Treviso)

CONTE VERGA FALZACAPPA
   (Treviso)

LITTORALE FRIULANA-AQUILEIA (Friuli Coast Wines)

This zone has not yet been stabilized but, as mentioned in the text, is likely to produce Tocai, Verduzzo, Merlot, et al.

Producers

ISOLA AUGUSTA
    (Palazzolo della Stella, Udine)
TENUTA SANTA MARGHERITA DI PORTOGRUARO
    (Portogruaro, Treviso)
CONTE VERGA FALZACAPPA
    (Treviso)

CHAPTER TWELVE

EMILIA-ROMAGNA

Emilia-Romagna

The great region of Emilia-Romagna separates Lombardy and the Veneto from Tuscany and the Marches; its northern boundary is the river Po. Despite its strategic position and its famous cities— Piacenza, Parma, Modena, Bologna, Ferrara, Imola, Forli, and Ravenna—which all date back to Renaissance times, it is not well known to the visitor to Italy except for its beaches, around Rimini and Cattolica.

Its landscape is mixed: starting from the Piedmont Hills, it passes to the alluvial plain of the Po Valley, the craggy Apennines, the foothills toward the sea, and the lagoons and swamps of the Po Delta. The climate is harsh and continental, but a more fruitful region, agriculturally speaking, scarcely exists. More than anything, the region is noted for its inspired pork-sausage making, its fruit growing (cherries, peaches, plums, pears, and apples), and its cheese making (Parmesan); but not its wine producing.

Emilia-Romagna produces twice as much wine as Lombardy, but its DOC-quality production, of 11 million liters, is about the same. There are said to be seventy-two different types of wine made, but only, I think, a small proportion reach the culminating point of being put in a labeled bottle. For the rest, we have three major wine-growing areas, the Piacenza Hills for Gutturnio, Modena for Lambrusco, and the Romagna Hills for Albana and Sangiovese, none of which are big producers or particularly prized for their quality, though I personally have a long-standing affection for a slightly aged, autumnally tawny Sangiovese from any of the better wineries, which wine-loving friends of mine seem to consider a perversity or perhaps a vanity on my part. In any event, I am impervious to their criticism: I like Sangiovese, and that is that.

The Gutturnio is the last extension of the Piedmont Hills and produces, as might be expected, a Barbera-cum-Bonarda wine. It has a fast-growing reputation as a quality table wine. I have no record of any attempts to age the produce of better years, though this should logically be both possible and worthwhile. At the moment, 1½ million liters are produced, while the DOC potential stands at 6 million.

The famous wine of Modena, the Lambrusco, has caused more controversy than any other. Connoisseurs, weaned on claret, are horrified as though they had never seen a sparkling red wine before. There are plenty of sparkling red wines in Italy; and, for that matter, in France too. The fact is that Lambrusco is not a wine of great quality, but it has its purposes. It no more goes with roast lamb than claret goes with fried eggs and bacon. Lambrusco goes with the Modena-Bologna food, which is based on very rich pasta dishes, zampone (a spiced and smoked sausage meat: heavy going but excellent), mortadella, and braised beans and lentils. Lambrusco cuts through the oils, fats, and béchamels like a knife, making digestion possible. However, let it not be said that I criticize Modena-Bologna cooking: it can be magnificent and not necessarily heavy. Try, for example, a chicken or turkey breast poached in champagne and browned in the oven, having been topped with a little melting cheese, raw ham, and a few slices of white truffle.

Lambrusco is at present having a remarkable renaissance: container-load after container-load is being shipped to the United

States. The producers have no idea where they finish up, but it is believed that it has become the party drink among young people: it has been ironically nicknamed Lambrusco Cola in Bologna. However, the young consumers in this case should not be criticized: perhaps they have started a new fashion for drinking sparkling wines, which, as long as the price can be kept within bounds, should make for the gaiety of nations: for *liberté, fraternité,* and *égalité,* as well as facilitating the search for happiness.

Though most people think of the Sicilians as being the most passionate of Italians, they are not altogether right. The Sicilians are a glum lot in comparison with the Romagnoli, who enjoy controversy and drinking as much as the Irish do: Sangiovese and Grappa are their Guinness and whiskey. They say that if you stop at a farm and beg a glass of water to quench your thirst from the lady of the house and she gives you wine, you can be sure that you are in Romagna.

On the south side of the road that leads from Bologna to Imola and the coast, is the hill country, which, extending to the Republic of San Marino, produces the best Sangiovese, Trebbiano, and Albana.

Albana is essentially a Romagna wine: no other region has ever made anything like it. One distinguished producer described it to me as "an odd wine, not to everybody's taste": the dry type has a bittersweet undertone, and the sweet is distinctly sweet. However, 6 million liters are made, and presumably sold, per annum, which is half as much again as is sold of Barolo, and, surprisingly, gets the highest prices of all the Emilia-Romagna wines.

The Sangiovese is another story. It is one of the basic wines of central Italy: it makes up over half of every liter of Chianti. The Romagnoli are fighting a vigorous battle to prevent, let us say, a Marches or an Abruzzese winery from making, bottling, and selling non-DOC Sangiovese. They insist that the only real Sangiovese is theirs. As far as the DOC Sangiovese produced in central Italy goes, each variety has its own name. In truth, even a Brunello is a Sangiovese variety, the Rosso di Piceno too—very different wines of very different quality. In any event, the Romagnoli are defending the good name of Romagna Sangiovese, fighting off all boarders; and, in the name of an eighteenth-century bandit, they have set up a high-spirited, rustic gastronomic society called the Passatore, which is dedicated to the diffusion and consumption of the 4 million bottles of Sangiovese di Romagna produced each year.

The Trebbiano vine is grown widely throughout the whole region from Gutturnio to the sea, but only in the Sangiovese-Albana hills is it likely to be approved as a DOC wine.

PIACENZA HILLS WINE

GUTTURNIO DEI COLLI PIACENTINI

This Gutturnio, made from Barbera (60 per cent) and Bonarda (40 per cent) grapes and grown on hills south of Piacenza, is not widely known nationally, being as yet mostly consumed locally. Its characteristics are an intense red color, a dry or abboccato taste, a pleasing aroma, and 12 per cent alcohol: a well respected table wine with a future.

There is some good Trebbiano white made in this area, but it does not seem to have made or to be making the DOC listing.

Producers
AZIENDA AGRICOLA GIUSEPPE MOLINELLI
  (Ziano Piacentino, Piacenza)
CAGNONI
  (Niviano Castello, Piacenza)

MODENA WINES

LAMBRUSCO DI SORBARA

The Sorbara red sparkling wine is considered the best of the Modena Lambruscos. Its classic growing area is on the plains in the immediate vicinity of Modena and to the north. However, due to a curious botanical phenomenon, the yield is very limited, and the Sorbara is therefore mixed with 40 per cent Salamino di Santa Croce, which comes from a zone just to the north of the classic zone.

Since it is not a hill wine, it does not come into the category of fine wines, but, at the same time, its price is always contained within the most reasonable limits. For decades, Lambrusco has been denigrated, often because all sorts of strange, bubbling, CO_2-assisted liquids labeled Lambrusco have been marketed; also, the idea of a sweetish, effervescent table wine was unacceptable to traditional drinkers. In fact, Lambrusco is a special-category wine that, since DOC legislation, has been selling better than ever at home and abroad. The Sorbara is dryish, fresh, and sparkling with a lively, red effervescence; it has an alcoholic content of between 10.5 and 12 per cent.

Producers
CANTINA TELEFORO FINI
    (Bomporto, Modena)
CANTINA SOCIALE DI SORBARA
    (Bomporto, Modena)

Producer
CHIARLI E FIGLI
(Modena)

LAMBRUSCO GRASPAROSSA DI CASTELVETRO

This delimited zone lies in the plains to the south of Modena. Its wine is similar to that of the classic Sorbara zone in all characteristics except that its color has some violet tints; it is slightly weaker alcoholically but has a more accentuated bouquet.

As with the Sorbara, it is produced both dry and amabile, and in both cases it is a full-bodied wine. The vine used is the Grasparossa variety of the Lambrusco and is so called because the grape stalks (graspi) are red.

Producers
CAVICCHIOLI
(San Prospero, Modena)
CHIARLI E FIGLI
(Modena)
CANTINA SOCIALE DI CASTELVETRO
(Castelvetro, Modena)
CANTINA SOCIALE DI SETTECAN
(Settecani, Modena)

LAMBRUSCO SALAMINO DI SANTA CROCE

The other member of the Lambrusco trio of wines (Sorbara, Grasparossa, and Salamino) is the Salamino. Just as the Grasparossa describes the red stalks, this grape is sausage-shaped, like a small salami; hence its name, in the diminutive form, Salamino.

The growing area is to the north of the classic zone, and the wine closely resembles the Sorbara, though it is a little more full-bodied. It is a vivid red wine with a lively effervescence, dry, slightly sharp and with a strong vinous aroma: between 10.5 and 11 per cent alcohol. To be drunk young.

Producers
SEVERI VINI
    (Baggiovara, Modena)
NEDO MASSETTI
    (Cibemo, Carpi)
CANTINA SOCIALE DI CARPI
    (Carpi, Modena)
CANTARELLI
    (Gualtieri, Modena)

TERRA CALDA SCORZA AMARA

This is a non-DOC Lambrusco of special repute. It is an intense red in color and has a tart tannic taste; it is often preferred to the other Lambruscos, which have a tendency to sweetness.

Producers
REMIGIO MEDICI
    (Villa Cadè, Reggio-Emilia)
CANTINE COOPERATIVE RIUNITE DELLA PROVINCIA DI REGGIO-
    EMILIA
    (Reggio-Emilia)
INA MARIA PALLERANO
    (Reggio-Emilia)

ROMAGNA HILLS WINES

SANGIOVESE DI ROMAGNA

The Romagna Sangiovese is cultivated on the hillsides flanking the south side of the road leading from Bologna to Rimini. This is prime wine land that has been cultivated since time immemorial. The excellent, robust product, which improves well with bottle age, does honor to the equally good food of the region. When young, the wine is even drunk with seafood with pleasing results. It may be labeled riserva after two years' maturing, though the DOC ruling does not say how much of this must be in the wood and how much in the bottle. In any event, it requires a year in the cask, and by the fourth year is perfect, often taking on a lovely tawny color: it is very dry, with a taut aftertaste. A wine of character.

Producers
TONINO E EDO PANTANI
    (Mercato Saraceno, Forlì)
PRIMO BALDINI
    (Crocetta di Longiano, Forlì)
CONTE G. B. SPALETTI
    (Savignano sul Rubicone, Forlì)

Producers

TENUTA AMALIA
   (Villa Verucchio, Forlì)

CONTE GUIDO PASOLINI DALL'ONDA
   (Monterricio, Imola)

RAVAGLIA
   (Ravenna)

CO.RO.VIN
   (Forlì)

C.I.A.A.D
   (Via Morgagni 10, Bologna)

ALBANA DI ROMAGNA

Albana white is first recorded in history by the enologist Pier de'
Crescenzi, in the thirteenth century, as being cultivated on the
hills south of Imola and Forlì toward the sea. It is produced from
grapes of the Albana vine, which is not grown in any other part
of Italy. Though this DOC wine may be produced as either dry
or abboccato, it seems always to be the latter. It is a fairly heavy
wine, golden yellow in color and with a generous 12.5 per cent
alcohol, yet fresh and with a highly individual personality in
taste and bouquet.

Producers

CONTE GUIDO PASOLINI DALL'ONDA
   (Montericcio, Imola)

CO.RO.VIN
   (Forlì)

C.I.A.A.D.
   (Via Morgagni 10, Bologna)

TREBBIANO DI ROMAGNA

The Trebbiano vine, along with the Sangiovese, have been the pillars of wine production in central Italy for centuries. The new DOC zone for Trebbiano will include vineyards around Forlì, Ravenna, and Bologna. The wine is a straw yellow, dry, well balanced, and with a light tannic taste and a minimum of 10 per cent alcohol, though 12 per cent is more customary.

Producers
CONTE GUIDO PASOLINI DALL'ONDA
    (Montericcio, Imola)
CO.RO.VIN
    (Forlì)
C.I.A.A.D.
    (La Morgagni 10, Bologna)

CHAPTER THIRTEEN

TUSCANY

Tuscany

Tuscany inevitably means Chianti, of which there are over 100 million liters of DOC wine produced each year. But there are other Tuscan DOC wines that are more than just worthy of note; in particular, the Brunello of Montalcino, the Vino Nobile of Montepulciano, the Montecarlo, the Vernaccia of San Gimignano, and La Parrina; there are also the Elba wines, those of the Lucca Hills, those of Pitigliano; and there is an enormous production, of 300 million liters, of non-DOC wine.

But to return to the DOC Chianti, classic or otherwise. Here we come across further divisions: Chianti of Montalbano, of Rufina, of the Florentine Hills, of the Siena Hills, of the Arezzo Hills, or the Pisa Hills, and more recently, of the Pistoia Hills. There is nowadays talk of subdividing the classic zone so that the areas of Castellina, Gaiole, and Radda form a sort of classic-classic zone. The famous wines of Montalcino and Montepulciano are from the Chianti zone, but their producers prefer, on the whole, to maintain their individuality and prestige, though each of them does produce fine Chianti. Carmignano, northwest of Florence, was a separate wine area by decree of the Grand

Duchy of Tuscany in 1716: today the producers of this area are trying to regain their independence from Chianti and establish themselves as a separate DOC entity.

The classic zone is, of course, considered the best, though there are plenty of parts there—valley bottoms, northern-aspect hillsides, etc.—that produce worse wine than is produced in the other, non-classic zones in more ideal circumstances. But, on the whole, the most distinguished producers are in the classic zone, and this means that the choice of grape, the vinification, and the aging are superior.

I have made no distinction between the various Chianti zones in my list, though the vast majority of the recommendations are in the classic zone and are, with few exceptions, not very large producers of fine wines; in the case of the big names, these produce and bottle one or more types of top-quality wines. Over and above the DOC protection of the consumer, the old classic Chianti consortium continues to put on each bottle its neck label, which shows a black cockerel on a red ground; less widely known is the use of the same style of label showing the same cockerel on a silver ground, meaning that the wine has been aged for two years, and on a gold ground, meaning that the wine has been aged for three.

Although it is laid down that Chianti shall be made from certain wines and in certain proportions, there is a considerable margin of diversity allowed. For example, the Sangiovese may fluctuate from 50 to 80 per cent; the black Canaiolo from 10 to 30 per cent; the Trebbiano and Malvasia from 10 to 30 per cent; and up to 5 per cent of Colorino or other grapes may be used. Some producers alter these ratios according to whether the wine is to be sold young or aged. If the wine is to be sold young, it will probably be treated with the governo system, but not necessarily. Some producers, on the other hand, do this with all their wines, and only several months after fermentation has finished, decide which are to be aged and which sold young. The governo process consists in gathering choice grapes a week or so before the big harvest, semi-drying them on mats, and pressing them about a month after the first fermentation of the big harvest; this strong wine is then added to the vats to the extent of 5 to 10 per cent of the total bulk. This causes a second fermentation, which matures the wine in the traditional Chianti manner, giving it its characteristic youthful sparkle. A Chianti made to be drunk young will probably have a greater percentage of Canaiolo than one to be matured, since the Canaiolo mitigates the asperities of the Sangiovese; in the case of an aged Chianti this service is not required, as the Sangiovese becomes smooth with time in the cask. Equally, the addition of white Malvasia and Trebbiano is sharply reduced for a wine to be aged, since these are added to make the Chianti drinkable six months after fermentation.

Every Chianti zone produces good young DOC Chianti, but the number of producers who have refined the art of making a fine old austere Chianti, a wine that fears no rivals, are relatively few.

In the past, there was considerable swapping of Chiantis between the various consortiums; for example, a poor growth from one zone might be strengthened by a coupage from some Chianti from the Arezzo Hills, which is a very tannic wine. Nowadays, both must stand on their own. Those who like a wine with a tannic tang will buy Arezzo Chianti or satisfy themselves with a softer wine from another zone.

But it cannot be repeated often enough that the Chianti that upholds the reputation of Tuscany as a producer of fine aged wines is not the wine to be found in raffia-covered flasks or in the 1.8-liter (½ gallon) Toscanella or other, new-style bottles, though some of these are wines of considerable quality. It is the Chianti bottled in Bordeaux bottles, well matured in the wood and refined in the bottle before being offered to the public, that can face criticism serenely.

In many other parts of Italy, as well as in Tuscany, the cru spirit is alive: this includes a desire to differentiate one's production inside one's winery, but also to differentiate it from one's competitors. The putting aside of the best wine for maturing has always been part of wine making, but this cru spirit has been accentuated in recent years, encouraged by Italy's top wine writer and critic, Veronelli. I mentioned the Cantina Club of Treviso, in the Friuli-Venezia Giulia, as an organization that "collects" fine crus. Of recent years, Count Roberto Pandolfini, whose family has produced fine Chiantis for decades and more on their estates, has returned to what really interests him: Italian wine—after having lived and worked in the United States representing a major Italian industry for a few years. He has set up an organization that purchases the best casks from producers and leaves them to age in their cellars. His enterprise, Selecru (see Chianti listing), is as yet young but is spreading its interests throughout Italy. This seems to me to be the trend for the future. The individual producers are not big enough to publicize themselves: the producers of great wines are usually small producers, and any effort to make their names famous is likely to be quite disproportionate to the possible financial return. It is therefore up to the wine writers to make the names famous and the cru experts and foreign importers to search out the best barrels and make the wines available on an international level.

In Part One of this book, I wrote that soldiers of various nations looted the wine cellars of Italy. Some wine was saved. Villa di Capezzana of Contini Bonacossi auctioned 1925 Chianti in London in 1967 for high prices. Roberto Pandolfini (though he was only a child then) told me how his father gathered together the best barrels and bottles of all the local producers and put them in his cellar and walled it up in such a way that no thirsty soldier would find it; his plan also included removing the risk of any of his rivals betraying him, since they, too, had an interest in the security of the cellar. There are still a few hundred bottles left, which have been rebottled and recorked because the wartime corks were of poor quality and the only bottles available were Fernet-Branca bottles, with the seal of that distinguished firm impressed in the glass.

Really fine wines can be drunk best at home rather than in a restaurant, except by prior arrangement, since they must be brought from the cellar, tenderly, as much as two or three days before they are due for the final sacrifice, a period in which they adapt themselves to room temperature, which should be as much as 70° F. They should be uncorked an hour or two before being served at table to bring out the full flavor and aroma. Franco Biondi Santi recommends from four to twenty-four hours for a fifteen-year-old Brunello and more if the wine is older. But how long should you give an 1888 vintage, a week or two? On the contrary, it should be decanted and served immediately and should be consumed inside a half hour, as it can fade away while you are still admiring it. I know nobody with the courage to make a graph based on the vintage and the "breathing time" recommended. There are still a few bottles of Brunello 1888 in existence, recorked every twenty-five years in the presence of a notary public, that sell for around five hundred dollars and have miraculously retained both body and bouquet.

Though not as long-lived as the Brunello, the Vino Nobile of Montepulciano is among the great wines of Tuscany. It comes from grapes grown between seven hundred fifty and two thousand feet up in the hills near Chianciano.

The great Chianti, Brunello, and Vino Nobile producers usually make a vin santo, in the traditional manner of long fermentation in sealed barrels, that reaches a smooth, rich 16 per cent alcohol when matured for five years. Particular care should be taken in choosing the producer of a vin santo, as some have found means of abbreviating this time-consuming process to the detriment of the wine. Vin santo comes both dry and sweet, the latter being more common, but a dry, such as made by the Prince Ginori Conti winery, is profoundly memorable.

One of the Brunello producers, Colombini, makes a unique sort of Brunello red vin santo called "Brusco dei Barbi." This is encouraged to ferment all through its first winter with the addition of yeast and passito Brunello till it reaches 16 per cent of dry wine of a dominating character. The process is more or less a secret patent. Like all the other Brunello wines, it sells easily on the Italian market at good prices, and in this case at appreciably higher prices than a regular wine.

Tuscany has changed much due to the DOC regulations and also much due to the exodus of farm hands and share-croppers. The vineyards have been semi-mechanized where possible and the interspersed olive trees uprooted to facilitate this, thus changing the traditional silver-gray landscape. All sorts of traditional customs have gone by the board; in the abundance of farm labor, for example, beans were often grown next to the vines, and instead of being picked, were dug under where they fermented and passed their protein content to the vines. This, for economic reasons, is no longer possible, and, in any event, is not required by DOC regulations.

Despite difficulties, and these have often included even the expropriation of land, wine production is not diminishing. After a major expropriation of land from the La Parrina estate, near Orbetello, on the coast, the owners were left with only the hills, which were not considered of much value. Over the past quarter century, these hills have produced magnificent peaches and fine Sangiovese wine, and, to the astonishment of the owners, their wines, now well established, are winning prizes and gold medals wherever they are presented. This Maremma area of Tuscany was malarial, but is no longer. The hills were mostly used for cattle raising, and the *butteri* were and are reckoned to be as good horsemen as any cowboy from the Great Plains.

A little inland is the Pitigliano white, a wine of lesser breed but not to be scorned, as it comes from the Trebbiano vine grown on good volcanic soil.

Following the coast to the north, we find the island of Elba, which specializes in white wine, of which only 500,000 liters are produced. This white is, as usual, a Trebbiano. The Elba red is closely related to Chianti, but the production is very small: only 50,000 liters. The official books say that the permitted production is five times as much, but one major Elba producer says the contrary: i.e. there is no vineyard land available, and Elba must aim only for the top-quality market if it is to do other than sell locally on the island. He also pointed out that mainland wines were being marketed as Elba wines without any DOC mention on the label. He stressed the importance of the DOC regulations for a small production zone of quality wines as their best and only protection from fraudulent practices.

Though Napoleon is said to have had negligible palate for food and wine, his name is linked to cognac and a few wines, presumably because he was a chance customer. In any event, during his exile on Elba he seems to have found more time to cultivate his tastes and his garden, since he is known to have personally planned and planted a vineyard there. In his memory you will find Elba wines with such names as Bianco dell'Imperatore and Vieux Rosé della Walewska, which are not only nostalgic for far-off Napoleonic times, but also very good wines today.

The soil of the Lucca Hills is almost too good to make wine: it produces a young Chianti-style wine to which the producers, being small, can give their full attention and assure that it is well made. Equally, the Vernaccia of San Gimignano, the town with the medieval towers, has a small production of good-quality whites that, like the Sardinian Vernaccia, ages well, but are not so strong.

Another small-production white is the Montecarlo; it has been produced for a hundred years and is unique in Italy. Its component parts are Semillon, Pinot Grigio, Pinot Bianco, Sauvignon, Rousanne, and Vermentino. None of this is exported: there just is not enough to go around, as it is. The *gran riserva* is a particularly fine wine and *secchissimo* (very dry).

To wind up this panorama, there are the non-DOC Tuscan whites, mostly made from Trebbiano and Malvasia; these are most acceptable wines, but rarely fine ones. The Valdichiana, near Cortona and south of Arezzo, I believe to be the source of much of this. Now, this Chiana Valley has its own co-operative and is bottling its own wine under a DOC label in a limited way. I tasted an excellent aged Sangiovese there in the small viticulture institute, so can agree with the Common Market gentlemen in Brussels who, having declared the area to have a vocation for wine production, are, through the FEOGA organization, investing funds in vineyards and processing plants, the local authorities having improved the land and put in the infrastructure.

I think we shall hear more of this area and a similar DOC area in nearby Umbria (Torgiano) in the future: up to now, both have been treated as colonial suppliers of raw materials.

CHIANTI

Chianti is a name that needs little introduction, though it is not widely known in its higher forms, i.e. when well aged.

Chianti production is documented back six hundred years and, for the past three centuries, has been exported from Italy. In the fourteenth century the confines of the classic Chianti zone were first laid down; by the seventeenth century the Antinori wines were well known; in the eighteenth century the Ricasoli barons were exporting Chianti; and by the nineteenth century Baron Bettino Ricasoli finally defined the vines and cultivation methods, after which Chianti spread throughout the world.

The classic Chianti zone lies between Florence and Siena, around which there is a strip as broad as the classic zone that hosts the other six Chianti denominations: Montalbano, Rufina,

Colli Fiorentini (Florentine Hills), Colli Senesi (Siena Hills), Colli Aretini (Arezzo Hills) and Colline Pisane (Pisa Hills).

The regular formula for fine Chianti is 70 per cent Sangiovese red wine, 15 per cent Canaiolo black, and 15 per cent white Tuscan Trebbiano or Malvasia, while for the young Chianti there is an addition of 5 per cent of Colorino red for the governo process, with minor alterations of the percentages of all the other wines.

There has been considerable abuse of the name Chianti in the past, and many of the producers of the finest Chiantis prefer not to stress the word Chianti so much as their specific proprietary names, thus leaving to some extent the name Chianti to the younger and lesser breeds.

It should be made abundantly clear that there are basically two types of bottled Chianti: the flask or Toscanella-bottle Chianti is to be drunk young; it is a prickly, lively beverage wine made with the governo process, which encourages quick maturation; it is a very good all-purpose luncheon wine. Then there are the fine riserva Chiantis, which are sold in Bordeaux-style bottles and age well. The latter, after two years' maturing in the cask, may be called *vecchio* (old), and after three, riserva. The producers of reputation mature their vintage years much longer before putting them on the market, by which time Chianti is comparable in quality to any fine wine.

The classic Chianti denomination requires that the wine be at least ½ percentage point stronger in alcohol than the others: and this, in turn, requires a more studied choice of the grapes being picked. However, this has little to do with the vastly higher standards maintained by the distinguished Chianti makers, many of which you will find listed subsequently. The other six Chianti areas vary appreciably in quality and characteristics from classic Chianti, due to differences of terrain and to some extent even of climate. But more than anything, Chiantis vary according to the producer and their maturing; a description of characteristics is therefore impossible and meaningless. A list of the more distinguished producers is much more valuable. As elsewhere in this book, the lists are in no order of merit, nor of alphabetical order or any other.

CHIANTI

Producers	Additional Description
MARCHESA M. L. STUCCHI GIUNTINI (Gaiole, Siena)	BADIA DI COLTIBUONO
BARONE RICASOLI (Florence)	BROLIO RISERVA CASTELLO DI MELETO
CONTESSA M. G. CASTELBARCO ALBANI (Greve, Florence)	CASTELLO DI UZZANO
MELINI (Pontassieve, Florence)	STRAVECCHIO MONNA LISA
PRINCIPE GIOVANNI GINORI CONTI (Radda, Siena)	PIAN D'ALBOLA
MARCHESI L. & P. ANTINORI (Florence)	VILLA ANTINORI SANTA CRISTINA
CONTI SERRISTORI (Val di Pesa, Florence)	MACHIAVELLI
GINO MILANESE (San Gusmè, Siena)	ROSENNANO
LUIGI CAPPELLINI (Greve, Florence)	VERAZZANO
CONTESSA ELENA SANMINIATELLI (Greve, Florence)	VIGNAMAGGIO
PIERINO DE CARLI (Greve, Florence)	VECCHIOMAGGIO
LAPO MAZZEI (Castellina, Siena)	FONTERUTOLI
CONTE GIOVANNI LORO (Tavernelle, Val di Pesa, Florence)	BADIA DI PASSIGNANO

Producers	*Additional Description*
VITTA	IL POGGIALE
(Val di Pesa, Florence)	
CONTE FILIPPO PANDOLFINI	TIZZANO
(San Polo, Florence)	
GIOVANNI CAPPELLI	LA QUERCIA
(Greve, Florence)	
ELEONORA RUSPOLI BERLINGUERI	LILLIANO ROSSO
(Castellina, Siena)	
MARCHESA FERDINANDA QUINTAVALLE	MANGIACANE
(Val di Pesa, Florence)	
MARCHESI CORSINI	MONTEPALDI
(Sancasciano, Val di Pesa, Florence)	
LETIZIA RIMEDIOTTI MATTIOLI	NOZZOLE
(Greve, Florence)	
RENZO OLIVIERI	PALAZZO AL BOSCO
(Val di Pesa, Florence)	
EMILIO BERTONI	VILLA A SESTA
(San Gusmè, Berardenga, Siena)	
FATTORIA DI ARTIMINO	
(Artimino, Florence)	
MARCHESE EMILIO PUCCI DI BASENTO	CASTEL DI CERRETO
(Firenze)	
PRINCIPI GUICCIARDINI-STROZZI	CUSONA
(San Gimignano, Siena)	
BIONDI SANTI	
(Montalcino, Siena)	
CONTE CONTINI BONACOSSI	CAPEZZANA
(Carmignano, Florence)	
CONTE AUGUSTO GOTTI LEGA	CAPANNOLI
(Capannoli, Pisa)	
MARCHESI DE'FRESCOBALDI	POMINO
(Florence)	NIPOZZANO

Producers	Additional Description
AMEDEO DI SAVOIA, Duke of Aosta (San Giustino Valdarno, Arezzo)	IL BORRO
CONTI BORGHINI BALDOVINETTI (San Fabiano, Florence)	SAN FABIANO
CONTI CAPPONI (Greve, Florence)	CALCINAIA
FATTORIA CARPINETO (Greve, Florence)	
CONTE G. PASOLINI DALL'ONDA BORGHESE (Barbarino, Elsa, Florence)	BARBARINO
I. L. RUFFINO (Pontassieve, Florence)	RISERVA DUCALE
SOCINI GUELFI (Castel Nuovo Berardenga, Siena)	LA CASACCIA
SPALETTI (Rufina, Florence)	POGGIO REALE
MARIA VICO BONELLI-VANNI (Poggibonsi, Siena)	MONTEMORLI
MARCHESE ANTONIO ORIGO (Chianciano, Siena)	LA FOCE CASTELUCCIO
CONSORZIO AGRARIO PROVINCIALE DI SIENA—ENOPOLIO DI POGGIBONSI (Siena)	
FRANCESCO GIUNTINI (Rufina, Florence)	SELVAPIANA
ENOTECA DEL CHIANTI CLASSICO (Greve, Florence)	a sales office for classic Chianti
G. VANNUCCI ZAULI (Poggi d'Ormicello, Empoli)	
CONTE ROBERTO PANDOLFINI (Via San Gallo 74, Florence)	SELECRU

BRUNELLO DI MONTALCINO

Produced from the Brunello grape (a large Sangiovese), this wine is a close relative of the Chianti family; its reputation and perfection, however, have a history of only a hundred years, but it is a history such as to have made Brunello the most sought-after and expensive wine in Italy.

It is grown in the Siena Hills (up to two thousand feet) around the country town of Montalcino; it has been the Biondi Santi family that has been chiefly responsible for Brunello's fame.

This wine cannot be marketed until it has matured in the wood for four years. After five years' maturing it may be called riserva; however, with care it can take fifty years of aging in the bottle, and more. Its characteristics are an intense ruby-red color with orange tints increasing with aging, and a dry, tannic, warm, robust, and lively taste that mellows and softens with bottle age. It has an intense aroma and between 12.5 and 13 per cent alcohol. It is recommended that this wine be uncorked as much as twenty-four hours before serving.

Producers	*Additional Description*
BIONDI SANTI	IL GREPPO
(Montalcino, Siena)	
GIOVANNI COLOMBINI	FATTORIA DEI BARBI
(Montalcino, Siena)	BRUSCO DEI BARBI
FRANCESCHI	COL D'ORCIA
(Montalcino, Siena)	

VINO NOBILE DI MONTEPULCIANO

This historic red wine traces its origin back to the fourteenth century. The adjective noble in its name is believed to be derived from the fact that it was produced (and drunk by?) the noble families, rather than from its noble qualities.

Montepulciano is in the Chianti world, just north of the spa Chianciano. Vino Nobile is produced with the same grapes as classic Chianti, but with minor alterations in the proportions and without the governo process. It is a wine to mature, not to drink young. The vines are cultivated on the hillsides between seven hundred fifty and two thousand feet above sea level.

By law, Vino Nobile must have three years' maturing, of which two must be in the wood. If it is given three years in the cask, it may be labeled riserva, and after four years, riserva speciale. It is accordingly a wine that welcomes further nurturing in the form of bottle aging.

When young, it is a deep garnet, taking tawny tints with maturity. It is dry, lightly tannic, but soft, warm, and generous. It has a delicate bouquet with age and all of 12–13 per cent alcohol. A most satisfying and elegant wine.

Producers	*Additional Description*
ADAMO FANETTI	SANT'AGNESE
(Montepulciano, Siena)	
FRATELLI BAIOCCHI	
(Montepulciano, Siena)	

VIN SANTO

Vin Santo is made in many parts of Italy, always in relatively small quantities. In Tuscany, the grapes, usually Trebbiano and Malvasia, are laid out to dry on gratings from October to January; they are then pressed, filtered, and passed to small barrels, which, instead of being cellared, are put in an attic, where the winters are colder and the summers are hotter. With the heat of the summer, the wine ferments; with the cold of the winter, it reposes. Usually Vin Santo is left to work out its own fate for five years, after which it is filtered and bottled. Vin Santo then improves with bottle age. The result is a very strong, velvety, and well-balanced dessert wine, sweetish but with a dry aftertaste, with around 15 per cent alcohol. There are bone-dry Vin Santos to be found, but not many.

Producers	*Additional Description*
MARCHESI L. & P. ANTINORI (Florence)	
BARONE BETTINO RICASOLI (Florence)	BROLIO
A. CONTINI BONACOSSI (Carmignano, Florence)	CAPEZZANA
GIOVANNI COLOMBINI (Montalcino, Siena)	MONTALCINO
MARCHESI DE'FRESCOBALDI (Florence)	NIPOZZANO
PRINCIPE GINORI CONTI (Radda, Siena)	DRY
BIONDI SANTI (Montalcino, Siena)	MOSCADELLO
MARIA VICO BOELLI-VANNI (Poggibonsi, Siena)	

LA PARRINA

The Parrina "Etruscan" wines are produced in the hills behind Argentario, Orbetello Peninsula, in Grosseto province. The wines are called Etruscan by the only major producer, because they are produced on land where the Etruscans lived and built their cities. The Parrina wines, however, bring no surprises: they are traditional for the area. The red is a Sangiovese (80 per cent) with the addition of Canaiolo, Montepulciano, and Colorino; the white is Tuscan Trebbiano, with the addition of a little Malvasia.

The red, particularly when aged, is a big wine, ruby red, smooth, well balanced, dry, and with 12 per cent alcohol. At over six years of age it takes on a delightful autumnal color. The white is a straw yellow, tending to be golden, dry, smooth, and with a pleasing bouquet and sharp aftertaste. Alcohol 11.5 per cent.

Producer	*Additional Description*
MARCHESA GIUSTINI SPINOLA	ETRUSCO
(Albinia di Orbetello, Grosseto)	

BIANCO DI PITIGLIANO

Pitigliano wine is as little known as Pitigliano itself, a country town in a bleak volcanic area to the west of Lake Bolsena toward Grosseto, in southern Tuscany. The wine, which is white, is obtained from Tuscan Trebbiano (also called Procanico), which, through the centuries, has provided good wine; to this may be added Tuscan Malvasia, Greco, and Verdello, provided none of these reaches over 15 per cent of the total.

The vines grow on a lunarlike landscape up to one thousand

feet in the hills around Manciano, where there are sulphur springs much used for general health purposes. The resultant wine is a medium straw color with green tints; it has a light body and is smooth but rather sharp. In all, an inexpensive table wine, not for aging.

Producer

CANTINA COOPERATIVA DI PITIGLIANO
   (Villagrande Pitigliano, Grosseto)

ELBA

The Island of Elba, from the times of ancient history, is known to have produced wine. It is said that Napoleon Bonaparte, during his exile there, having procured some land, devoted much of his time to viticulture. The Tuscan Trebbiano (Procanico) is the most prevalently cultivated vine, but there is also the Sangiovese, from which good reds and rosés are obtained.

The white Elba is a pale-straw-colored wine with a dry, harmonious taste and a minimum of 11 per cent alcohol, which in practice runs as high as 13.5 per cent.

Elba is an island of iron ore, which was first mined and worked by the Etruscans well over two millenniums ago. This iron soil, of course, has its effect on the wine, and though iron is not a required component of wine, DOC or otherwise—in fact it can cause oxidization—it has a tonic effect.

Producers	*Additional Description*
TENUTA ACQUABONA	
(Portoferraio, Elba)	
MARCHESI ANTINORI	PODERE CASAROSSA
(Portoferraio, Elba; Florence)	
PODERE LA PIANELLA	ROSSO DELLA GUARDIA
(Proccio, Elba)	VIEUX ROSÉ DELLA WALEWSKA
	BIANCO DELL'IMPERATORE

ROSSO DELLE COLLINE LUCCHESI (Lucca Hills Red)

This red wine from the Lucca Hills comes from immediately north of the city of Lucca. Unlike so much wine land, this is particularly luxuriant and verdant, and, since time immemorial, much the same wines as have been cultivated in the Chianti zone have been grown in nearby Lucca. In fact, today the Lucca red has the same components as Chianti: Sangiovese, Canaiolo, Trebbiano, Tuscan Malvasia, and Colorino, and with much the same result. The wine is a ruby red, dry, prickly, and with 11.5 per cent alcohol. A wine to drink young, usually.

Producers	*Additional Description*
BARONESSA CARLA GIUSTINIANI	FORCI
(Pieve, San Stefano, Lucca)	
LEONI	SAN GENNARO
(San Gennaro, Lucca)	

VERNACCIA DI SAN GIMIGNANO

Produced near San Gimignano, in Tuscany, from the second half of the thirteenth century, and perhaps much earlier, from Vernaccia grapes on the sandy-clay hillsides rising to fifteen hundred feet, the Vernaccia di San Gimignano is a golden-yellow wine of considerable distinction.

After a year in the wood, it may be labeled riserva. Such a wine should then be given at least two more years of repose in the bottle, when it takes on all the characteristics of a fine wine.

Unlike its Sardinian cousin, its alcoholic content is more normal, 12 per cent.

Producers	Additional Description
CONTESSA ALBA BALBI VALIER	PIETRAFITTA
(San Gimignano, Siena)	
GIUSEPPE RENIERI	
(San Gimignano, Siena)	
PRINCIPI STROZZI E GUICCIARDINI	GUICCIARDINI STROZZI
(San Gimignano, Siena)	

MONTECARLO

Montecarlo is a small town behind Lucca toward Montecatini, in what might be considered an extension of the Tuscan Chianti area; and in fact the Montecarlo red is made of the same grapes as Chianti and in the two traditional manners; with the governo process for drinking young, and reserve for aging. This red is not in the DOC listing, though it is an excellent wine.

The white starts off traditionally, being made up of Trebbiano up to 70 per cent; but the balance, for Italy, is very exotic: Semillon, Pinot Grigio and Bianco, Sauvignon, Rousanne, and Vermentino.

Though it is not stipulated by the DOC regulations, the white is usually made from selected grapes and aged for two or three years before being marketed, by which time it has become a very superior wine; also, it will have greater alcoholic content than is required by law and greater capacity for aging in the bottle.

Producers	Additional Description
N. D. FRANCA MAZZINI FRANCESCHI	GRANDE RISERVA
(Montecarlo, Lucca)	MONTECARLO
FATTORIA BUONAMICO	
(Montecarlo, Lucca)	

BIANCO VERGINE VALDICHIANA (Virgin Chiana Valley White)

The Chiana Valley has always been a great producer of white Trebbiano, most of which in the past was sold in bulk to the big négociants for bottling in Florence as Tuscan white under proprietary names. The producers now are struggling to make a reputation on their own. The Valdichiana is 80 per cent Trebbiano and 20 per cent Malvasia, this latter softening the asperities of the Trebbiano to make a more widely acceptable wine. They also make a Sangiovese red in the area, which is not listed for future DOC-ing. However, one, bottled under the label Manzano and aged for five years, that I drank there was exceedingly pleasing.

Producer
CANTINA SOCIALE DI CORTONA
(Camucia, Cortona, Arezzo)

TUSCAN WHITES

Tuscan Whites, or white Chiantis as they are sometimes called, are not from specific DOC areas, though the better brands are made with Tuscan Trebbiano and/or Tuscan Malvasia from Tuscany. They are not generally considered great wines, but they are not, by any means, to be underestimated, at least when they come from the more distinguished wineries. They were, in fact, the traditional wine of Tuscany, but were superseded by red Chianti in Renaissance times. The Trebbiano-Malvasia partnership produces a fine wine at all times. It is fresh, dry, well balanced, and with a pleasing bouquet—a wine that appreciates a little bottle age.

Producers	*Additional Description*
MELINI (Pontassieve, Florence)	LACRIMA D'ARNO
GIUSEPPE VANNUCCI ZAULI (Empoli)	STIGLIANO
MARCHESI DE'FRESCOBALDI (Florence)	POMINO
MARCHESI L. & P. ANTINORI (Florence)	VILLA ANTINORI
CONTE FILIPPO PANDOLFINI (San Polo, Florence)	TIZZANO
GIOVANNI COLOMBINI (Montalcino, Siena)	BIANCO DEL BEATO

CHAPTER FOURTEEN

MARCHES

Marches

The Marches is an isolated region in many ways, even though it is close to Rome. It has poor communications, both road and rail, and is cut off from the west by the Apennines. Only now has a six-lane highway been built along its coast, linking it with Bologna in the north and Puglia in the south, and a route—via L'Aquila, the mountain capital of the Abruzzo—to Rome to the south is nearing completion. Historically, the Marches have looked to the Adriatic Sea as their line of communications, and in consequence, have the best fishing fleet in Italy.

Though detached from Rome, Rome's fate always depended on who controlled the Marches: it was therefore one of the first pieces of land the Romans, as early as the third century B.C., felt they had to own. Hannibal tried to encircle Rome via the Marches, but his troops got so drunk on the local Verdicchio wine that they were heavily defeated; the Romans—so the story goes—pronounced Verdicchio a faithful Roman ally.

The real history of the Marches is that it was a part of the Papal States till the unification of Italy, just over a hundred years ago. Surprisingly, the Marchigiani, in contrast to most people in this increasingly agnostic world, do not expect manna to drop from heaven but, rather, are industrious individualists who believe that God helps those who help themselves. But, quite unexpectedly, now a little manna has come their way.

Until ten or twenty years ago, there were dozens of types of wine made in the Marches: every farmer made his own, even if the lay of his land was unsuitable. The essence was to be self-supporting, and this implied complex mixed farming with vines growing up fruit trees. It was all very pretty, but not the best way to make fine wines.

Of all the citizens of the Papal States, those of the Marches best learned the Christian lessons about the mischief into which idle hands can get. Theirs is the land of piecework, but not the squalid, sweatshop immigrant sort of the big cities. The Marchigiani, in their homes, work with their own modern semi-automatic machinery making shoes and sandals, knitwear and boutique clothing, and bijouterie. They are a people unwilling to leave their land and, at the same time, unwilling to live on its meager offerings—a people of determination and character.

As I said, a little manna has come their way or perhaps it is God helping those who have always helped themselves. In any event, a regional development corporation, partly funded by the Common Market, has been making substantial low-interest loans to tidy up the vine growing and to set up modern processing and bottling plants. The plan has not yet reached halfway mark, though profound changes have been brought about.

Nobody may know much about the Marches, but there are few who drink wine who have never heard of Verdicchio, whose 6.5 million liters are sold throughout Italy and exported to all the world. It is a wine of character, and experts agree that it is one of the very best in the world to accompany fish dishes.

The first glass of Italian wine I ever tasted was from these parts: it was a rough young red wine, strong, tannic but not acid: I recall it as though it were yesterday, as it made a profound impression on me at the tender age of ten—yes, forty years ago. It opened my eyes to completely new horizons, many of which I have subsequently visited.

The production of DOC wine in the Marches runs to 14 million liters, of which almost half is Verdicchio, closely followed by Piceno red. The other three categories, Bianchello del Metauro, Verdicchio di Matelica and Cònero red, share the modest balance. The reds are basically Montepulciano grapes plus Sangiovese, which is a close relative. The Bianchello and Matelica are equally close cousins of the Verdicchio di Jesi: the Matelica has a particularly high reputation for quality. As a general rule to be followed also in other areas, the purchaser should choose the superiore and classico categories, which mean that the wine is the best available. This is particularly important when a whole zone is in evolution, as is the Marches, rather than firmly settled in its habits and traditional experience.

To the fury of the Passatore Society of Emilia-Romagna, the Marchigiani have registered a DOC Sangiovese dei Colli Pesaresi (Pesaro Hills), though I doubt that it will be a rival for many a year yet. There is also a Falerio Trebbiano, which has recently applied for recognition as a DOC wine, but this equally has no broad reputation. As for the Vernaccia di Serrapetrona, this rustic, frothy wine does not justify the DOC category it holds.

VERDICCHIO WINES

VERDICCHIO DEI CASTELLI DI JESI
(Jesi Castles Verdicchio)

Though the Marches are little known even to Italians, there must be few who have not drunk the famous Verdicchio dei Castelli di Jesi. The Verdicchio vine was known in ancient Roman times and praised by Pliny the Younger and Juvenal; it is still one of the pillars of Italian wine. The spelling of Jesi with an "I" or a "J" seems optional.

It is produced in a relatively small area in the hinterland of Ancona, to the west of the town of Jesi. By law, it must be obtained from 80 per cent Verdicchio grapes; the remaining 20 per cent may be made up of local Trebbiano or Malvasia. The majority of the area is considered classico, the remainder may only call itself Verdicchio.

The wine is sold in unusual shaped bottles considered frivolous by sober-minded wine lovers and experts, but, at all times, the content is taken very seriously. It is a pale-straw-colored wine, dry, pleasantly astringent with a delicate aroma and at least 12 per cent alcohol.

Producers

GIOACCHINO GAROFALI
    (Loreto)

CANTINA SOCIALE DI CUPRAMONTANA
    (Cupramontana, Ancona)

Producers
CASA VINICOLA FAZI-BATTAGLIA
   (Castelplanio Stazione, Ancona)
STAPHILUS DI BARTELUCCI E FANTONE
   (Via Simonetti 2, Ancona)
DINO DOTTORI "AURORA"
   (Cupramontana, Ancona)
UMANI RONCHI
   (Osimo Scala, Ancona)

VERDICCHIO DI MATELICA

The Verdicchio dei Castelli di Jesi is not only the best-known wine from the Marches, but far better known than the Verdicchio di Matelica, its neighbor from the hills in the hinterland of Ancona.

This wine is made mainly with the Verdicchio grape (80 per cent) but may be cut with Tuscan Trebbiano and Tuscan Malvasia, like its more famous cousin. The Matelica is a pale-straw-colored wine and closely resembles the Jesi wine. The producers have a fast-rising reputation and are beginning to export their wine.

Producers
DINO DOTTORI "AURORA"
   (Cupramontana, Ancona)
ITALO MATTEI
   (Matelica, Macerata)

BIANCHELLO DEL METAURO

The Bianchello is found just south of the Republic of San Marino and of Rimini, on both sides of the river Metauro in its last few miles before it reaches the Adriatic Sea at Fano.

This white wine, made from grapes of the Bianchello (or Biancame) vine, with a very modest percentage of Tuscan Malvasia added, has been fast gaining a reputation both at home and abroad.

In the not very distant past, it was a very secondary 10 per cent wine; one can only assume that better selection of the grapes has brought it into the higher-quality bracket of having 11.5 per cent alcohol. Perhaps the improvement is due to the new regional development corporation's labors in the vineyard. For the rest, it has the customary characteristics of a good table wine: a dry, fresh, and well-balanced taste and a pleasing and delicate aroma.

Producers
ANZILOTTI-SOLAZZI
    (Fano, Pesaro)
CONSORZIO AGRARIO DI PESARO
    (Pesaro)
GUIDO GUERRIERI
    (Piagge, Pesaro)

CÒNERO ROSSO

The small mountain behind the port of Ancona on the Adriatic, Mount Cònero, is the delimited zone for this worthy red wine; the production is modest in quantity and most of it is drunk

locally. However, being based on the Montepulciano and Sangiovese grapes, the Cònero red is a good, robust, dry wine, ruby
in color and with a pleasing vinous aroma and at least 11.5 per
cent alcohol. It ages usefully, losing its fruitiness and becoming
quite an elegant wine.

Producers
UMANI RONCHI
 (Osimo Scala, Ancona)
CASA VINICOLA GAROFALI
 (Loreto, Ancona)
AZIENDA VINICOLA ROBERTO BIANCHI
 (Osimo Scala, Ancona)

PICENO ROSSO

The medieval market town of Ascoli Piceno, the home of the red
Piceno wine, is in an obscure part of the Marches. This
Piceno Rosso, it can be said, is produced over almost the whole
territory of the Marches, from Ascoli Piceno in the south to
Macerata and Senigallia in the north, with the exception of the
area immediately around the port of Ancona, which has its own
Cònero DOC red.

A classic Piceno is produced in a small area running from
Ascoli Piceno to the sea, and this, provided it has been aged for
a year before being marketed, may be called superiore.

There is little surprise about the choice of vine used: as in
adjacent Tuscany and Emilia-Romagna, it is the reliable Sangiovese that is mostly employed, along with a little Montepulciano,
which is closely allied to it.

Particularly in the case of the classic superiore Piceno, the wine
appreciates aging in the bottle and justifies the trouble. Here, as

with any Sangiovese, we have a light-ruby wine that softens with
time both in taste and color till it is a fit accompaniment to roast
meat dishes.

Producers	*Additional Description*
CONTE GIOVANNI VINCI GIGLIUCCI	BOCCABIANCA
(Cupra Marittima, Ascoli Piceno)	
CANTINA SOCIALE DI CUPRAMONTANA	
(Cupramontana, Ancona)	
GIUSEPPE PENNESI	
(Sant'Elpidio a Mare, Ascoli Piceno)	
ENOPOLIO, CONSORZIO AGRARIO PROVINCIALE	
(Macerata, Ascoli Piceno)	
EMIDIO COSTANTINI BRANCADORO	LA TONACCIA
(San Benedetto del Tronto, Ascoli Piceno)	
UMANI RONCHI	
(Osimo Scala, Ancona)	

SANGIOVESE DEI COLLI PESARESI (Pesaro Hills
Sangiovese)

This wine, produced from 90 per cent Sangiovese, 7 per cent
Montepulciano, and 3 per cent Tuscan Malvasia or Trebbiano is
in the tradition of central Italy. The DOC zone includes the hills
around Pesaro and Fano, which lead toward the Romagna, famous
for its Sangiovese. The wine itself is a garnet red, harmonious,
with a fairly tannic base and a minimum of 10.5 per cent alcohol.

Producer

AZIENDA AGRICOLA ELIGIO PALAZZETTI
(Pesaro)

FALERIO BIANCO

This wine is on its way to DOC-ing. Like the other Marches wines, it provides no surprises. It comes from 80 per cent Trebbiano, 5 per cent Malvasia, and 15 per cent either Verdicchio or Pinot Bianco. Such a composition of wines inevitably produces a satisfactory table wine—the strong character of the Trebbiano, with the mitigating influence of the Malvasia, and the fragrant elegance of the Verdicchio or the Pinot.

Producer

EMIDIO CONSTANTINI BRANCADORO
    (San Benedetto del Tronto, Ascoli Piceno)

VERNACCIA DI SERRAPETRONA

This unusual wine—and it is particularly unusual for the Marches —has had centuries of fame and is even mentioned in Dante's *Divine Comedy.*

Nowadays its effervescent character is made by the highly contemporary charmat process in large sealed vats. It has a purplish color, an intense aroma, a sweet, earthy flavor, and sharp aftertaste. It is said to become more harmonious and balanced with bottle age.

It is a dessert wine—and a rather rustic one—that is more often used outside of mealtimes as an apéritif.

Producer

ATTILIO FABRINI
    (Serrapetrona, Macerata)

CHAPTER FIFTEEN

UMBRIA

Umbria

Orvieto wine is, like Chianti, Verdicchio, Frascati, Soave, and Valpolicella, one of Italy's best-known wines abroad. For a long time, however, it has not been nominated a DOC wine. This was, I think, due to the fact that a few of the major producers, with the notable exception of the Marchesi Antinori, who have their plant and cellars in Orvieto, did their processing and bottling outside the growing zone; and this, by DOC regulations, is not permitted. Wine must be made in the immediate area in which the vine is grown, and only a few very minor exceptions have been made to this rule. This anomaly has now been overcome.

As everywhere else in central Italy, the Trebbiano and Sangiovese grapes rule supreme. Orvieto, however, has some minor differences that give it its unique character. Basically it is a Trebbiano (60 per cent); then there is some Malvasia to make it sweeter and smoother, followed by smaller quantities of Verdello and Greco, which give it its je-ne-sais-quoi and its gentle perfume. Most Orvieto is abboccato, slightly sweet, but a sweetness that is very limited and such as can be tolerated by one accustomed to drinking dry wines. You might say that it is the ideal wine to share while initiating a young lady into Bacchic delights. With time, you may be able to wean her onto the dry Orvieto, which is better.

The countryside of Umbria is as gentle as the Orvieto wine it produces, and dotted with famous medieval towns such as Assisi, Spoleto, Todi, and Gubbio; its capital is at Perugia, where can be found the only other approved DOC zone of the region. This is Torgiano (or Torre di Giano), where there are many small producers and one well-established one. It is this last, just as with the Marchesa Franca Spinola Giuntini's La Parrina zone in Tuscany, that sets the standards, and they are very high. Dott. Giorgio Lungarotti, over the past thirty years, has restructured the whole operation of the rolling hills that belonged to various members of his family and himself and built up a centralized and rational system of cultivation, processing, maturing, bottling, and marketing. The Torgiano red is a fine Sangiovese with a little Canaiolo and Trebbiano and a drop of Montepulciano: not far from a Chianti. It is a wine that ages magnificently for ten years and probably much more, but already, in 1972, there were no more bottles of 1964 left in the cellar.

The white is a Trebbiano and Grechetto, to which may be added small quantities of Verdello and Malvasia; that is to say, it is similar in formula to an Orvieto. Yet this Torre di Giano is very different and as dry as a bone; and it ages to a decade comfortably, refining all its qualities admirably. The fact is that, except for a number of wines that have been established over the generations, whose habits are well known, so many Italian wines, due to new plantations or new processing or just new personal enterprise, have not a documented history that goes back a century or even three decades with assurance. We say a wine will last ten years, but this is because it is a known fact. It may well last fifty years, but there is no way of knowing till another forty years have passed, and then only if someone stands guard over the wine during this period.

The total Torgiano production is modest: just 200,000 liters of white and much less of red. The rolling hills of Umbria are ideal vine-growing land; they have lacked only capital investment to make them more famous. A few miles to the west, another zone is being delineated: the Trasimene Hills. Over the years, I have drunk, many times, fresh, young wines produced near Lake Trasimeno. The problem, however, lies not in producing fresh young wines, which is relatively easy; it lies in the investment and the enological processing necessary to make that fresh young wine a traveler and, perhaps, allow it to mature in suitable circumstances; this, too, costs money. I wish the Trasimene Hills good luck in raising the capital, as the raw material is most pleasing.

ORVIETO

The well-known Orvieto wine is produced south and southeast of Orvieto, around Terni, and north of Viterbo: just north of the Est! Est! Est! zone. It is obtained from the equally well-known Tuscan Trebbiano grape with an admixture of Tuscan Malvasia, Verdello, and Grechetto.

Orvieto comes in two types: dry and abboccato. Both are fairly intense, straw-colored wines, well balanced and smooth. The dry has a pleasant, astringent aftertaste, whereas the abboccato has a delicate, caressing farewell. Both have a minimum alcoholic content of 11.5 per cent, though in practice the dry usually runs to 12 per cent and the abboccato to 12.5 per cent. There is a small classic zone, whose wines are the best for cellaring, as a good Orvieto can take even up to ten years of bottle age. There is a small production of Orvieto red, which, unlike the white, is non-

DOC: not a wine of great reputation, but a Sangiovese, which is always a sound basis for a good, lasting wine.

Producers   *Additional Information*

BARBERANI E CORTONI
  (Orvieto, Terni)
ACHILLE LEMMI
  (Montegabbione, Orvieto)
LUIGI BIGI
  (Orvieto, Terni)
PETRURBANI
  (Orvieto)
CONTE VASELLI
  (Castiglione in Teverina, Viterbo)
MARCHESI L. & P. ANTINORI   CASTELLO LA SALA
  (Florence)
AZIENDA AGRICOLA "LE VELETTE"
  (Orvieto)

TORGIANO (Torre di Giano)

The Torgiano wines are little known but have a long reputation, which is now growing widely. They come from a small zone south of Perugia, toward the country town of Torgiano. The quantity produced is by no means large.

The red is made, much like a Chianti, chiefly of Sangiovese with a little Canaiolo and Trebbiano. The white is obtained from between 50 and 70 per cent of Trebbiano and the remainder of Grechetto. Both are full-bodied wines of pronounced taste and alcoholic strength: 12 to 13 per cent for the red, 12 per cent for the white.

The white is a straw-colored wine that, when young, is slightly fruity and sharp. However, it takes a lot of bottle age, refining away all its asperities and youthful roughness. Equally, the red ages very well indeed. It is excellent at six years old, three in the wood; it is perfection at eight, when it has disposed of all its excess tannin.

The Lungarotti winery makes a broad range of fine wines, including a Vin Santo and Soledad Dry; this latter being a fortified sherry-type apéritif wine that is most acceptable.

Producer	*Additional Information*
CANTINE GIORGIO LUNGAROTTI	RUBESCO (red)
	TOR DI GIANA (white)
	CASTELGRIFONE (rosé)

COLLI DEL TRASIMENO (Trasimene Hills)

As in the Chiana Valley, in Tuscany, the wine producers of the hills around Lake Trasimene have in the past sold their wines in bulk to more famous négociants, who have sold the wine under their own labels. Now these producers are beginning to bottle their own wines. As elsewhere, there are no great surprises here: the white is a Tuscan Trebbiano with the addition of some Tuscan Malvasia, some Verdicchio, and some Grechetto. The red is a Sangiovese with the addition of some Tuscan Trebbiano, some Tuscan Malvasia, and, a little oddly, some Gamay. Everything is in order for the making of fine table wines and a reputation. DOC nomination is in the offing, after which it will depend on the farmers and the enologists whether that reputation is made.

Producer
CANTINA SOCIALE DI CASTIGLIONE
    (Castiglione sul Lago, Perugia)

CHAPTER SIXTEEN

LAZIO

Aprilia Wines

Lazio

Wine has been important in Rome from the beginning of history and even before. The main supplier was always the Alban Hills, fifteen miles to the south of the city. A logistics problem existed: how to shift the barrels from the hills to Rome. This was solved by the farmers' becoming part-time carters, who, over the centuries, became also a colorful part of the folklore of Rome.

In the seventeenth century, to the best of my knowledge, occurred the first piece of real Keynesian-New Deal economic policy, though it turned out to be more durable and people still like it today. It seems that there was a failure of the grape harvest due to the famous noble rot, and much hardship was being felt by the countrymen of the Alban Hills. Pope Urban VIII, one of the most civilized and intelligent of popes, solved the problem in a most surprising way.

Some ten years before, he had put aside in his desk drawer some architectural plans as being rather grandiose as well as expensive. This urbane Barberini pope got them out, dusted them off, and called for Gian Lorenzo Bernini, whose designs they were. He told him to go ahead with the building of the colonnade and the square in front of St. Peters and to put the farmers and carters to work bringing blocks of travertine marble down from the Alban Hills quarries. This decision saved the day for them, and often makes it for us; it also makes the famous saying, "What the barbarians didn't do, the Barberini did," look a trifle silly and perhaps malicious.

The Alban Hills wine is best drunk up in the Alban Hills straight from a barrel in a cool cellar; it is then a still, golden liquid that, accompanying roast lamb and wild asparagus, is one of those Arcadian pleasures that one remembers forever. But the world is not notably Arcadian any more.

Castelli Romani wines (this is the generic term for the whole zone) have never been great travelers: when the barrels are brought to Rome, they must be kept in cold cellars or the wine plays tricks. But nowadays the production is far too small to supply the restaurants and wine shops of a city of nearly three million inhabitants, particularly as an appreciable quantity is bottled and sold throughout the world. And this includes all the DOC and DOC-ing categories: Colli Albani, Colli Lanuvini, Frascati, Marino, Cori, Velletri, Montecompatri, Colonna, and Zagarolo.

The "best" of the taverns of Old Rome and Trastevere still stock *sfuso* (from the cask or demijohn) Castelli wine, but I have observed (and followed suit) that many of the old hands, particularly in winter, prefer the Cesanese di Olevano red, which comes abboccato and is very much a wine to roll around one's tongue. They also like red Cesanese del Piglio, which, over recent years, has been brought from modest origins to an excellent bottled table-wine status: it ages very nicely for four or even five years. But reds do not raise the problems that whites, and particularly Roman whites, do. The makers of Castelli wines are in the avant-garde of enological stabilization, though the optimum, when reached, somehow seems to get a long way from the wine as drunk under a tree at Frascati. However, the characteristics of these Roman wines are such that they are essentially wines to be drunk young; only the Fiorano of Prince Boncompagni Ludovisi, and the Winefood's Fontana Candida superiore are designed for a longer life. Castelli wines are unobtrusive, yet play their part admirably in enhancing most dishes, except the more piquant ones, which require a stronger and, perhaps, red one.

You will read in most books on Italian wine about "noble rot," a condition that is encouraged or at least allowed to proceed under control with Sauternes and some German wines; less is said of *pourriture gris,* which is the next stage and means that the grape has degenerated badly, losing liquids, tannin, and sugar, as well as picking up all sorts of bacteria that drive the enologist to desperation. The dividing line between the noble and the gray rots is a matter of opinion.

Grapes with noble rot are discarded in all of Italy save the Roman hills: they would be thrown away there too if the condition were not so prevalent due to the humidity and other factors. The enologists smile when wine enthusiasts talk nostalgically and knowingly about noble rot, because, when the grapes arrive at the winery, they take rigorous action to be rid of it.

The grapes are lightly pressed, and the nobly rotting skins are thrown away: the juice is then given a dose of sulphur and a flash pasteurization (80° C. for a few seconds), after which there is no more noble rot. A lot of other things have gone too, but they at least can be replaced.

The enologists say that noble rot was the cause of Castelli wine being an unstable, non-traveler, that it caused maderization (oxidation) and continuous "wild" fermentations whenever the wine was shaken or there were temperature increases, especially in summer. On the credit side, they say that the noble rot produced a sort of penicillin, Botriticina, which might have been the reason for the long conservation of some sweet wines in the past, but that the disadvantages vastly outweigh the advantages in every other way, and that, above all, noble rot, if not cultivated under clinical conditions, can reduce the yield of the crop by as much as 40 per cent.

The enologists "admit," if that is the proper word to describe their confident statements, that the Castelli wines are not the Arcadian wine you drink at Frascati made from selected grapes, but a wine that is now enjoyed throughout the world. Here they pragmatically rest their oars and cheerfully add, "Well, Castelli wine scarcely got to Rome before we worked on it; now it will travel to the moon." They have a lot of right on their side, since fashion-preference-taste in wine has continuously changed throughout history; in the past fifty years, for example, we have seen the virtual extinction of the taste for sweet table wines, and a rise in preference for fresh, light, dry ones—much as they make in the Castelli Romani.

Another proof-of-the-pudding DOC zone is that of Aprilia, in the province of Latina, just south of Rome. The whole area was, for two thousand years, called the Pontine Marshes, though much land was, if soggy, well above sea level. The draining of the malarial swamps was one of the best-known public works of the penultimate king of Italy, Victor Emmanuel III. In the past forty years, a territory that once "farmed" only water buffaloes has become a major agricultural success and the site of much light industry.

That it should have turned out to be good land for vineyards is something of a surprise. An old friend, a retired diplomat, having learned how to make claret in France, bought a few acres there, set to work with a will, and was soon producing a most pleasing young wine. He did not live long enough to bottle a "Pontine Claret," which is a great pity. He complained that the only snag he had run up against was that the Cabernets were far too strong, often having over 15 per cent natural alcoholic content.

The Aprilia DOC zone, then, is generous with its yield, rather too generous. At present, the wines, entirely made by a co-operative, stand by themselves. They say that the processing differs from ordinary Italian practice and leans more on Tunisian French methods. The three wines, Merlot, Trebbiano, and Sangiovese, that they make are very popular and remarkably cheap; they seem tailor-made to meet a large consumer public.

The Maccarese Castel San Giorgio wine is grown on the plains just north of Fiumicino Airport. The estate produces inexpensive, honest-as-the-day, and most pleasing reds (Sangiovese) and whites (Trebbiano and Malvasia) under first-class conditions. I am told that everything belongs to the I.R.I. (the mixed-economy holding company that owns half of Italy's industrial productive capacity) and that the I.R.I. permits this estate to run at a deficit. I have the added pleasure, therefore, when drinking a glass of Maccarese, of getting more than my money's worth, since I am convinced that it has been subsidized by the I.R.I.'s more successful ventures. This is a non-DOC wine, but a most worthy one.

This leaves us with Est! Est! Est!, the wine that so delighted the worthy German prelate Monsignore Reverendissimo Hans Fugger that, in the year 1110, he drank himself to death with it at Montefiascone, near Lake Bolsena. I do not think that anybody would do that today; in any case, the much beloved wine of the bishop was a Moscadello, while today's is a Trebbiano. But the distinguished Antinori company of Florence has recently entered the lists, producing their own Est! Est! Est!, so who can tell if history will not one day repeat itself?

As a tailpiece, I would like to add a mention of a well-educated Sangiovese, which has been made only in the past decade from carefully selected grapes in the Sabine Hills, an area in the north of Lazio, near Rieti, which previously had no reputation for its wines. This San Vittore degli Uccellatori* is a fine table wine, which requires two years' aging in the wood and one in the bottle, after which it is in its prime and with no acerbities.

* Cantine San Vittore in Torri, in Sabina, Rieti

CASTELLI ROMANI WINES (Roman Castles Wines)

COLLI ALBANI (Alban Hills Wines)

The Alban Hills white comes from the area around Albano, Ariccia, and Castel Gandolfo, to the west of Lake Albano and south of Rome.

The papal summer palace is at Castel Gandolfo, and the local wine has been served to the popes for centuries. This "Roman" wine is made from the Malvasia and Trebbiano grapes and is a highly regarded light and dry table wine: it is amber-colored and has a delicate aroma, full body, and at least 12 per cent alcohol.

If the grapes are selected well and the wine reaches 12.5 per cent, it is classified superiore, which also means that it will take a year or two of bottle aging. The Fiorano will take several more years of nursing to good effect.

Producers	Additional Description
PRINCIPE ALBERTO BONCOMPAGNI LUDOVISI DI VENOSA (Capannelle-Roma) CANTINA SOCIALE COOPERATIVA COLLI ALBANI (Fontana di Papa Cecchina, Albano)	FIORANO BIANCO

COLLI LANUVINI (Lanuvian Hills Wines)

This white comes from just past Lake Albano, toward Genzano, Velletri, and Lake Nemi, going south from Rome. It is made from the Malvasia and Trebbiano grapes, to which is added a little Bonvino. Here there is more Malvasia than Trebbiano used, as in the Alban Hills, which makes a "richer" wine with more body and a touch of sweetness. It is a straw-colored wine with a minimum alcoholic content of 11.5 per cent. Like the other Castelli Romani wines (Albano, Frascati, Marino, etc.), it has enough character to accompany most luncheon dishes.

Producers
SANTARELLI
   (Via Stazione Tuscolana 104, Roma)
CANTINA SOCIALE DI GENZANO
   (Genzano)

FRASCATI

Frascati wine, which is always a white, comes in three types: dry, amabile, and *cannellino* (sweet). The dry Frascati is the one best known in Italy and abroad. Frascati has been produced since Renaissance times, when the popes and cardinals made the Alban Hills their summer residence.

Frascati is made with grapes from the Malvasia vines of Candia and Lazio, the Tuscan Trebbiano, and the yellow Trebbiano (also called Greco). The soil is volcanic and, therefore, good for vine growing. However, the climate is humid, and this produces the famous—or infamous—noble rot, which is mentioned in the introduction to this chapter; it is considered a necessity for making the sweet and abboccato Frascatis.

Frascati is normally not a long-lived wine, though a 12 per cent superiore can improve with a few years in the bottle. At any time, it is an enjoyable table wine, smooth, harmonious, and with a pleasing aroma.

Producers	*Additional Description*
CONTE ZANDOTTI	SAN PAOLO
(Roma)	
CANTINA PRODUTTORI FRASCATI "SAN MATTEO"	
(Frascati)	
FONTANA CANDIDA	
(Frascati)	
TRIMANI	
(Via Goito 20, Roma)	
SANTARELLI	
(Via Stazione Tuscolana 104, Rome)	
A. DE SANCTIS	
(Frascati)	

MARINO

Marino wine is one of the Castelli Romani wines and comes from the north side of Lake Albano, above the shores of which is the pope's summer residence at Castel Gandolfo.

Romans, on the whole, count Marino as the best of their local wines, particularly when it is served directly from the barrel in the wine shops of the city.

Both a red and a rosé are also to be found, but these are basically Cesanese wines, which are better from their native habitat, near Frosinone, to the south. The white, which is the traditional product, is a dry Malvasia of golden color to which has been added some Tuscan Trebbiano and a little Bonvino to make the conventional warm but slightly sharp Castelli wines. Like the others, the Marino is not the greatest of wines, but it is one that one can live with very happily, without wearying of its company.

Producers

SOCIETA LEPANTO
    (Frattocchie di Marino, Rome)
CANTINA SOCIALE COOPERATIVA DI MARINO
    (Ciampino, Rome)

MINOR CASTELLI ROMANI WINES

VELLETRI
MONTECOMPATRI
COLONNA
ZAGAROLO
CORI

These are small towns with long, distinguished, and fascinating histories. Each of them soon will have its own DOC wine-producing label, though with minor differences the wines align themselves with the more famous Castelli Romani wines, being obtained from the same Malvasia and Trebbiano grapes.

Producer
CONSORZIO AGRARIO ROMANO
     (Via Urbana, Rome)

CESANESE WINES

CESANESE DEL PIGLIO
CESANESE DI OLEVANO ROMANO
CESANESE DI AFFILE

There are three types of Cesanese wines, produced around Rome and to the south toward Frosinone. Particularly the Piglio (dry) and the Olevano (abboccato) are popular among the Romans; the sweet Affile seems little known. Of the first two, neither is a great wine, but they are both very acceptable, and, after all, nobody wants to drink great wines twice a day.

The Piglio, over recent years, has been improved immensely, and larger quantities have been laid down for maturing by the local producers' co-operative. The result is a deep-red wine, dry, full-bodied, full of taste, not excessively tannic or fruity: in all, far more than just a satisfactory table wine. Rather, a wine with a future.

The abboccato of Olevano is picnic wine, a little frizzante

when young, which makes a ham sandwich a gourmet luncheon without the aid of mustard.

Producers

CANTINA SOCIALE COOPERATIVA CESANESE DEL PIGLIO
    (Piglio, Roma)
CANTINA SOCIALE DI OLEVANO
    (Olevano, Roma)
CANTINA SOCIALE DI AFFILE
    (Affile, Roma)

APRILIA WINES

TREBBIANO DI APRILIA
MERLOT DI APRILIA
SANGIOVESE DI APRILIA

The Aprilia area has no viticultural tradition; in fact, for centuries it was called the Pontine Marshes, which were drained only during the 1930s. In the post-World War II period, a number of Italian enological experts and farmers were expelled from formerly French Tunisia and settled there; already during the prewar period considerable numbers of war veterans from the Veneto had been given reclaimed land there and the agricultural exploitation of the area was well under way.

As a wine-producing area, it has always been one using non-Italian methods. For some time, till his death, in the 1960s, an Italian ex-diplomat made his version of claret, using French vines, which was widely appreciated. The Aprilia co-operative, which handles most of the local production, is using French Tunisian methods to produce smooth and pleasing table wines. The Trebbiano is a clear, pale-straw-colored wine with the customary dry Trebbiano taste, a fresh bouquet, and 12 per cent

alcohol. The Sangiovese is a rosé, dry and strong. The Merlot—
probably the best of the trio—is a full-bodied garnet-red wine,
with a tannic tang, a fair bouquet, and 12 per cent alcohol.

Producer
COOPERATIVA ENOTRIA
   (Aprilia, Latina)

ALEATICO DI GRADOLI

This remarkable but little-known wine, the Aleatico di Gradoli,
comes from a growing area to the west of Lake Bolsena, toward
Pitigliano. This unusual wine, red and sweet, is made from the
Aleatico grape, which, having been semi-dried, offers a 16 per
cent wine, garnet-colored, velvety, round, and with a strong fruity
bouquet.

   It is also made as a *liquoroso* wine, when it reaches a minimum
of 17.5 per cent alcohol.

Producer
CANTINA SOCIALE DI GRADOLI
   (Gradoli, Viterbo)

EST! EST! EST! DI MONTEFIASCONE

Produced in volcanic soil around Lake Bolsena, south of Orvieto,
the Est! Est! Est! is obtained from the usual well-known white
wines of central Italy: The Trebbiano (65 per cent), the Malvasia

(20 per cent), and the golden Trebbiano, locally called Rossetto (15 per cent).

The original wine of this country, so much loved by Abbot Hans Fugger, was from the Moscatello vine. However, the present-day wine is a very satisfactory table wine—brilliantly clear, straw yellow, dry, rounded, and with a pleasant, fresh finish.

A fuller story of Abbot Hans Fugger's tragic end is that he was on his way to Rome to be present at the coronation of his Emperor, Henry V, by the Pope. Martin, his servant, traveled a day ahead to scout out the best wine for his master: on finding it, he would write with chalk on the door of the inn EST! At Montefiascone, he found the wine so much to his taste that he wrote EST! EST! EST! on the door. His Most Reverend Excellency was of the same opinion and, one tale says, after a three-day drinking bout, gave up the ghost.

Another story says that he actually went to the coronation ceremony in Rome and rushed back to Montefiascone, where he lived till his dying day, though whether this was three days or thirty years it is not stated, though it was probably for many years, both because his name became Italianized to Gianni DeFuk, as was the custom with residents with impossible foreign names, and also because it takes a long time to kill oneself drinking too much good wine.

In his will he is said to have left funds with the municipality for a barrel of wine to be poured over his tomb every year on the anniversary of his demise. It is said that this practice was carried out until a certain Cardinal Barbarigo converted this liquid legacy into a distribution of wine to the local seminarists. Though much doubt may be cast on this story, there is none about the existence of the most reverend gentleman whose bones lie in the church of St. Flaviano Martyr in a tomb on which is inscribed HIC IACET J. DEFUK/DOMINUS MEUS/QUI PROPTER NIMIUM EST EST EST/ MORTUUS EST. This also brings up the consideration that perhaps Cardinal Barbarigo's decision was not so much based on social justice as due to the trouble the sacristan of the church had cleaning up after this yearly bucolic ceremony.

Producers

CAV. G. MAZZIOTTI
      (Bolsena, Viterbo)
CANTINA COOPERATIVA DI MONTEFIASCONE
      (Viterbo)
L. & P. ANTINORI
      (Florence)

CHAPTER SEVENTEEN

ABRUZZI

Abruzzi

In all my twenty-five years' drinking in Italy, I have never heard a good word put in for the Abruzzi wines. Certainly it never dawned on me even to buy a bottle. I thought of those forbidding mountains, open to at least three of the four winds, and often so rocky that not even shrubs would grow, and concluded that it was not wine land.

I was right and wrong. Looking at the subject from Rome, the mountains are unwelcoming, but, tucked away on the other side, there are fertile valleys running down to the Adriatic that produce far from rustic wines. My knowledge of and affection for the Abruzzi have grown in the past two years, and it no longer seems so awesome and forbidding.

Recently, at a wine tasting, I met a young Italo-American and his wife who were doing a grand wine tour of Italy and France. They were taking a couple of days out to visit the land of his parents. He seemed downcast at the prospect, fearing to be shamed in front of his wife, finding the Abruzzi natives sleeping with the pigs under their beds and hotels with running water only in the yard. I was able to reassure him that the Abruzzi not only had fine hotels and excellent wine but that, after Sabatini's, in Florence, one of the best restaurants in all Italy was the Tre Marie, in the capital, L'Aquila ("the eagle," which sits on a mountaintop), a most elegant and lively city. With my encouragement and a few addresses, he gained the confidence that his trip was not only not doomed to disastrous failure, but that it might even be a personal success.

The Abruzzo region is one of evolution, transformation, and injection of new blood in the form of huge sums of investment capital from the Cassa per il Mezzogiorno, the governmental corporation for the development of southern Italy. Only a few years ago, it took several hours to drive to the capital, with a thousand hairpin bends. Today, you get there in an hour by autostrada, driving past magnificent scenery, tunneling through mountains, and leaping across great valleys: the highway is no mean engineering feat and was incredibly expensive. By the end of 1974, the second part, which will link Rome with the Adriatic via L'Aquila, should be finished. These profound changes in the economy and in communications will have their effect also on the wine. Already Pescara, the Abruzzi's Adriatic seaport, is a boom town, with a consequently greater demand for finer wines. The whites of Chieti already are very good and will surely be better.

It is demand and capital investment that give the producer the incentive to employ a good enologist, replace his old vats, buy some good casks, and all the rest needed to improve his wines: these conditions are already existing, though it is not likely that the producers will be looking for foreign agents for many a year yet.

MONTEPULCIANO D'ABRUZZO

The Montepulciano vine was introduced into the Abruzzo region early in the nineteenth century and now is the most widely cultivated red-grape vine. The wine-producing areas are entirely on the eastern slopes of the Apennines, toward the Adriatic Sea, around the towns of Sulmona, Vasto, Pescara, Teramo, and Chieti, and in the valleys leading up toward L'Aquila.

The Abruzzo is not noted for fine wine, though appreciable improvements have been noted in recent years, particularly with the whites of Chieti.

This Montepulciano is produced in a rosé, called Cerasuola, which is quite widely known even outside of the Abruzzo region: it is a cherry-colored wine with a pleasing dry taste. The red is a ruby red, tending to orange with age; it is a dry, tannic wine with a strong aroma and 12 per cent alcohol. It requires some aging and, if matured for two years in the wood, it may be labeled *vecchio* (old), at which time it becomes a well-balanced as well as robust wine.

Producers
CANTINA SOCIALE MADONNA DEI MIRACOLI
   (Casalbordino, Chieti)
CAMILLO VALENTINI
   (Loreto Aprutino, Pescara)
DI PROSPERO
   (Pratola Peligna, L'Aquila)
CANTINA SOCIALE DI ROSETO
   (Roseto degli Abruzzi)
CASAL THAULERO
   (Roseto degli Abruzzi)

TREBBIANO D'ABRUZZO

This is a new DOC category, as yet to be approved. The growing area is the hillsides behind the coastal strip from Pescara north to Teramo and south to Chieti. The Trebbiano is well adapted to this terrain and offers an excellent rounded white wine with as much as 12–13 per cent alcohol. In sum, a wine likely to demonstrate greater worth if honored with a few years of bottle age.

Producers

DI PROSPERO
    (Pratola Peligna, L'Aquila)
EDOARDO VALENTINI
    (Loreto Aprutino, Pescara)

CHAPTER EIGHTEEN

CAMPANIA

Campania

The Campania means Naples, Capri, and Ischia, along with mandolins, pizzas, and, of course, a view of Vesuvius: the tourist run par excellence. But it does not ring much of a bell on the subject of wine, even though there are 300 million liters produced in the Campania region every year. This is 20 per cent more than the production of Lombardy, yet Lombardy has nearly 2½ million liters of DOC wine, against the Campania's ½ million.

Plainly, the Neapolitans cannot work up much enthusiasm for all this Common Market nonsense: just more forms to fill in and, as everybody knows, when you start filling in government forms, you never know where they will finish up or what you will find yourself committed to doing. Some officious functionary might quite unreasonably even assume that you sold wine for money and made a profit, which, again, might involve taxation and other repressive vexations that were finally consigned to past history when the Bourbon kings were overthrown a century ago.

Fortunately there are half a dozen pillars of society who have filled in the forms and thus have exposed themselves for the good name of the Campania's wine and whose courage merits, at the very least, warm recognition and perhaps a tax rebate.

In any event, they are D'Ambra of Ischia, Marchese Patrizi of Capri, Michele Mastroberardino of Avellino, Saviano of Ottaviano-Vesuvius, Giuseppe Scala, and the Vinolearia Company of Formia. There may be more; if so, I ask their forgiveness. I recall a Ravello Gran Caruso wine with great pleasure and also a Furore Divina Costiera also of the Amalfi Coast, but these are non-DOC. I also recall a producer called Tucci, to whom I am eternally grateful for his modestly priced and honest wine; but where is his winery? At Solopaca near Caserta? Or perhaps in Avellino? I cannot remember.

In the Campania, we move into another world, a world where the Sangiovese and Trebbiano are not welcome. It is a wine world that started when the Greeks landed at Cumae, just north of Naples, at the beginning of history, to found a colony, bringing with them their seed grains and vines and presumably much else to make their life comfortable. After all, we must remember that another of their colonies, the one at Sybaris, in the arch of the Italian boot, had quite a reputation for the good life. It seems they brought vines to produce white wine and red wine; the former, to this day, is called Greco; the latter, with etymological corruption over the millenniums, worked its way from Hellenic to Aglianico, and thus it has remained. Whatever truth there is in this astonishing lineage, the important factor is that both, given the right soil and exposition and subsequent loving care—because both need a good rest in the barrel—produce wines of exceptional quality.

In early historical times, both vines were grown on the coastal strip between Terracina and Formia and farther south along the Bay of Gaeta. This area was very important in Roman times and in the French, Spanish, and Bourbon periods (from the fourteenth to the nineteenth centuries); both towns were ports with lively traffic. However, Terracina was in the Papal States and Formia (and Gaeta) in the Neapolitan Kingdom. As a frontier area like the Friuli, it suffered more than any other from marauders and the battles culminating in the unification of Italy. The

South suffered badly in this unification, inasmuch as it was, in a wry way, "defeated." The southerners were not under foreign domination, as was North Italy under the Austrians. Naples was an independent kingdom with a capital city many times bigger than Rome and second only to London and Paris: the ruling Bourbons, who were a mixture of Spanish, French, and Austrian blood, had become as much Neapolitan as the Neapolitans. The Kingdom of the Two Sicilies (as southern Italy and Sicily were oddly called) was as progressive as any state in Europe: it had industry, shipyards, and rail transportation before such things had reached other countries. The only people who were unwelcome (and usually jailed) were republicans. For the rest, the Neapolitans were as happy as the citizens of any other kingdom. They welcomed the conquest of the Bourbon authority by Garibaldi and, later, by Piedmont troops, as one might welcome the conquest of any authority in the hope of getting a milder one in replacement. Many southerners lived to regret their hopes, which were dashed as their industries collapsed and their agriculture failed, faced with the more active and better established northern enterprises. Emigration, as everybody knows, to the United States and all the world was the southerners' only recourse. Only in the past few decades has an effort been made to repay the moral, physical, and financial damage done a hundred years ago.

The demoralization of the South has still not been overcome, but many of the prestige products and natural beauties of the land, which Norman Douglas wrote about before World War I, are at last being recognized. Grinding poverty is, finally, a rarity, but this is also due to the emigration of not tens but hundreds of thousands of southerners to central and northern Europe in the past twenty years.

Only in the past decade can one say that the southern Italian quality wines have started to become interesting on an appreciable scale. Just as much as a supporter of French or German wines will not say a good word for an Italian wine, the northern Italians do not say a good word for southern wines. It may take northern and central Italy ten years to overcome the prejudices against their wines, but it may take southern Italy thirty years, unless there are a large number of people who are quite open-minded and simply looking for honest wine at the right price, rather than needing a well-known label and publicity on the back of buses to reassure their uncertain souls.

After the wine-growing area centered on Formia, where in the past hundred years an Aglianico and a Greco have been produced under the Roman names of Falerno (Falernian) and Cecubo, there are four other areas of importance: the islands of Capri and Ischia, Vesuvius, and Irpinia.

Though Capri is very small, there is a remarkably large production, of 600,000 liters; but, of this, only a small part is marketed, as it is mostly made by smallholders who drink it or sell it in their own bars and restaurants. Cantine Patrizi is the major producer, with 35,000 bottles of white and 7,000 of red, both of which are matured for a year in the cask and improve in the bottle.

The Casa D'Ambra has been, for decades, the standard-bearer of Ischia wines: recently it has joined the Winefood group of Milan, a holding company having a major interest in half a dozen excellent wineries in Italy. Due to an enlightened management, these wineries and their vineyards are being newly capitalized to increase and improve the quantity and quality of their DOC wines. This entry of a major international firm into the Neapolitan world of mostly outdated business practice should be beneficial, and perhaps will even arouse others to raise their ambitions and emulate Winefood's standards. Over and above the DOC Ischia wines, Winefood will be continuing the other three well-known D'Ambra wines, the Biancolella, the Forastera, and the Per' 'e Palummo, which do not fit into DOC categories.

The wines of Ischia and Capri, like those of Ravello, are, on the whole, lightweights, but none the worse for that: they reflect the sun and the sea in their bouquets. Perhaps the only surprise on the Bay of Naples is the Gragnano red, a full-bodied, rich wine that comes from the northern-aspect slopes of the southern arm of the bay, above Castellamare di Stabia. I used always to buy Gragnano when passing this little town, as it was always the real thing; elsewhere I found strange wines masquerading under that name. My only recommendation for a source for Gragnano is Saviano of Ottaviano-Vesuvius, who buys and bottles.

This leads to Vesuvius wines, which, in ancient times, were sold in nearby Pompeii and Herculaneum until the eruption engulfed both these cities and the volcano's vineyards. Throughout history, Vesuvius has destroyed the vineyards, and, throughout history, Neapolitan man has put them back again, because volcanic soil makes good wine. In this century, some vineyards were completely out of production until 1948 due to the 1906 and 1945 eruptions: these included the best Lacryma Christi lands. Here again one finds many wines masquerading under a well-known name. Many small producers put out Lacryma Christi, some of which are very nasty and sticky—or were in the past—to the extent that one feels badly deluded and gives up the search. Here Saviano and Mastroberardino are the major producers of repute. To my mind, the dry rosé, rather than the red, the white, or the sweet varieties, is the Lacryma Christi most worthwhile. Saviano produces a champenoise rosé, *mirabile dictu,* on the slopes of Vesuvius that enlivens a dish of grilled shellfish in a way that is quite extraordinary. The reds and rosés are made with Aglianico and Piedirosso grapes and the white with Greco.

Moving inland, we leave the territory of the Greeks and Romans and visit the ancient Samnites of Irpinia. Here we find some of the finest wines of southern Italy, wines that can hold up their heads in any company, though they are made of the same grapes as the Vesuvius wines; the difference lies in the particularly favorable land (it is also volcanic soil) and Mastroberardino's care.

The Samnite land of Irpinia is 60 per cent mountain and 40 per cent hills. Benevento lies to the north, Foggia to the east, Naples to the west, and Salerno to the south. It was ravaged during World War II, and subsequently, due to grim unemployment, there was a huge exodus of farm hands. Postwar reconstruction, based on giving quick work, was unsuccessful in the long run, since the plans were ill-conceived. Only in more recent years has the enological institute managed to redirect government plans and spending into more practical channels so as to increase the quantity and quality of the traditional Aglianico, Greco, Piedirosso, and Coda di Volpe vines and eradicate the Trebbiano and Sangiovese.

The Aglianico, as produced in the Taurasi area, needs at least four years in the cask and one in the bottle: its asperities are softened by the addition of the Piedirosso grape. The Greco di Tufo, a wine with a fine bouquet and an elegant nature, is given a little more body with grapes from another historic vine, the Coda di Volpe, the fox's tail, so called because of its shape. There is also the Fiano, a distinguished white dry wine of which very little is made.

This region may not scintillate with names of famous wines and wineries like those of Piedmont and Tuscany but, at the same time, it is by no means the national calamity that many would have one believe.

BAY OF NAPLES WINES

ISCHIA

Wines have been produced on the island of Ischia since the sixth century A.D. The soil is of volcanic origin, which is noted for making a good wine. In the past, much white wine from other parts of Italy has been sold under the Ischia label; today there are three DOC-controlled Ischia wines: white, red, and superior white.

The characteristics of the white must be: a brilliant straw color tending to golden, a rich, round, dry, and harmonious taste, a pleasing light bouquet, and a minimum of 11 per cent alcohol. This wine is obtained chiefly from Forastera and Biancolella grapes. The superior white differs in that it has a richer bouquet and 12 per cent alcohol and is treated like a red wine, with the grapeskins in the fermentation vat for forty-eight hours, after which a governo process may be carried out. The red must be ruby red, dry, lightly tannic, and with 11.5 per cent alcohol; it is made from Guarnaccia, Piedirosso, and Barbera grapes.

Producer
CASA D'AMBRA
    (Porto d'Ischia, Ischia)

CAPRI

Capri wine is not on the DOC list, though it seems that it may be nominated in the future. This delay is perhaps because much mainland wine sails under Capri colors, especially during the summer season. However, the major firms making Capri wine have disciplined themselves, and I suspect that, at most, some local wine comes across the narrow channel from the Sorrento area, which, in terms of climate and terrain, is identical to Capri.

The Capri white is obtained from Greco, Fiano, and Biancolella grapes and is a straw-colored, dry wine with a very pleasing aroma and a fresh aftertaste. It ages a few years most creditably.

The red comes from the Aglianico with a little Guarnaccia added; this, too, improves appreciably with bottle age, of which it is known to take up to ten years.

Producer
MARCHESE ETTORE PATRIZI
    (Capri, Naples)

VESUVIUS LACRYMA CHRISTI

This famous wine, which has had too many imitators—at least imitators of its label—has come from around fifteen hundred feet up Mount Vesuvius, above the towns of Ottaviano and Boscotrecase, for millennia. The red is obtained from the Sciascinoso and Caprettone varieties of the Aglianico vine, and with admirable results. The white is from the Greco and is of a golden amber, rich, dry in taste and bouquet, and with a considerable alcoholic content. My preference is for an aged rosé, though all these wines can take many years of bottle age to good effect. They are all, as yet, non-DOC wines; it will be a great day when the name Lacryma Christi is properly protected.

In 1892, at the Vienna world wine competition, Lacryma Christi was adjudicated "the best in the world." In the postwar period, Lacryma Christi has won several gold medals at wine contests at national and international trade fairs. The leap from 1892 to 1948 is due not only to volcanic eruptions but to Vesuvius spewing forth sulphuric acid to complete the ruin during that period. Sparkling reds, whites, and rosés, both sec and demi-sec, are made by the champenoise method.

One myth as to the origin of this ancient name is that Jesus wept tears, observing the Devil's (successful?) attempts at corrupting innocent souls: the tears fell on Vesuvius, irrigating the vineyards. Another, more evolved myth is that the Devil, on being ejected from Paradise, grabbed a slice, which fell to earth; it became, believe it or not, the Bay of Naples—though this, of course, occurred long before they built the petroleum-cracking plant. God then came to earth in human form and wept over the loss of his piece of heavenly real estate, but, every cloud having a silver lining, his tears watered the vineyards to give us the famous Lacryma Christi wine.

Producers

DITTA SAVIANO 1760
   (Ottaviano, Naples)
MICHELE MASTROBERARDINO
   (Atripalda, Avellino)

IRPINIA WINES

TAURASI

Taurasi red wine comes from just south of Benevento, a city that flourished under papal rule in medieval times, and toward Avellino. The soil is volcanic, being only some thirty miles from Vesuvius; also, being near a major ecclesiastical city such as Benevento is a favorable augury for finding good wine.

Taurasi's history is said to go back much further, to the ancient Greeks, who brought to southern Italy their Aglianico vine, which is widely cultivated throughout what was Magna Graecia, the Greek colony consisting of Calabria, Puglia, and eastern Sicily.

Taurasi wine is made from 70 per cent or more of Aglianico and 30 per cent of Barbera, Piedirosso, or Sangiovese, though Piedirosso is preferred. If the wine is matured for four years, of which one is in the wood, it may be called riserva and usually offers 12.5 per cent alcohol.

As with many other red wines, with age it takes on orangy amber tints and greater smoothness and personality. However, all Taurasi has to be matured for over three years (one in the wood) before being marketed, and this in itself is a sign of a fine wine. It can take ten years of bottle age with ease and to good effect, but it is ready to drink and in fine form from its fifth year. It is a strong, robust red wine and, when aged, a distinguished, well-balanced one with an intense bouquet. A wine well worth investigating.

Producers
MICHELE MASTROBERARDINO
    (Atripalda, Avellino)
ISTITUTO DI ENOLOGIA E VITICOLTURA
    (Avellino)

GRECO DI TUFO

To the north of the Taurasi zone and close to the city of Benevento, it is said, the Greco di Tufo has been cultivated since the first century B.C. In the middle of this zone is the little town of Tufo, whose name, of course, comes from the volcanic tufa rock on which it is built. The Greco (of Tufo) refers to the vine that supplies 80 per cent and more of this white wine, the remainder being made up of Coda di Volpe. It is a straw-colored wine tending to be golden, dry, delicate, and well balanced, especially after three or four years of bottle age. Minimum 11.5, usually 12 per cent alcohol.

Producer
MICHELE MASTROBERARDINO
    (Atripalda, Avellino)

CHAPTER NINETEEN

BASILICATA (Lucania)

Basilicata (Lucania)

The Basilicata, also called Lucania, has about the most unrewarding soil of Italy, with the notable exception of Cervinia, in Piedmont, which is covered with snow twelve months of the year. Mount Vulture is a burned-out volcano, and its slopes, which are unfit for any other cultivation, provide the necessary nourishment for the vine, which is noted for its willingness to produce fine grapes from the rockiest and most despised soil: in fact, it is almost a case of the worse the soil, the better the grape.

Basilicata is noted for being the most depressed area of all Italy. Visiting its capital, Potenza, I expected to find crumbling façades, rows of pensioners sunning themselves or playing bocce in the piazzas, a complete absence of children, and an uncomfortable and threatening silence in empty streets—all the motifs of a modern Italian movie. I knew that wealth had reached the provincial cities of Italy, even the southern ones, in an extraordinary manner in the past decade—there seems to be far more folding money about in Cagliari, Foggia, and Bari than in Rome—but I was astonished to find, instead of grim-faced peasants in black corduroy suits traveling by mule, a bustling modernity, modern buildings, smart shops and cafés—and heavy traffic. But it is something of an oasis in a desert. The trunk road to Potenza from Matera is pretty lonely, and if one goes north or south of it five miles, one arrives in a world of primordial solitude fit for hermits. In fact, only in the past decade, a courageous younger generation has been investigating completely desolate hills and finding dozens of Byzantine churches and monasteries, inhabited a thousand years ago by Basilian monks: the curiosity is that they are entirely in caves, with external façades and with pillars and frescoes inside in the style of the Ajanta cave temples of India. In this incredible lost land, they make one great wine, the Aglianico del Vulture, which has an all-Italy reputation and has now been approved for its DOC appellation.

On the same volcanic hillsides, from seven hundred to twenty-two hundred feet up, a Malvasia and a Moscato dessert wine are produced; both are high in alcohol but low in sugar, that is to say, they are slightly sweet rather than very sweet, as are the dessert wines of nearby Puglia.

The remaining wines of the Basilicata, mostly cutting wines, vanish to the "North," as do all cutting wines, without leaving a forwarding address.

AGLIANICO DEL VULTURE

The Aglianico del Vulture is the only wine of note in the Basilicata; however, its reputation throughout Italy over the decades led the way to a broader appreciation of other southern wines.

Obtained from the Aglianico grape and grown in the still-warm soil of the foothills of the extinct volcano Vulture, the Aglianico is a vivid-garnet-red, dry, astringent, full-bodied wine which with age becomes austere and dominating. With two years in the wood and one in the bottle, it may be labeled vecchio (old): the selected wine for maturing usually has 13 per cent or more alcohol. If bottle aging is continued for another two years in the cellar (i.e. five years in all), the Aglianico can be called riserva.

Producers

FRATELLI NAPOLITANO
  (Rionero in Vulture, Potenza)
PATERNOSTER
  (Barile, Potenza)
MARTINO E FRANCESCO MIALI
  (Martina Franca, Taranto)
CONSORZIO AGRARIO PROVINCIALE
  (Potenza)
CENTRALE CANTINE COOPERATIVE DELLA RIFORMA FONDIARIA
  (Bari)

CHAPTER TWENTY

PUGLIA

Puglia

In comparison with the Basilicata, Puglia is a Garden of Eden, flowing with milk and honey, though it suffers from a harsh, continental climate; the Adriatic Sea, which flanks it, seems to do little by way of mitigating the summer heat and the winter cold. Nevertheless, Puglia bursts with wine, oil, wheat, and fish.

And yet Puglia has also known grinding poverty and emigration. Today the grinding poverty is a thing of the past, but not the emigration. It does seem that the science of producing large-scale wealth is a distinctly postwar and even more recent phenomenon. Investment, of course, is necessary, but in itself is insufficient; new methods and marketing are the real essence. In the past decade, Puglia has acquired a fast-growing industrial area between Bari, Brindisi, and Taranto of great oil refineries, petrochemical plants, and steel foundries. But even these, of themselves, are not enough. It is a complex meshing in of agriculture and industry, a city market for the former and big production of the latter, that makes for a general well-being of a region. This new balance of the economy has changed the whole way of life of Puglia and also the pattern of wine production, which has always been enormous:

1000 million liters—as much as Piedmont and Lombardy combined.

The bulk of this great sea of wine is cutting wine: *coupage,* or *taglio,* as it is called in French and Italian. A wine that serves as a transfusion of rich, alcoholic, and strongly colored plasma into the paler wine of the "North" to produce a well-balanced table wine.

The operative word here is "North." The Puglia wine producers are as secretive as armaments manufacturers. Nobody really knows where the wine finishes up; perhaps not even the producers themselves, since the furnishing of end-use certificates, as in the arms trade, is not the practice. But espionage reports circulate: a French tanker ship loads at Barletta; tanker trucks with Verona plates leave the Salento, perhaps for Germany, perhaps for Verona. Of course the exports turn up in the trade figures provided by the government statistics office, but one's curiosity as to precisely where all this wine goes is never satisfied. The reds are mostly 15 per cent Troia of Barletta and 18 per cent Primitivo (or Primativo) of Gioia, which northerners deprecatingly describe as ink. The Pugliese call them black wines and even drink them young, but they are not wines for aesthetes and weaklings, though they might do both a lot of good. The wines of Puglia are, as yet, uncomplicated: they are either brute masculine or lush feminine. The 'tween sexes are now being invented to meet the new domestic demand for quality table wines, and, to give an idea of the complexity of the chromosomes of one of Puglia's best 'tween-sex table wines, the Torre Quarto, this is a list of its components: Troia, Barbera, Pinot, Sangiovese, Aglianico, and Malbec. This is a San Severo wine from near Foggia, and a first-class wine for anybody's money.

Perhaps the most interesting domestication or emasculation of these formidable wines has been done, over the past two decades, in the Castel del Monte area, which is noted for its Troia, black Bombino, and Montepulciano cutting wines. Even the Sangiovese and Montepulciano vines change their character on the torrid plains of Puglia, to become black ink. The Rivera Company, choosing grapes grown on the hills between a thousand and fifteen hundred feet up, has produced most civilized wines. This cultivation in the hills prevents the overquick ripening of the grape, and with an early harvest, a wine with lower alcoholic content and greater delicacy is obtained.

One of the great problems in producing quality wines in the South is the heat, which not only gives the wine a heavy, earthy taste, but during fermentation accentuates this through excessive "boiling." Temperature control, then, of the musts is, one might say, a must; it is done either by air conditioning or deep cellars.

Here lies the essence of the problem: An early harvest, before the grape gets too full of sugar and still has greater acidity, is necessary. Cultivation in the hills to mitigate the heat, preferably with pergolas rather than in low bushes. A selection of the "hidden" bunches of grapes, which have not felt the full brunt of the burning sun. In no case is there any risk of the wine being too weak. And temperature controls that give the wines a "northern" climate, once they are in the winery, in the height of a southern summer. Incredible as it may seem, the grape harvest is in August in Puglia. The grapes of northern France and Germany never really ripen, and this gives them their high acidity, which is so valuable for stabilizing and aging a wine, particularly a white. Though these northern wines have a low alcoholic strength, this is easily made up with chaptalization. The producers of central and northern Italy would like to harvest early for the acidity value, but the loss of alcoholic content would be such as to require chaptalization, and this is illegal. Italian producers, however, say that, particularly with whites, Italy would produce more elegant and more stable wines with this system.

The Rivera company makes red, white, rosé, and a *stravecchio* (old-age) red. The rosé is their masterpiece, and the stravecchio is ample proof of the virtues of the Bombino Nero grape when grown in the hills.

Then there is the Renna firm's Squinzano, which I came across

quite by chance. It is made from the Negro Amaro (or Negro-
maro or Negramaro) grape in the Salento, the heel of Italy. It is
also called the "double red" because of its violent color. But it
relaxes over ten years into a black wine with no asperities: a rich,
round wine of great dignity and immense personality, fit to accompany such dishes as jugged hare, pheasant in salmi Tuscan
style, or a roast haunch of venison.

There is a new Matino DOC category, close to Squinzano,
which uses the same Negro Amaro grape with the addition of
Sangiovese and Malvasia; this is presumably of a similar nature,
but I have never found any on the market. The DOC Primitivo of
Manduria, equally an "ink" wine, is said to age magnificently,
but I have found none of this available either, and none of the
people to whom I have written hopefully asking if they have anything to tell me or to sell me have replied. It, therefore, seemed an
extravagance to go and knock on the front door of such wineries
as I could find and say, "Excuse me, but I am writing . . . ,"
since they are unlikely to reply to anybody who might be interested. The Primitivo is essentially a cutting wine, and any maturing is likely to be for local and private consumption. There is, however, one non-DOC Primitivo, called Marchese Santeramo in Colle
and produced by Prince Francesco Caracciolo Carafa at Viglione,
thirty miles south of Bari and not far from Matera, that is exceptional not only as a southern wine but as a European one. First,
the vines are grown between 1,200 and 1,500 feet in the hills;
then every method for producing a distinguished wine is employed
including maturing in casks for six years before bottling. The result is not a tamed wild wine, but one that has all the characteristics of a fine, aged northern one.

A lot of authorities and writers seem concerned as to what will
happen to all this violent wine from the South now that DOC does
not permit its use. They have forgotten that throughout Europe
there is at most only 25 per cent of VQPRD wine; the rest can
still have a transfusion of brute male wine. And many distinguished
VQPRD producers maintain non-appellation lines for their less

privileged grapes, which welcome a shot of Primitivo, Bombino, or Troia.

The second great production in Puglia is that of wines for the vermouth and apéritif industries of Turin and Milan. This is centered around Locorotondo, Ostuni, Martina Franca, and Alberobello, in the fairyland of the Trulli, the cone-shaped whitewashed houses unique in Italy. These wines are not ferocious ones, like the reds, but heavy, full-bodied ones, some of which, particularly Martina Franca and Locorotondo, are processed as table wines. A wide variety of white grapes—Bombino Verdea, Alessano, Pampanuto, Palumbo, Malvasia, and the Neapolitan Pagadebiti (it pays your debts)—all seem to produce much the same wine, which is dry, smooth, golden-greenish, and with a healthy but not exaggerated alcoholic content.

Choice grapes (probably hidden ones) are processed separately and bottled under the label Torre Sveva (Swabian Tower) in memory of Frederick II of the Swabians, who, in the thirteenth century, ruled Puglia. This is a most acceptable wine whose major characteristic is its fullness not so much of taste but of body: the sort of wine that can accompany a highly flavored bouillabaisse without being overwhelmed.

Some of the Salento wines have been domesticated; particularly, those of Leone de Castris have a reputation throughout much of Italy. The Squinzano black, I mentioned earlier, comes from this area, but I would not say that it was a domesticated wine. Rather, it is an old warrior, one that has seen its battles of love and war and, with the years, overcome its youthful barbarity.

Finally, the lush, feminine wines of Puglia: these are Moscatos with the incredibly high sugar content of 15 per cent and as much as 17 per cent of naturally produced alcohol. These are the Moscato of Trani, the Aleatico of Puglia, and the Moscato of Salento. Over and above those of the De Castris winery, the Ruffino company of Pontassieve, in Florence, bottles some of these. Though the modern world has little use for dessert wines to wind up a meal, I have noted that they are now most welcome at midmorning and cocktail hour.

SAN SEVERO

The San Severo white, red, and rosé wines, produced around Foggia, are fairly well known in Rome and, to a lesser degree, in the North, and were among the first of the Puglia wines to gain recognition.

The whites are made with Tuscan Trebbiano and white Bombino, approximately half and half; whereas the reds and rosés are Montepulciano d'Abruzzo with the addition of up to 30 per cent of Sangiovese. All three, due to the torrid summer weather, are of a high alcoholic content and are noted for being good for aging: a red can take a decade or more in its stride.

The white is a straw-colored, dry, sincere wine; the reds tend to brick color with age and the rosés to ruby.

The bulk of San Severo wines go for cutting duties in the North, but the d'Alfonso and Farrusi wineries are producing wines of considerable distinction. The Torre Quarto is a fine red by any standards which is mature at four, excellent at six, and better at ten years of age.

Producers	*Additional Description*
LUDOVICO D'ALFONSO DEL SORDO	
(San Severo, Foggia)	
MARCHESE CIRILLO FARRUSI	TORRE QUARTO
(Cerignola, Foggia)	

CASTEL DEL MONTE

The Castel del Monte wines come from around Bari and particularly from the towns of Trani, Andria, and Bisceglie to its north. The castle on the mountain they are named after was built there by King Frederick II in 1240. These wines, particularly the rosé, have led the way in advancing the reputation of Puglia table wines over the past quarter century.

The white, made with Pampanuto and the addition of Trebbiano, Bombino, and Palumbo grapes, offers a straw-yellow wine dry, fresh, and well balanced, with a modest 11.5 per cent alcohol. From a good winery, such a wine can take five years of bottle age.

The rosé and the reds come from the Bombino Nero with a little Montepulciano added. The rosé is a fairly deep rosé, rather tannic when young and with a delicate bouquet and 11.5 per cent alcohol. The reds are 12.5 per cent wine, ruby tending to orange with age, dry and tannic. If matured for a year in the wood and two in the bottle, they may be called riserva; eight years is a normal life span, but twelve to fifteen is by no means exceptional, particularly for the Rivera wines.

Producers
RIVERA
    (Andria, Bari)
GIUSEPPE STRIPPOLI
    (Bari; Piazza Virgilio 3, Milan)
SEBASTIANO DE CORATO
    (Andria, Bari)
CENTRALE CANTINE COOPERATIVE DELLA RIFORMA FONDIARIA
    (Bari)

PUGLIA WHITE WINES

LOCOROTONDO

The Locorotondo zone is adjacent to that of Martina Franca but to the east, toward the Adriatic Coast. It forms part of the picturesque Trulli world. Locorotondo and Martina Franca produce an almost identical table wine: it is straw-colored with strong greenish reflections, dry, vinous in aroma and with a not excessive alcoholic content but a great fullness of body. It is produced in large quantities for the vermouth industries of the North, but of recent years a most acceptable table wine has been produced by some wineries.

Producers	*Additional Description*
PREMIOVINI	TORRE SVEVA
(Brescia, Lombardy)	
CANTINA EMMIGI	TORRE SVEVA
(Locorotondo, Bari)	
CANTINA SOCIALE DI LOCOROTODO	
(Locorotondo, Bari)	

MARTINA FRANCA

Martina Franca wine is, to all intents and purposes, the same as Locorotondo, which equally comes from this hill land between the Gulf of Taranto and Brindisi and Bari, on the Adriatic Coast.

Much of the production from the Verdeca and Alessano vines goes to make the Turin vermouth, but, as in so many areas in the South, considerable effort has been made by producers to overcome the undignified secondary role of producing cutting wine and bulk wine by enhancing the qualities of their wines for the table under their own labels through a careful selection of the grapes, skilled blending, and improved processing. With the growing wealth of Puglia, due to industrialization, a large local demand for quality wines has arisen and is being supplied by local wineries.

Producers
GIUSEPPE STRIPPOLI
    (Bari and Piazza Virgilio 3, Milan)
MARTINO E FRANCESCO MIALI
    (Martina Franca, Taranto)
CENTRALE CANTINE COOPERATIVE DELLA RIFORMA FONDIARIA
    (Bari)

SALENTO WINES

MATINO

Matino is a small town in the province of Lecce, on the Salento Peninsula, the heel of Italy. It overlooks the Gulf of Taranto, the arch of Italy. As a DOC category it includes only red and rosé wines, both made from the potent Negro Amaro, which is a cutting wine by origin that requires some aging before being fit for the table, preferably being softened by some red Malvasia or Sangiovese. The government agency that regulates the wine zones is unable to supply the names of those who make Matino wine, stating that they only lay down the law and the boundaries within which it is made. In view of this general vagueness, I list those wines I have come across, and can only add that Leone De Castris makes a very fine rosé; Renna, a remarkable aged red; and Ruffino bottles in Tuscany a variety of aged reds and sweet dessert wines.

Producers
RUFFINO
    (Pontassieve, Florence)
RENNA
    (Squinzano, Lecce)
AZIENDA AGRICOLA CALÒ
    (Sandonaci Alezio, Lecce)

Additional Description
VECCHIO SALENTO
STRAVECCHIO

CHAPTER TWENTY-ONE

CALABRIA

Calabria

Calabria's wine production is less than a tenth of that of Puglia, though it has two wines that are possibly more distinguished than anything produced in Puglia, and among the best in all Italy.

Calabria just is not ideal agricultural country; it is harsh, dry land, impossible to irrigate, subject to flash floods, rocky, mountainous, and even suffers from earthquakes. The vine, however, as usual, hangs on by its fingernails even to the most unwelcoming soil.

Calabria is waking up to the fact that it has been ignored and maltreated for centuries and is rather bad-tempered about it: the six-lane Sun Highway has reached Calabria, and this, more than anything, has accentuated the frustration with and resentment of the Mafia pressures on city-hall administration that bring no good to anybody—except the Mafia. With this new spirit abroad, perhaps the traditional view that there is not much point in doing anything well, as you will not reap the rewards, will be overcome, particularly among the tens of thousands of young men who have learned to work in the factories of Germany.

I know an elderly Calabrian gentleman who must be very rich. He has been the proprietor of a northern engineering firm for some forty years, but he dearly loves his Calabria, where he owned a huge villa and farm. Plainly, he had been offended everywhere he turned when trying to sell the wine he produced. He does not need the money; it was just a matter of honor with him. It is a red wine with considerable body, but it is a trifle too sharp. Then, one day some five years ago, he resolved his problem. He saw how he could sell his wine not for one hundred fifty lire a liter, but for one thousand lire for three quarters of a liter. With a capital investment of something over $1 million, he converted his old villa into a luxury hotel; he engaged a staff in Rome and instructed the headwaiter to serve his wine only. He has succeeded admirably; he makes a magnificently long profit on his wine, though I doubt that he will see much of his capital investment back during his lifetime.

Such Quixotic methods are not for everybody. But, one day, Calabria will return to what it was two thousand years ago, the land of luxury and delights of the Sybarites; a Magna Graecia of civilization and Bacchic pleasures.

Calabria has only one DOC wine, the Cirò, which is alleged to have been first planted back in Grecian times. It is named after a little coastal town thirty miles south of the ruins of Sybaris. The growing area is fairly extensive up and down the coast and the grape is the Gaglioppo (also called Magliocco), which is found outside this area only in the Messina-Milazzo zone across the straits in Sicily. There is a small classic zone in the immediate vicinity of Cirò and Cirò Marina, the seaport.

The Caruso Brothers are the best-known producers, and their red Cirò riserva, aged three years in the wood, can take many more in the bottle. The Gaglioppo, in vintage years, surpasses its legal 13.5 per cent alcohol minimum and reaches as much as 17 per cent, when it is particularly noted for its very slow aging and for its great longevity.

The white Cirò is made from the Greco grape, which we previously met in the Campania, where it produces the fine Greco di Tufo. This is grown more to the south of Cirò, toward the Gulf of Squillace.

It is over twenty-five years since I first heard mention of Squillace—a more obscure place in all Italy would be hard to find. In Killarney, a young Irish priest, a former Vatican diplomat, told me that should I ever weary of the world, I should retire to Squillace and enroll myself in the monastery there, which overlooks the valley.

Though I bear his counsel in mind, to date I have not wearied of the world. But, now that I know about the excellent wines there, the prospect is more attractive. I am sure that the good farmers do not let the monks go to bed without a glass of Greco and, perhaps, a bottle of Gaglioppo on the feast days of the Church.

A little farther south from Squillace comes the formidable Greco di Gerace, a wine born in the hills of poor, dry soil under a broiling sun. It is a miracle that the vine manages to draw nourishment and liquid out of this crumbling clay; and, in fact, it takes two vines to make a liter of wine and the price is consequently at least five times that of wine produced in happier circumstances. To make up for its lack of quantity, the vines give quality and an astounding 17–19 per cent alcohol that is so smooth that one does not feel its strength on the palate. The producers are very proud of their wine and have two antique tales about it. One is that ten thousand of their ancestors, in the sixth century B.C., faced an army of a hundred and thirty thousand warriors from nearby Krotōn: they drank heavily of Greco, engaged the enemy, and put them all to flight. The other tale is that, in Imperial Rome, it was generally agreed that if drinking Greco di Gerace did not arouse your amorous instincts, then there really was something wrong with you!

Umberto Ceratto of Bianco also makes a Mantonico, which

resembles his Greco; but it is not quite as strong and is slightly
sweet when young. The Greco is a wine to drink in its first few
years of life; the Mantonico ages more and becomes completely
dry.

CIRÒ

This land of Cirò, overlooking the great Gulf of Taranto and the
Ionian Sea, is among the oldest civilized parts of Italy: it was
colonized by the Greeks in prehistory and is particularly noted
for the nearby dolce-vita city of Sybaris, which only now is being
excavated, and a temple of Bacchus, which demonstrates that
the cult of wine was practiced there some two and a half millennia ago.

The best Cirò wine is produced in a small area around the town
of Cirò on a little headland north of Crotone (Greek Krotōn),
called Punta Alice. If it is produced from grapes grown in the
vicinity of Cirò and has an alcoholic content of at least 13.5 per
cent, the Cirò may be called classico. If the wine is then aged for
three years, it may also be called riserva. It, in fact, usually has an
alcoholic content of 14–15 per cent, and in exceptional years it
hits the 17 per cent mark. This is a wine that has made its reputation throughout Italy, not for its strength, but, rather, for its talent
in reaching a great age with dignity, though it turns sweeter in its
second decade.

A much larger, non-classic growing area produces wines that
are more modest in their offerings, though they meet the DOC
requirements of being made with the Gaglioppo grape. They are
ruby red, turning darker with age, full-bodied, warm, and harmonious; and, with maturing, they become well balanced and
velvety.

The Cirò white is a Greco, straw-colored, full-bodied, and

strong in personality, and with at least 12 per cent alcohol; a fine wine, but not in the same category as the red.

Producers

FRATELLI CARUSO
(Catanzaro)

CANTINA SOCIALE "CIROVIN"
(Cirò Marina, Catanzaro)

VINCENZO IPPOLITO
(Cirò Marina, Catanzaro)

CAPARRA E SICILIANI
(Cirò Marina, Catanzaro)

CANTINA SOCIALE DI SANBIASE
(Catanzaro)

GRECO DI GERACE

Gerace is a small town under the big toe of Italy, looking out onto the Ionian Sea. The Greco wine is mostly produced in the hills south of Gerace and Locri, around Bianco, a small town by the sea. The demand for it has made it rather hard to find and relatively expensive, since the production is small.

It is a remarkably delicate wine, despite its ebullient natural 17–18 per cent alcohol. When young, it tends to the abboccato, but with some bottle age attains a subtle dryness, a fragrant bouquet, a soft amber color, and a most elegant finish.

The Mantonico is a 16 per cent dessert wine, which, after four years in the wood, becomes dry and generous. This, too, is in short supply and consequently at fairly high prices.

Producer

UMBERTO CERATTI
(Caraffa del Bianco, Reggio Calabria)

CHAPTER TWENTY-TWO

SICILY

Sicily

It is well documented that the Dionysian cult was established in Sicily in the seventh century B.C., which means that wine existed too, as this was the essence of Bacchic rites. The wine maker, therefore, we may conclude, if certainly not the first profession in European civilization, comes high in the list, along with prostitutes, soldiers, priests, and kings.

The Sicilian wine maker today, twenty-six centuries later, produces 900 million liters each year; not as much as Puglia, but a good rival. Much of this is cutting wine, which is sold in the "North," along with wine-concentrates, vermouth, Marsala, and dessert wines: half the production is drunk on the island.

Like Calabria, nothing has ever gone quite right for Sicily. After a glorious page at the beginning of history with the Greeks and the Phoenicians, others—Romans, barbarians, Byzantines, Normans, Swabians, Angevins, Spaniards, Piedmontese, the French under Napoleon, and finally the Bourbons—took turns at ruling the island. None of them had the interests of the Sicilians at heart; it is not surprising that finally the Sicilians decided it was best to handle their own justice with the aid of a sawed-off shotgun.

The lack of sound government, even today, when the island is administered autonomously from Palermo, has caused considerable concern, especially in the wine business, which must now look to all Europe for its sales. Sicilian standards are mostly non-existent: farmers still plant what they like, harvest when they like, process the wine just how the fancy takes them, all quite independently of any regulation, technology, or local planning. Like the Taormina wine I mentioned in Part One of this book, it is basically honest wine, but too roughly made to command anything but wholesale prices.

There are only two DOC zones. One is Marsala, which has disciplined itself over a couple of centuries; the other is Etna, which is based on Catania, the most efficient and open-minded city of Sicily.

The producers of two groups of wines, Corvo and Regaleali, seem unwilling to take part in any co-operative movement, preferring to stand on their own, even if this means a possible loss of prestige on a national level and exclusion from any government-sponsored promotion of DOC-quality wines.

The red Faro* (from Messina) and the white Partinico† (from behind Palermo) are both well-respected wines, but produced in relatively small quantities. The former is obtained from the Nerello grape along with some Calabrian Gaglioppo and Mantonico: it is mature in two years, perfect in five. The Partinico needs three years to mature, after which it can improve another six or seven in the bottle; it is a 16 per cent dry apéritif wine.

The major production of bottled wines is in the field of sweet, dessert wines: Moscatos, passitos, Malvasias, and, of course, Marsala. The best known of these are the Moscatos of Noto, Syracuse, Zucco, Pantelleria, and the Malvasia of the Lipari Isles. These are all wines with 15 per cent alcohol and 15 per cent sugar, which, to say the least, is very sweet and very strong. As I said in the Puglia chapter, these wines, though called dessert wines, are rarely drunk with dessert; now, more often, they are midmorning

* Spinasanta (Messina).
† Salvatore di Giuseppe (Partinico, Palermo).

or cocktail-time drinks. There is an Albanello di Siracusa, a dry apéritif wine of over 17 per cent alcohol, that is highly recommended.

The major names in Sicilian wines are Barone di Villagrande (Etna), the Duke of Salaparuta (Corvo), and Count Tasca of Almerita (Regaleali). The Etna red is a very good table wine that improves with bottle age: the superiore white is a wine to drink young. The Salaparuta wines, from near Palermo, are very well known throughout Italy except for their special crus, such as Colomba Platino and the Prima Goccia, both thoroughbred dry whites. The Regaleali estate lies fifteen hundred feet up in the hills halfway between Palermo and Caltanisetta, and, since 1830, has produced fine wines under the strict surveillance of the various generations of the Tasca family. They won a first prize in Sicily in 1846 and, more recently, a first prize at Pramaggiore (Veneto) in 1969; with the aid of Italy's best enologists, the present Conte Tasca is aiming even higher than before in the current competition for prestige and quality.

To the west is Marsala, Sicily's No. 1 DOC wine, yet it is not having great success today. Perhaps, when the winery was English-owned, the English had more interest in importing it and victualing the warships of the Royal Navy with it, as Nelson is said to have done. Perhaps it has spoiled its reputation by turning out banana-, strawberry-, and coffee-flavored Marsalas, the very thought of which strikes horror into the heart of any wine lover. Marsala, without extraneous flavorings, is produced in a dozen different forms, most of them excessively sweet. Perhaps the Vergine, the Extra, and the Stravecchia are the best examples of what we think of as a choice, well-aged, dry Marsala.

MARSALA

This DOC category deals with Marsala wine, a 12 per cent golden-white wine which is the basis of the famous 18–19 per cent dessert wine: I doubt that anybody has ever tested it before it is turned into Marsala. It resembles the wines of Spain that are used for making Sherry, and first gained fame in 1772, when a Mr. Woodhouse shipped sixty pipes (large barrels of 105-gallon capacity) of it to England; to make sure it arrived in good form, he laced each barrel with two gallons of distilled wine, and the whole shipment was a roaring success. A few years later, Benjamin Ingham and Whittaker arrived in Sicily, bringing with them the already well-tried methods of making Madeira, Port, and Sherry, thus inventing a fourth fortified wine, Marsala.

All this came to a halt with Napoleon's conquest of Italy. After the Congress of Vienna and the restoration of the political status quo ante, Marsala, under the three British shippers, played a major role in drinking habits. However, the story of Nelson victualing the British fleet with Marsala is not highly plausible. Mr. Cyril Ray, in his *The Wines of Italy,* suggests that the British Navy took on ordinary wine rather than fortified Marsala. I would suggest that the reason for this was because the French had won their Italian Campaign, Malta had been taken, and Napoleon personally was in Egypt; so Nelson probably loaded up his ships with all the British shippers' barrels he could take aboard to save them from falling into the hands of the French or of looters. Mr. Cyril Ray also discounts the later myth of the Bourbon Navy discontinuing its bombardment of Marsala, after Garibaldi's landing, for fear of damaging British property.

The DOC regulations about Marsala as a dessert wine are not detailed, since the various houses settled on their methods, their symbols, and their trade names long before DOC was thought up. However, the basic wine must be from the Catarratto, Grillo grapes with up to 15 per cent of Inzolia.

In general, the turning of this wine into Marsala is done by adding a 6 per cent mixture (1½ per cent of wine alcohol and 4½ per cent of strong wine made from Mistella and Sifone grapes). Subsequently, a further additive of concentrated wine must, which has been "boiled," is poured in to give the wine its tawny color and added warmth. The result is a very sweet wine, but this high sugar content is burned up in the cask over the years. That is to say, the older the Marsala, the dryer it will be.

Marsala, by DOC legislation, may be labeled, according to age, Fine, Superiore, or Vergine; you will also find Stravecchia. Marsala is marketed under the name of Italia and Inghilterra (England). As with cognac, you will find letterings on the bottle such as SOM, OP, PG, COM, and GD: these mean Superior Old Marsala, Old Pale, Particularly Genuine, Choice Old Marsala, Garibaldi Dolce. The Extra and Stravecchia Marsalas are really well aged, probably by the Solera system. The less said the better about the strawberry and banana Marsalas; these, no doubt, are the joy of the Mafia, from whose unlimited territory the Marsalas come. However, it should be added that the distinguished and historic Florio winery, which is now part of a Turin industrial group, is making most pleasing brandy.

Producers
CARLO PELLEGRINO
    (Marsala)
FLORIO, INGHAM, WHITTAKER & WOODHOUSE
    (Marsala)
DIEGO RALLO E FIGLI
    (Marsala)
SCIASCIA
    (Marsala, Trapani)

ETNA

The Etna wines come from high above sea level—between twenty-five hundred and three thousand feet—on Mount Etna, where the vines grow in soil well fertilized by volcanic ash: they grow on a strip running from the north around the eastern slopes and to the south of the volcano, from the towns of Randazzo to St. Alfio and Brancavilla.

The white wine, consisting of grapes from the Carricante vine (60 per cent) and the Catarratto (40 per cent), is the best known, though the red is rather better. This white is straw-colored with green reflections and tends to turn amber with age; it has a dry, light, harmonious, and smooth taste, a fruity fragrance, and a minimum alcoholic content of 12 per cent. There is a classic zone around the town of Milo: wines from here, if made with 80 per cent Carricante and if they have more than 12 per cent alcohol may be called superiore.

The red and the rosé are identical, as far as the grapes used to make them are concerned (Nerello Mascalese 80 per cent and Nerello Mantellato 20 per cent), but differ in the processing. The red is a deep garnet, while the rosé is a light ruby; both are dry, warm, robust, and well-balanced wines with a strong aroma and at least 12.5 per cent alcohol. The reds age for a decade to good effect.

Producers
BARONE NICOLOSI DI VILLAGRANDE
    (Milo, Catania)
S.T.I.V.I.S.
    (Catania)

CORVO

The Salaparuta Corvo wines, of Casteldaccia, both white and red, are well known throughout Italy and almost standard wines at banquets at the Grand and Excelsior hotels and served automatically if you do not specify another brand.

Considering that these wines come from Palermo, in Sicily, it is surprising that they have succeeded so well: this does not detract from the quality, but only arouses admiration for the marketing talent.

The white is a warm, velvety wine that is usually served cold to enjoy its full body: the red is equally dry, round, and with a very satisfying aftertaste. This red, however, with a few years of bottle age can become a very distinguished wine. Both red and white have between 12 and 13 per cent alcohol.

The Colomba Platino would seem to be the Duca di Salaparuta's classic-zone white, selected grapes and superior processing offering a finer, tauter wine. The whites are obtained, much like Marsala, from the Inzolia and Catarratto grapes: the reds from Perricone and Catanese.

Producer	*Additional Description*
DUCA DI SALAPARUTA	PRIMA GOCCIA (white)
(Via Principe Belmonte 1,	Sherry Stravecchio
Palermo)	

REGALEALI

Produced on the Regaleali estate at a height of fifteen hundred feet in the south of Palermo province, the red, white, and rosé wines are of very high quality and all estate bottled by Conte Tasca's winery.

The red and the rosé are made from the Nero d'Avola and Nerello Mascalese grapes; the rosé being made with a light pressing and fermented without the grapeskins. Both are warm, smooth wines, harmonious and delicate and with sufficient acidity for aging. The white comes from the Catarratto and Inzolia grapes (like Marsala) and is a pale straw color with golden reflections. It has a lively bouquet and a dry, velvety taste. The white, which has 12.5 per cent alcohol, is recommended also as an apéritif wine. The red has 13 per cent and the rosé 12 per cent alcohol.

Producer
CONTE GIUSEPPE TASCA DI ALMERITA
    (Regaleali, Vallelunga, Palermo)

DESSERT WINES

MOSCATO DI SIRACUSA

The Syracuse Moscato dessert wine is well known, at least in Italy, and admired for its rich golden color, its generous warmth, and its 16 per cent alcohol. You may find the word "Pollio" on the bottle; this refers back 2½ millennia to King Pollius, who is said to have brought the wines to Sicily from Thrace, in Greece. The dry Albanello comes from Syracuse too.

Producer	*Additional Description*
GIOVANNI BONVICINO "ARETUSA" (Syracuse)	ALSO ALBANELLO

MALVASIA DI LIPARI

The wines of the Lipari, or Aeolian, Isles, just off the Sicilian coast, northwest of Messina, are most highly respected, particularly the sweet white Malvasia; some of it even comes from the small volcano island of Stromboli. As is to be expected from a Malvasia produced under a southern sun, it is a golden liquid, sweet, smooth, full-bodied, and with an intense aroma and between 14 and 16 per cent alcohol.

In the nineteenth century, very large quantities were made. But after the Phylloxera pest, when most of the vineyards were destroyed, the land was abandoned and the farmers emigrated. Due to antiquated equipment and the difficulties of making this wine, the production is now both limited and not notably profitable; that, however, does not make the wine any less desirable. It is just another of the eternal misfortunes against which the Sicilians have always battled.

Producer
CANTINA SPERIMENTALE DI MILAZZO
  (Milazzo, Messina)

CERASUOLO DI VITTORIA

This completely unknown wine is shortly to receive its DOC nomination. It is produced on the south coast of Sicily in the province of Ragusa and obtained from Frappata grapes with the addition of some Calabrese, Grossonero, and Albanello. It is a most unusual wine: when young it is a dry table wine, cherry-colored and with a bouquet of flowers. With age—and it can age, they say, as long as twenty-five years—it loses its redness to become pale and transparent, at which time it is customarily used as an apéritif rather than a table wine.

Producer
BUCCELLATO
  (Vittoria, Ragusa)

MOSCATO DI PANTELLERIA

To the southwest of Sicily is the island of Pantelleria, on the route to North Africa. On this hot, rocky island is cultivated the Moscato vine with magnificent results.

Two types of Moscato wine are produced: one a table wine (Moscato Naturale) and the other a 15 per cent dessert wine, made from semi-dried grapes (the Moscato Passito di Pantelleria), which is renowned throughout Italy.

Both wines are amber-colored, the passito being darker. Both are sweet, the passito being much sweeter, fuller-bodied, more velvety, and more generous. The passito, which is the wine to buy, reaches even 16 per cent alcohol and improves with aging in the bottle.

Producers

COSSYRA MACCOTTA
    (Marsala, Trapani)
CARLO PELLEGRINO
    (Marsala, Trapani)
DIEGO RALLO
    (Marsala, Trapani)

ALCAMO

Alcamo is produced around the town of Alcamo, to the west of Palermo; it is obtained from the Catarratto, Inzolia, and Gullo grapes, much like Marsala and Salaparuta. The light-colored white wine is dry, full-bodied, and agreeable. Normally, Alcamo wine is used for vermouth making and cutting: enormous quantities are exported. The DOC bottled Alcamo is a domesticated form but remains very potent, with its 14 per cent alcohol.

Producers

GIUSEPPE ABBATE
   (Viale Monza 43, Milan)
CANTINA SOCIALE DI SAN FRANCESCO DI PAOLA
   (Alcamo, Trapani)

CHAPTER TWENTY-THREE

SARDINIA

Sardinia

Sicily is the largest island in the Mediterranean; Sardinia comes a close second. Sicily you can reach in half an hour from continental Europe: there are train and car ferries continually making the crossing of the Straits of Messina. Even a bridge is being constructed; it will be the longest in the world but, as you can see, Sicily is in shouting distance of the mainland.

Sardinia has been a very different story. The boat from Civitavecchia (Rome's port) to Cagliari takes twelve hours: the car ferry to the nearest point of Sardinia takes eight hours. And these are brand-new ships, which make good time, and the service is most satisfactory. But today there are more than a half dozen DC-9 jet flights on the Rome-Cagliari route every day, as well as many other, subsidiary lines. Only ten years ago, Sardinia was difficult to reach; thirty years ago it was isolated.

This isolation has made Sardinia's history and character quite different from that of the rest of Italy. Sardinia is usually lumped together with southern Italy and Sicily, but it has nothing in common with either, not even the language.

Once upon a time, Cagliari was a stopover on the shipping route from Carthage to Spain; the Phoenicians and Carthaginians also worked the Sardinian mines for precious metals. Frightening, larger-than-life statues of Baal, a god who plainly required human sacrifice, have been dug up in Sardinia. Contemporaneously the Sardinians had their own, Etruscan-style civilization in the hills and the granite mountains, defended by a network of seven thousand little fortresses called Nuraghe. Marauders and settlers of all sorts came, but like the Carthaginians they stayed on the coastal plains.

The great curiosity of Sardinian civilization is what didn't happen. The Romans came, the Vandals came, but neither made much impression. Then the popes sent monks to civilize the island; let us allow that they succeeded.

The first foreign domination, if such it really was, was that of the Spaniards, who ruled for three centuries through a viceroy. But the Spanish Inquisition never came. Since Sardinia was attached to Spain and not to Italy, the Renaissance never came either, as it never reached Spain, and architecture remained Gothic. Sardinia was untouched by Napoleon's Italian campaign, which shook the whole political-philosophical structure of Italy with revolutionary ideas. Previously, by the Treaty of London in the early-eighteenth century, Sardinia had passed into the hands of the Dukes of Savoy, who became Kings of Sardinia but rarely visited their kingdom; thus, during the Risorgimento for the unity of Italy, the Sardinians were already on the winning side, of Garibaldi and Cavour, and there was no upheaval at all.

The Sardinians did not emigrate to America with the Neapolitans and the Sicilians at the turn of the century. World War I would have passed them by completely, had not a few battalions of Sardinian country boys gone to the Austrian front, where they covered themselves in glory as the best shots and the most unconventional infantrymen that the Italian Army had ever enrolled. During Fascism, Sardinia was used as a sort of punishment station for wayward or troublesome functionaries: in isolated Sardinia they could do no harm. Mostly, they married there and lived happily ever after. There was no Resistance either: no partisan movement against the Nazis. The German Army retired from Sardinia in correct military order without ill-feeling on either side and certainly no bloodshed. Sardinia again remained isolated.

It took the U. S. Army to dispose of the anopheles mosquito, the Aga Khan to build his Emerald Coast, and a DC-9 air service to show the world that Sardinia was a most desirable island. And people even learned that its wines are as different from all the others of Europe as are the people themselves.

The most important thing that linked Sardinia to the rest of Europe was that, fifty years ago, its vines suffered from the same Phylloxera plague, causing the loss of some 200,000 acres of vineyards.

Nobody seems to know much about where the vines of Sardinia come from, though it seems most probable that they came from Spain centuries ago, rather like the language spoken today in Alghero, which is eighteenth-century Catalan, a language no longer understood in its native Barcelona. The Vermentino of the Gallura may have come from Genoa originally, but it is thought to have arrived by way of Corsica, which stands a few miles to the north, across the Bonifacio Channel. Another of the curiosities of Sardinia is that it has similar ethnic and geological roots to nearby Corsica, but power politics have kept these twin islands apart throughout all history.

Almost all of Sardinia is good for wine producing, except the higher reaches of the Barbagia Mountains, which are fit only for grazing sheep and goats. The lower slopes, however, produce some of Sardinia's best wines, including the Oliena, the Jerzu, and the Perda Rubia.

My first visit to Sardinia was some ten years ago. It was midwinter; my hotel was empty, cold, and unwelcoming. I walked the streets of Alghero, which also were empty, cold, and unwelcoming. As I was lamenting my fate, I heard music: strange, oriental music. I traced it to a rustic wineshop filled with great black barrels, where a dozen men were drinking and singing— but unsmilingly. I entered timidly, bought a glass of wine, and sat in a corner. It was my introduction to Vernaccia, Sardinia's most potent white wine. With my second glass, my depression left me and I sang a little. I felt warmer, too.

Two of the singers, deciding that I was not a tax collector, invited me to drink and sing with them. Two or three Vernaccias later, one of my newfound friends said that there was better Vernaccia in a nearby wineshop. He turned out to be quite right, and it was improved with a few hard-cooked eggs. Apéritifs and hors d'oeuvres over, we walked down to the port in search of some seafood and Vernaccia, which were not difficult to find, and, since Vernaccia is a dessert wine, we later wandered back to the center of town to a café to wind up with coffee and Vernaccia as they hauled down the shutters. I was a trifle dizzy the next morning, but I had no actual headache. I had learned a lot about Vernaccia—it was something of a crash program—and also that the Sardinians were not as unapproachable as I had always thought.

Subsequently I have drunk almost all the wines of Sardinia, with the exception of some of the sweet malvasias, and I can say that I could live very happily with them. They have great strength of character and considerable elegance and bouquet; they are never unobtrusive little wines to ignore as you gossip at table.

The hills around Cagliari produce a number of so-called dessert wines that are excellent for cocktail hour or any between-meals drinking. Many of these are dry wines or slightly abboccato, unlike the Sicilian and Puglia dessert wines, which are usually very sweet. They do not sour easily, like so many wines, in a few days after being opened, so they can be kept, opened, in your bar. It is perhaps useful to know that beer offers between 3 and 8 per cent alcohol, a sherry between 16 and 18 per cent, and whisky and other liquors 43 per cent; most Sardinian wines lie in the 13–19 per cent bracket, but, unlike the sherries, are not fortified wines.

Of the dessert-type wines, the Girò, the Monica, the Moscato, the Nasco, and the Malvasia of Cagliari are the most famous: Monicas and Malvasias are also made in other parts of the island;

particularly, the Malvasia of Bosa and the Moscato of Sorso Sennori are famous.

The basic *vin du pays* of Sardinia is the Nuragus, a full-bodied and pleasing wine that, though not a cutting wine in the sense of a Barletta Troia, has always been sold in bulk to put some backbone into "northern" white wines, and is, at present, still exported for this purpose in large quantities. Selected grapes, processed mostly in Cagliari, produce a more than adequate table wine.

Another white, which is more elegant, is the Vermentino from the hills south of the Costa Smeralda. This flies two flags: Aghiloia when it is a 15 per cent apéritif wine and S'eleme as a 12.5 per cent table wine. Then there is the Torbato, from the west coast, which equally is a strong 15 per cent dry white and suitable as an apéritif or for accompanying well-seasoned fish dishes. But these formal "marriages" are altogether too fussy when one gets down to the strong whites of the Mediterranean. A good, full-bodied white goes admirably with hamburgers or roast turkey; and if it has real character, it can well stand up to roast pork or beef. It is the whites and rosés of the "North" that wilt when confronted with stronger fare.

Yet another curiosity of Sardinia is the Cannonau red. It turns up in many guises and forms, but whether due to processing, climate, soil, or different vine varieties, I do not know. There is the ordinary Cannonau table wine: dry, light, ruby red, and more than just acceptable. Then it becomes Dorato di Sorso, a strange, golden-pink wine, presumably processed *in bianco,* from red grapes of great delicacy and appreciable body. It becomes Mandrolisai, a smooth red wine from the mountains that is dry and with a most elegant finish. The more formidable Cannonaus, for which aging in the cask and the bottle is essential, are, first, the Capo Ferrato, almost a black wine, with a strong tannin content; second, come the Jerzu reds and rosés from the higher mountain valleys, which are very strong and have a rare bouquet, that redolent of a land still untrammeled by the myriad considerations of our industrial civilization. And finally the two masterpieces, Oliena and Perda Rubia, which are opened when you have a wild boar steak on the barbeque or some well-hung and plump quails or partridge on the spit. These are both black wines, though there is a Perda Rubia rosé which, if anything, is superior even to the red. The most suprising of all the Cannonau's transformations is that of becoming Anghelu Ruju, an abboccato and velvety dessert wine with a dry farewell and around 18 per cent alcohol, which can serve as an apéritif, in French style, or as an after-dinner "port," in English style.

VERNACCIA DI ORISTANO

The Vernaccia is Sardinia's most famous wine, coming chiefly from the west coast and around the town of Oristano. It is, like all good wines for aging, a bad starter. Only at the end of its second year does it begin to shape up: by its fourth year it is ready to drink, but can usefully take many more years of refining in the bottle. By law, it must be aged two years in the wood: if it is aged for three in the wood and has over 15.5 per cent alcohol, it may be labeled superiore. When fully matured, it is an amber-colored wine with an intense and lively bouquet, and a dry and masculine taste backed up by 15–17 per cent alcohol. It is not a wine to play with: only those with good heads can drink it as a table wine; more usually it is used as an apéritif.

Producers
GIUSEPPE FRANCESCO COSSU
    (Oristano, Cagliari)
SELLA E MOSCA
    (Alghero, Sassari)
SILVIO CARTA
    (Baratili San Pietro, Oristano)
CANTINA SOCIALE DELLA VERNACCIA
    (Oristano, Cagliari)

DESSERT WINES

GIRÒ DI CAGLIARI

Girò is one of the trio of unusual and, for those who know them, delightful dessert wines of Cagliari: the Girò, the Nasco, and the Monica. All of them come from the hills around Cagliari, where during a long summer the sun burns the earth and produces a grape full of sugar and character.

The Girò is a soft red, rich in bouquet and delicate in flavor, yet full-bodied and well balanced. It has 15 per cent alcohol. Most of the Girò to be found is sweet; a dry is also made, as well as a liquoroso that rises to 17.5 per cent alcohol. The liquoroso with three years in the wood may be labeled riserva.

Producers
CANTINA SOCIALE DI MONSERRATO
(Monserrato, Cagliari)
EFISIO MELONI
(Selargius, Cagliari)

MONICA DI CAGLIARI

The Monica vine, cultivated in the hills behind Cagliari, is believed to be of Spanish origin. It produces a "big" red liquoroso wine of 15–17 per cent alcohol: a wine that requires three years in the cask (when it may be labeled riserva) and reaches full maturity after three more years in the bottle. It is rich, generous, warm, sweet, and with a subtly dry aftertaste.

Producers
SELLA E MOSCA
    (Alghero, Sassari)
EFISIO MELONI
    (Selargius, Cagliari)
VINALCOOL
    (Cagliari)
CANTINA SOCIALE DI MONSERRATO
    (Monserrato, Cagliari)

MOSCATO DI CAGLIARI

The Sardinian Moscato comes mainly from the hills surrounding the Campidano plains behind Cagliari, but also from the Gallura in the north.

Both are obtained from the Moscatello grape, which offers a wine of between 14 and 16 per cent alcohol. It is a sweet dessert wine, golden in color, warm, smooth, and generous—one is tempted to say voluptuous, an adjective that admirably fits many Sardinian dessert wines. It is also made as a liquoroso wine, when it must be aged in the wood for a year to be labeled riserva and reaches 17.5 per cent alcohol and more.

Producers

CANTINA SOCIALE DI MONSERRATO
(Monserrato, Cagliari)

CANTINA SOCIALE DEL CAMPIDANO
(Quartu Sant'Elena, Cagliari)

EFISIO MELONI
(Selargius, Cagliari)

SELLA E MOSCA
(Alghero, Sassari)

NASCO DI CAGLIARI

The most distinguished of the Cagliari trio of fine dessert wines—Nasco, Girò, and Monica—is obtained from the Nasco grape and offers a golden wine. It is dry, with a minimal touch of sweet undertone and a pleasing aftertaste, much as with some sherries. Like the others, with its 14–17 per cent alcohol, it makes an excellent apéritif. It is a full, generous, and aristocratic wine, which DOC law insists be matured in the wood for three years. After which further, bottle age is more than worthwhile. This wine is said to resemble the traditional Hungarian Tokay.

Producers

CANTINA SOCIALE DI MONSERRATO
(Monserrato, Cagliari)

EFISIO MELONI
(Selargius, Cagliari)

SELLA E MOSCA
(Alghero, Sassari)

VINALCOOL
(Cagliari)

MALVASIA DI CAGLIARI
MALVASIA DI BOSA

These are two dry malmseys of notable personality: Bosa, perhaps, being the stronger. Though considered table wines and particularly suitable for serving with lobster and other shellfish, they are highly alcoholic wines (14–17 per cent), which make them also suitable as apéritifs.

In fact, they both have a resemblance to dry sherries, though they are not fortified wines. Both are golden, full-bodied wines with a rich bouquet and slightly dry aftertaste. They improve with bottle age—even ten years.

Producers
CANTINA SOCIALE DI DOLIANOVA
(Dolianova, Cagliari)
CANTINA SOCIALE DI MONSERRATO
(Monserrato, Cagliari)
VINALCOOL
(Cagliari)
SELLA E MOSCA
(Alghero, Sassari)

MONICA DI SARDEGNA

This is a new DOC category, under which any Monica that meets the laid-down minimum characteristics and produced anywhere on the island may be registered as appellation. The requirements are that the wine be ruby red, dry, and with a pleasing bouquet and a tart aftertaste. Should the wine's alcoholic content be 13 per cent instead of the minimum 12 per cent, and should it have been aged a year in the wood, it may be labeled superiore.

MOSCATO DI SORSO SENNORI

The Moscato of Sorso Sennori comes from around these two
small towns that lie between Sassari and the sea. This wine is
usually a rich, golden one, full-bodied, fragrant, and with a
high alcoholic content; it is sweet, but not aggressively so. A
dry, a liquoroso white, and a dry red Moscato are also made,
though these seem not widely known or available.

Producer
CANTINA SOCIALE DE SORSO SENNORI
  (Sorso Sennori, Sassari)

NURAGUS

This is *the* wine of Cagliari and has been so for centuries. The
Nuragus vine is widely cultivated in Sardinia, but it grows best on
the plains and hills of the Campidano. This wine from the
Campidano plains is the local carafe wine, and it is also sold
abroad and to the mainland to give that body that northern wines
(particularly second pressings) lack. The Nuragus from the hills is
bottled; in the spring of the following year it is ready to drink. But
a little bottle age for superior brands does no harm and much
good. The alcoholic content is high, rising to 14 per cent and
more.

Producers
ZEDDA PIRAS
  (Cagliari)
EFISIO MELONI
  (Selargius, Cagliari)

VERMENTINO DI GALLURA

This vine, which comes originally from Liguria, on the mainland, is cultivated on the northeast tip of Sardinia. It produces an elegant, golden wine, dry and astringent. It is a lively wine, and though it seems very light it usually has over 14 per cent alcohol and sometimes as much as 16 per cent, when it can be labeled superiore. It is a fine table wine with the lower alcoholic strength; otherwise it is best considered as an apéritif.

Producer
CANTINA SOCIALE VERMENTINO MONTI-TELTI
    (Monti, Sassari)

TORBATO

The Torbato comes from the west coast, mostly from around Arborea and from the best of the Vernaccia-growing land. It is, like the Vernaccia, the Vermentino, and the Dorato di Sorso, a sturdy wine that makes an excellent cocktail-hour drink. It is golden amber, well balanced, bone dry, and with 13–14 per cent alcohol. There is a Torbato passito, sweet and stronger.

Producer
SELLA E MOSCA
    (Alghero, Sassari)

CANNONAU WINES

CANNONAU DI SARDEGNA

The Cannonau is Sardinian red wine par excellence: it changes its character from vineyard to vineyard, from plains to hills, and from the variety of processings it is given. It makes a magnificent dry table wine at all times and places. Selected grapes from selected hillsides produce very fine wines: these include the Oliena, the Perda Rubia, the Jerzu, and the Capo Ferrato, which are wines of such strong personality that they are not easily forgotten.

On the whole, Cannonau is a strong, dark ruby-red tending to orange with age. It is dry, generous, and tannic and of sufficient character to marry with venison, wild boar, and the game birds of Sardinia. A wine to age. See also Jerzu, Oliena, and Perda Rubia, for three very special categories of Cannonau. Simple Cannonau is required by law to have a year's aging in the wood; if given three, it may be labeled riserva, and if it has more than 15 per cent alcohol, it may be called superiore.

Producers

CANTINA SOCIALE COOPERATIVA DI SORSO SENNORI
(Sorso Sennori, Sassari)

SELLA E MOSCA
(Alghero, Sassari)

VINALCOOL
(Cagliari)

DORATO DI SORSO

The Dorato (golden) wine of Sorso, with its pink tints, is another of the Cannonau specialties. The wine is robust and strong (15 per cent) yet light and fragrant with an ethereal bouquet. It somehow seems to have picked up a breath of fresh sea breezes from the Mediterranean, which is not far away. In all, a most unusual wine, best perhaps as an apéritif, otherwise with a lobster or other highly flavored seafood.

Producer
CANTINA SOCIALE DI SORSO SENNORI
    (Sorso Sennori, Sassari)

CAPO FERRATO

This so-called "ruby-red" wine comes from the mountains on the southeastern corner of Sardinia, to the east of Cagliari. It is a stern, almost black wine, dry and astringent; but, with due aging, it becomes harmonious and ideal for accompanying highly flavored meats such as venison, game, etc. Its customary alcoholic content is about 14 per cent; it is as yet non-DOC.

Producer
CANTINA SOCIALE CASTIADAS
    (Capo Ferrato, Cagliari)

JERZU

The Jerzu Cannonau is a unique wine. It has an indescribable ethereal bouquet, followed by a round, dry taste that recalls nothing one has tasted elsewhere. It comes as a red and as a rosé: in either case a strong wine fit to go with a roast kid or suckling pig on a chilly day, though this is not to suggest that it is a rustic wine. It is, in its strange way, most elegant.

Producer
CANTINA SOCIALE COOPERATIVA DEL MANDROLISAI
    (Sorgono, Nuoro)

OLIENA

In the mountains of the Barbagia around Nuoro, where sheep graze, bandits hide out in the maquis, women weave tapestries and linen, and hunters shoot wild boar, they make some magnificent and big wines. Here again we find the Cannonau, but this time producing a formidable black wine, quite unsuited to dainty palates. The Oliena is a full-bodied, tannic wine with around 15 per cent alcohol. Its taste and aftertaste are exceptional, both of which improve with bottle age, of which the Oliena can take many years. The best of the matured wines, with 16 per cent and more, cannot be compared with any other wine, except their next-door neighbor, the Perda Rubia (red stone).

Producers
CANTINA SOCIALE DI OLIENA
    (Oliena, Nuoro)
SEBASTIANO DEIANA
    (Oliena, Nuoro)

PERDA RUBIA

Also made from the Cannonau grape, to my mind this wine is even more formidable than the Oliena. It comes in red and rosé form. The red is a dark wine, as mysterious as the Sardinian mountains: it is warm, "tarry," rich in taste and aftertaste, and often with 17 per cent alcohol. With aging, it takes on orangy tints and softens some of its untamed nature, though this is never of the violent sort found in Puglia among the Negro Amaros and Troias. There is a rosé of much the same characteristics that, though no weaker, is more delicate and slightly more suited to conventional tastes, though one should not expect to find a rosé of the type that one finds at Lake Garda.

Producer
COMM. MARIO MEREU
    (Tortoli, Nuoro)

ANGHELU RUJU

This means "red angel," and its name is not unjustified. It is a ruby-red wine, warm, rounded, harmonious, and very strong (17 per cent alcohol). It enjoys a few years' maturing in the wood and refining in the bottle; four years is more than sufficient. It is consumed as a cocktail, as a between-meals drink, and as a "port" after dinner. Some drink it at table, but it is for most people too strong and also rather too sweet. It might go well with a kidney pie, liver alla veneziana, or a lamb curry.

Producer
SELLA E MOSCA
    (Alghero, Sassari)

APPENDIX A
A Foreign-Language and Technical Glossary

ABBOCCATO	Slightly sweet
AMABILE	Sweeter than abboccato
AOC	Appellation d'origine contrôlée—the French equivalent of the Italian DOC wine category
AUTOCLAVE	See Charmat
BRUT	Very dry—usually referring to French champagne or Italian Pinot spumante made by the champagne method
BUXBAUM	A German enologist, who invented the 20-point system for judging the quality of wines —a system nowadays considered unsatisfactory though still in use till a better one is invented
CANTIMPLORE	A Renaissance-designed bottle for serving wine cool. See rinfrescatoio
CANTINA SOCIALE	A wine-producing plant run by a co-operative of farmers
CHAPTALIZATION	The adding of sugar to wine during its fermentation to increase the alcoholic content; a system named after Count Chaptal de Chanteloupe in 1800

CHARMAT | A system to make sparkling mousseaux wines and spumantes in bulk at a lower cost than by the traditional *méthode champenoise*

COUPAGE | See Taglio

CUVE CLOSE | See Charmat

CUTTING WINE | See Taglio

CRU | A superior wine made from grapes produced on a limited area particularly suited to viticulture; usually translated "growth"

DEMIJOHN | A large glass bottle usually covered with plaited straw and usually containing fifty liters

DOC | Denominazione d'origine controllata—the Italian equivalent of the French AOC category for regulating the various types of vines, their grapes, their processing, and the aging of the wines

DOLCE | Sweet

ESTATE BOTTLED | A wine that has not only been made from grapes grown on a specific estate, but also processed and bottled there

FEOGA | A Common Market fund raised by taxes on agricultural imports from non-EEC countries and spent on improving or subsidizing Common Market agriculture

FRIZZANTE | Sparkling, effervescent, or prickly; petillant

GOVERNO | A system used chiefly in Tuscany in the processing of young Chiantis

HECTOGRADE | A metric system for measuring the alcoholic content of wine

LIQUOROSO | A strong, sweet wine that may or may not be fortified

MADERIZATION | The oxidation of wine, which causes its deterioration

MALMSEY | The old English word for malvasia

MÉTHODE CHAMPENOISE | The system used in making French champagne and many Pinot-based brut spumantes in Italy

MEZZOGIORNO The South of Italy, including Sicily, Sardinia, and other, smaller islands

MOUSSEUX French sparkling wines made by the charmat system

MUST Unfermented grape juice

NÉGOCIANT One who bottles wine he has purchased in bulk: he may also do all the mixing of wines and maturing in the wood to produce specific appellation wines that are carried out for estate-bottled AOC wines

NOBLE ROT *Muffa nobile* in Italian, *pourriture noble* in French, and *Edelfaule* in German; the mold or mildew that attacks certain grapes to beneficial effect (sweet whites)—others, not

OÏDIUM Powdery mildew

PASSITO A wine, usually sweet, made with semi-dried grapes

PERONOSPERA Downy mildew

PÉTILLANT See Frizzante

PHYLLOXERA A vine pest; a genus of plant lice

POURRITURE GRIS See Noble rot

RINFRESCATOIO A glass carafe blown in such a way that there is a pocket into which crushed ice may be placed to cool the wine

RISERVA Wine made from selected grapes and matured for one or more years, according to legislation or tradition

ROSOLIO The prototype of liqueurs, first produced in Renaissance times from distilled wine, herbs, and spices

SECCO Dry

SUPERIORE A wine made from selected grapes and usually matured in the wood for a year or more

SPUMANTE Usually, the Italian equivalent of the French mousseaux wines; however, brut spumantes are made with Pinot grapes with the same method as used for champagne

STRAVECCHIO	Very old
TAGLIO	*Vino da taglio* means cutting wine; in French, *coupage*. These wines are all from the Mezzogiorno and usually of high alcoholic content, and of vivid color (in the case of the reds) or much body (in the case of the whites), which are added in modest quantities (rarely as much as 15 percent) to more northern wines to correct deficiencies.
TEARS	A generous wine will turn its surplus alcoholic strength into glycerine, which can be observed on the inside of the glass when the wine is swirled.
VIN DU PAYS	Local wines, normally not bottled and labeled, but sold in demijohns or by the barrel
VITIS VINIFERA	The grape-bearing vine
VDQS	Vin délimité de qualité supérieure; a broader and less demanding category than DOC or AOC and the equivalent of the Italian "semplice" (simple) appellation, which, however, is little used
VQPRD	Vin de qualité produit en régions déterminées; a Common Market classification meaning quality wines produced in specific areas

An Explanation of DOC Legislation

Rather than translate the governmental prose of the DOC legislation, I have taken the Torgiano DOC category and put its recognition decree into simpler terms as an example. It is as follows:

No. 35 and 36 VINI A DENOMINAZIONE DE ORIGINE "CONTROLLATA" (DOC wines) are Torgiano white and Torgiano red, recognized by the Presidential Decree of March 20, 1968, and the official Gazette of May 25, 1968.

The decree opens with a nine-line general-information paragraph which says that the name of the wine comes from that of a medieval tower, the Turris Jani, and gives details of its location. It goes on to say that a fine red Sangiovese and white Trebbiano wine have been produced in this area for many centuries and that, in the past few decades, these wines have been gaining a reputation beyond the confines of Umbria.

The decree of recognition is divided into four Articles and the production regulations into eight Articles.

ARTICLE ONE
Torgiano wines are hereby recognized as DOC, and the following production regulations are hereby approved. The denomination is re-

served to red and white wines that fulfill the conditions according to
the rules that came into force on November 1, 1968.

ARTICLE TWO

Producers who propose to sell their wine as DOC Torgiano, beginning with the 1968 vintage, must report the locations of their vineyards
and their yield within four months of the publication of this decree.

ARTICLE THREE

Further, until the sixth year from the entering into force of the Torgiano DOC decree, vineyards may be registered provisionally even if
other vines than those permitted are grown in them, provided that these
do not yield more than 15 percent of the total production of the
winery.

At the end of the sixth year, these vineyards will be struck off the
register if the producer has not brought them into line with the discipline of ARTICLE TWO and if they have not been duly inspected by
the provincial agricultural authorities.

ARTICLE FOUR

If producers of red and white Torgiano wine, at the time of the
coming into force of the DOC legislation, have wine already bottled
or in course of bottling (provided not in bottles of over five liters
capacity), they are permitted to sell these with the following time
limitations:

1. within 12 months for wines in stock at winery
2. within 18 months for wines with wholesalers, agents, and the like
3. within 24 months for wines in shops, restaurants, bars, etc.
4. within 6 months for wine sold in bulk or in bottles, barrels of
   over 5-litre capacity. (I.e., bulk wines must be disposed of
   quickly and not bottled and labeled—Au.)

PRODUCTION REGULATIONS

ARTICLE ONE

DOC may be used for Torgiano red and white wines that conform
with the following regulations.

ARTICLE TWO
Torgiano red must be made of grapes from the following vines and in the proportions stated:

Sangiovese	50–70 percent
Canaiolo	15–30 percent
Trebbiano toscano	up to 10 percent
Ciliegiolo or Montepulciano	up to 10 percent.

Torgiano white must be made of grapes from the following vines and in the proportions stated:

Trebbiano toscano	50–70 percent
Grechetto	15–35 percent
Malvasia toscana, Malvasia di Candia, or Verdello	up to 15 percent.

ARTICLE THREE
Grapes used for making red or white Torgiano must be grown in the limits of the commune of Torgiano (Perugia), excluding all the lands damaged by the recent floods, the land close to the banks of the rivers Tiber and Chiaschio and all valley bottoms, as well as all hollows and low ground on the north side of Bufa Hill.

ARTICLE FOUR
Torgiano vines must be cultivated in traditional manner and in traditional conditions, so as to provide the traditional characteristics. Therefore, all vineyards sited in valley bottoms or other flat or damp land are to be excluded.

The system of cultivation, or pruning, etc. must be traditional to the area or be such as not to alter the characteristics of either the grapes or the wine.

All forms of "forcing" (irrigation, etc.) are prohibited.

The maximum yield permitted for grapes to be used for DOC red and white Torgiano is 120 and 125 quintals per hectare respectively. In particularly favorable years, the yield must be reduced by selection so that it does not exceed the above figures by more than 20 percent. The maximum yield of wine from the grapes should not exceed 65 percent for both red and white Torgiano.

ARTICLE FIVE

The vinification must be carried out within the territorial limits of the commune of Torgiano. The grapes for making red and white Torgiano wine must be such as to ensure 11.5 percent and 11 percent respectively of alcoholic content.

The vinification of Torgiano red must be done by partial immersion of the grapeskins; that of Torgiano white must be done by normal methods.

ARTICLE SIX

Torgiano wines, on being marketed, must have the following characteristics:

Red Torgiano
clarity   brilliant
color   ruby red
aroma   vinous, delicate
taste   dry, harmonious, and of good body

minimum alcoholic content   12 percent
total acidity   from 5 to 7 per 1000
net dry extract   from 20 to 25 per 1000
ashes   from 1.7 to 2.2 per 1000.

White Torgiano
clarity   brilliant
color   straw yellow
aroma   vinous, light, and pleasing
taste   lightly fruity but pleasantly sharp

minimum alcoholic content   11.5 percent
total acidity   from 5 to 7 per 1000
net dry extract   from 15 to 20 per 1000
ashes   from 1.5 to 1.8 per 1000.

ARTICLE SEVEN

The addition of any qualifications, such as *superiore, extra, fine, scelto, selezionato,* and the like, to Torgiano DOC wines, either red or white, is prohibited.

ARTICLE EIGHT

Whoever offers for sale or otherwise distributes Torgiano wine that does not conform to the above discipline and conditions will be punished in accordance with Article 28 of Presidential Decree No. 930 of July 12, 1963.

A sharp eye will note that there is a divergence between the minimum requirement of the grape and a minimum of the wine as far as alcoholic content is concerned. Anything below the minimum possible alcoholic content of the grape cannot be DOC, though 11 percent is vastly higher than broad European standards. However, to market a "poor" crop, it must be enhanced with wine concentrates (either neutral concentrates of southern cutting wines or concentrates made from the same wine) by ½ percentage point. This is three or four times as expensive an operation as chaptalization, and consequently a producer will worry about his comparative costs; it should also be noted that the permitted enhancement is minimal in comparison with that permitted in northern Europe.

However, with wineries that own prime land and have a first-class technical and field staff, this problem arises only with a rare rainy, cold summer.* Torgiano, for example, even with the generally bad 1972 crop, escaped damage and has 12.2 percent alcohol; normally Torgiano produces wine with 12.2–12.6 percent alcohol.

Further, though this is not insisted upon by DOC regulations, a Torgiano Rubesco, for example, is normally matured for three or four years: two to three in the wood and one in the bottle, though these proportions may be altered according to the quality of the vintage.

The DOC regulations, therefore, put a lower limit on the quality of wines: many of the better wineries produce wines that are likely to enter into the new category of Guaranteed DOC, as mentioned on page 44.

* In February 1973 the vast majority of the Barolo and Barbaresco growers, observing that their 1972 wine could not meet DOC conditions due to the poor summer and a consequent 10 percent alcoholic content, voted to declassify the whole vintage. Those who contended that they had small quantities that might reach DOC standards were invited to present them, within thirty days, to the provincial authorities for analysis.

APPENDIX C
A Note on Monastic Rosolios and Elixirs

Some twenty-five Italian monasteries and convents still produce rosolios, health elixirs, and herbal tonics. Normally visitors buy a bottle
along with a holy medal and a rosary as a souvenir. If they like the
elixir, even in Italy they will have a hard time finding a bottle on the
open market. There is one way out of the problem if, for example,
you get hooked on rosolio! The Trappist Fathers have a small store
close to Piazza Navona, in Rome, called Ai Monasteri (Corso Rinasci-
mento 72, Rome; telephone 652-783) which carries over sixty varieties of the herb-based liqueurs that vary from 25 percent alcohol to
95 percent—i.e. over double that of Scotch. This store can handle
English-language correspondence and has some experience in exporting, particularly inside Europe, where the customs barriers are down
and no import permits are required. They not only sell wines and liquors of monastic production, but also real honey, jams, and "Chantal"
cosmetics, these last being made by the Trappist Sisters at Pisa according to a French formula.

The monasteries and convents best known in this field are:

San Giovanni di Dio (Florence)
Trappist Fathers (Rome)
Casamari (Frosinone)

Camaldoli (Arezzo)
Trisulti (Collepardo, Frosinone)
Monteoliveto Maggiore (Siena)
Vallombrosa (Florence)
Santa Trinità (Florence)
Chiaravalle della Colomba (Alseno Piacenza)
Certosa di Firenze (Galluzzo)
Benedettini Silvestrini (Frascati)
Trappist Sisters (Guardastallo, Pisa)
Benedictine Fathers of Monte Vergine (Avellino)
Madonna delle Vertighe Sanctuary
Franciscan Fathers of Montesenario (Florence)
Abbadia San Benedicti (Seregno)
Carmelitani Scalzi (Roma)
Novacella Abbey (Bressanone)
Muri-Gries Abbey (Bolzano)

Each of these has its specialties. I do not profess to have tried a large number. Those I have, I have enjoyed.

Index

Abbate, Giuseppe, 356
Abbazia dell'Annunziata (Barolo), 138
Abbazia di Novacella, 185, 194, 195
Abbazia di San Gaudenzo, 146
Abboccato, 107, 375
Abruzzi, 307–11. *See also* Montepulciano
Acidity, 28. *See also* Aging
Acquabona, Tenuta, 268
Acqui, 145–46
Aeolian Isles. *See* Lipari Isles
Affile, Cesanese di, 301–2
Africa, 75, 76
Aghiloia, 363
Aging, 56ff., 81–84. *See also* specific wines
Agliarico, 314, 316ff., 320, 322, 330; del Vulture, 326–27
Air, 8, 26. *See also* Oxygen and oxidation
Alba, 125, 142. *See also* Barbera; Nebbiolo
Albana (A. di Romagna), 241, 242, 249; vintage charts, 58–59, 62–63
Albanello (A. di Siracusa), 348, 353, 354
Alban Hills (Colli Albani), 291–92, 296
Albano, 296
Alberobello, 333
Alberti, Fratelli, 143
Alcamo, 355–56
Alcoholic strength, 27n, 39–42ff.
Alcholism, 78–79, 108–9
Aleatico, 81, 304, 333
Alessano, 333, 337
Alfonso del Sordo, Ludovico d', 334
Algeria, 34, 39, 40, 50, 72, 75
Alghero, 361
Alsace-Lorraine, 42
Alto Adige (South Tyrol), 10, 23, 34, 53, 61, 69, 72, 98, 176–78ff., 188–90 (*see also* specific wines); museum, 127; 1947 vintage, 56
Amabile, 107, 375
Amalfi, 8, 17, 19
Amalia, Tenuta, 249

Ambra, Casa d', 314, 316, 319
Ambrosi, Giulio, 167
Americans. *See* United States and Americans
Amerine, Maynard, 17
Andria, 334
Anemics, 98
Angheli Ruju, 364, 374
Angoris Sacta, 223, 227, 228, 230
Antinori, Marchesi L. & P., 259, 261, 266, 268, 272, 284, 287, 295, 306
Antoniolo, Mario, 132
Anzilotti-Solazzi, 279
AOC, 35, 37ff., 44, 375
Aosta, 123
Aosta, Amedeo di Savoia, Duke of, 263
Aosta Valley, 15, 53, 122–24, 128–30
Apéritifs, 106. *See also* Dessert wines
Aprilia, 294–95, 303–6
Aquileia, 225
Arborea, 370
Arezzo Hills (Colli Aretini), 252, 254, 260
Ariccia, 296
Armagnac area, 42
Arquà, 208
Arteries, 96
Artimino, Fattoria di, 262
Asaldo, 173
Ascoli Piceno, 280
Asia, 76
Asti, 125, 127, 148–49. *See also* Barbera; Malvasia
Asti Spumante, 106, 126, 148–49
Attemis, Sigismondo, 229
Attimis Maniago, Conte Gianfranco d', 223, 227, 229, 233, 234, 236
Australia, 75, 76
Austria(ns), 24, 72. *See also* Austro-Hungarian Empire
Austro-Hungarian Empire, 34, 222
Autoclave. *See* Charmat
Avellino, 49, 53, 69, 314, 322; Istituto di Enologia e Viticoltura, 323
Azienda . . . *See* specific surnames

The Great Wines of ITALY

SWITZERLAND

AUSTRIA

YUGOSLAVIA

ADRIATIC SEA

LIGURIAN SEA

CORSICA

VALLE D'AOSTA
Aosta Wines
AOSTA

PIEDMONT
Novara Hills Wines
NOVARA
Central Piedmont Wines
Vermouth
TURIN
Oltrepò Pavese Wines
MILAN
LAKE MAGGIORE

LOMBARDY
Valtelline Wines
LAKE COMO
Lake Garda Wines
BRESCIA
LAKE GARDA
Gutturnio
PIACENZA
PARMA
MANTUA
PO R.

TRENTINO-ALTO ADIGE
Alto Adige Wines
MERANO
BOLZANO
Trentino Wines
TRENTO

VENETO
Verona Wines
VERONA
River Piave Wines
Padua Hills Wines
PADUA
Venetian Wines
VENICE

FRIULI-VENEZIA GIULIA
Gorizia Hills Wines
GORIZIA
Eastern Friuli Hills Wines
Grave del Friuli
Friuli Coast Wines
TRIESTE

EMILIA
BOLOGNA
Lambrusco
Trebbiano
FERRARA
FORLI
Albana
Sangiovese
RIMINI
PESARO

LIGURIA
Cinqueterre
GENOA
LA SPEZIA
Rossese di Dolceacqua
VENTIMIGLIA

TUSCANY
Lucca Hills Wines
LUCCA
PISA
FLORENCE
Chianti
Brunello
SIENA
Vin Nobile
Val di Chiana Wines
La Parrina
ORBETELLO
Elba

UMBRIA
Trasimene Hills Wines
L. TRASIMENO
PERUGIA
Torgiano
Orvieto
TERNI
L. BOLSENA
Est! Est! Est!
TIBER R.

MARCHES
Pesaro Hills Wines
Bianchello
Rosso Conero
ANCONA
Verdicchio
Rosso Piceno
ASCOLI

LAZIO

ABRUZZI
TERAMO
Montepulciano
PESCARA

SEA